Michael Coyle is a code breaker. In this book he reminds us that our discussions of crime and criminal justice—even our own understandings of fairness and social justice – tend to occur only in code. With his carefully situated ethnographies of criminal justice language, Michael Coyle builds [a] bridge across a variety of locations—the everyday language of politicians and criminal justice practitioners, the premeditated language of press conference and public reports, the perceptions proffered through public discourse—and so pushes ahead the project of cultural criminology.

> Jeff Ferrell, *Professor of Sociology, Texas Christian University, USA, and Visiting Professor of Criminology at the University of Kent, UK*

This path-breaking book offers an innovative way of understanding justice discourse in the current political economic era. As Coyle reminds us, words do matter and language has a major impact on societal reactions to crime. Certainly, no progressive criminology library is complete without *Talking Criminal Justice*.

> Walter S. DeKeseredy, *Professor of Criminology, University of Ontario Institute of Technology, Canada*

By using the tools of ethnography and cultural criminology to decode the language of moral entrepreneurs and political operatives that inform policies of social control and punishment in the United States, Michael Coyle provides a *tour de force* in the social construction and reproduction of justice in everyday theory and practice. This book should be required reading for academics and students of media and crime justice alike.

> Gregg Barak, *Professor of Criminology and Criminal Justice, Eastern Michigan University, USA*

Michael J. Coyle provides a model for empirically-informed inquiry into the meaning, construction, and consequences of employing

the concept "justice," including the oft used "victim." This paradigm shifting analysis affirms the value of critical qualitative media analysis for examining burning theoretical and practical issues. I welcome this tour de force.

David L. Altheide, *Emeritus Regents' Professor,*
Arizona State University, USA

Michael Coyle makes a plain and compelling case that talking about getting "tough on crime" implies support for "criminal justice" that is inherently unjust. You can't read this book without watching the way you talk about crime and justice and noticing how others do. That's something even we who call ourselves critical criminologists all too often overlook.

Hal Pepinsky, *Professor Emeritus, Indiana University, USA*

Talking Criminal Justice

The words we use to talk about justice have an enormous impact on our everyday lives. As the first in-depth, ethnographic study of language, *Talking Criminal Justice* examines the speech of moral entrepreneurs to illustrate how our justice language encourages social control and punishment.

This book highlights how public discourse leaders (from both conservative and liberal sides) guide us toward justice solutions that do not align with our collectively professed value of "equal justice for all" through their language habits. This contextualized study of our justice language demonstrates the concealment of intentions with clever language use which mask justice ideologies that differ greatly from our widely espoused justice values.

By the evidence of our own words *Talking Criminal Justice* shows that we consistently permit and encourage the construction of people in ways which attribute motives that elicit and empower social control and punishment responses, and that make punitive public policy options acceptable. This book will be of interest to academics, students and professionals concerned with social and criminal justice, language, rhetoric and critical criminology.

Michael J. Coyle, Ph.D. is Associate Professor in the Department of Political Science at California State University, Chico, USA.

Routledge studies in crime and society

Talking Criminal Justice

Language and the just society

Michael J. Coyle

Routledge
Taylor & Francis Group

LONDON AND NEW YORK

First published 2013
by Routledge
2 Park Square, Milton Park, Abingdon, Oxon, OX14 4RN

Simultaneously published in the USA and Canada
by Routledge
711 Third Avenue, New York, NY 10017

Routledge is an imprint of the Taylor & Francis Group, an informa business

© 2013 Michael J. Coyle

British Library Cataloguing in Publication Data
A catalogue record for this book is available from the British Library

Library of Congress Cataloging-in-Publication Data
Coyle, Michael J.
Talking criminal justice : language and the just society / Michael J. Coyle.
pages cm. – (Routledge studies in crime and society)
Includes bibliographical references.
1. Criminal justice, Administration of. I. Title.
HV7419.C697 2013
364.01'4–dc23   2012033583

ISBN: 978-0-415-69704-0 (hbk)
ISBN: 978-0-415-81523-9 (pbk)
ISBN: 978-0-203-08339-0 (ebk)

Typeset in Times New Roman
by Cenveo Publisher Services

To my family:

To my father who taught me that we are both hindered by and greater than pain and misfortune.

To my mothers who taught me that both error and reason lead to compassion.

To my partner, sisters and nieces who continuously teach me that the most important lesson and gift is love.

To my four-legged brother who taught me relatedness and responsibility.

To all these for teaching me that anger and desire for retribution have no limit and that moving through them each time matters.

Human beings do not live in the objective world alone, nor alone in the world of social activity as ordinarily understood, but are very much at the mercy of the particular language which has become the medium of expression for their society. It is quite an illusion to imagine that one adjusts to reality essentially without the use of language and that language is merely an incidental means of solving specific problems of communication or reflection. The fact of the matter is that the "real world" is to a large extent unconsciously built up on the language habits of the group ... We see and hear and otherwise experience very largely as we do because the language habits of our community predispose certain choices of interpretation.

Edward Sapir
As quoted in, Benjamin Lee Whorf, Language, Thought, and Reality

In our time, political speech and writing are largely the defense of the inde-fensible. Things like the continuance of British rule in India, the Russian purges and deportations, the dropping of the atom bombs on Japan, can indeed be defended, but only by arguments that are too brutal for most people to face, and which do not square with the professed aims of political parties. Thus, political language has to consist largely of euphemism, question-begging and sheer cloudy vagueness. Defenseless villages are bombarded from the air, the inhabitants driven out into the countryside, the cattle machine-gunned, the huts set on fire with incendiary bullets: this is called *pacification*. Millions of peasants are robbed of their farms and sent trudging along the roads with no more that they can carry: this is called *transfer of population* or *rectification of frontiers*. People are imprisoned for years without trial, or shot in the back of the neck or sent to die of scurvy in Arctic lumber camps: this is called *elimination of unreliable elements*. Such phraseology is needed if one wants to name things without calling up mental pictures of them.

George Orwell
"Politics and the English Language"

Contents

Foreword

Jeff Ferrell

Michael Coyle is a code breaker. In this book he reminds us that our discussions of crime and criminal justice—even our own understandings of fairness and social justice – tend to occur only in code. Now this is of course the nature of the social reality that we construct for ourselves; as the symbolic interactionists taught us, the social transactions by which we shape our lives are also and inherently cultural transactions, conducted through the codes of shared symbolic discourse and attributed meaning. Michael Coyle is well aware of this, and in fact more than adept at revealing the subtleties of such discourse. But in this book he's up to something more, and more troubling: showing the ways in which such everyday transactions regularly occur not within codes of our own making, but within the carefully coded discourse handed down to us by moral entrepreneurs and political operatives. Worse yet, save for the Michael Coyles among us, these codes aren't generally noticed, much less broken. Because of this, they retain their power to shape crime discourse as a machinery of subconscious social control and insidious social reproduction. And so, another of Coyle's revelations: to talk critically about crime talk, to write incisively about public writings on criminal justice, is to engage in something well beyond an academic exercise; it is to reveal the cultural dynamics by which the social order is maintained and social injustice is perpetuated—but also the dynamics by which a better world might be brought about. So, like I say, Michael Coyle is a code breaker—and as he shows, once you break the code, both existing ideologies and alternatives to them come spilling out for all to see.

In this code-breaking effort Coyle makes a major contribution to two related bodies of work in sociology and criminology. The first is that of Howard Becker and what we might call the second-wave symbolic inter-actionists who first began to reinvent sociological criminology a half century ago. Becker's subversive notion of 'moral entrepreneurs'—persons of power who work to insinuate their moral agendas into the everyday fabric of society—not only suggested a critical sociology of social morals, but offered a healthy dose of sociological cynicism to those who would believe that the moral order is somehow consensual and organic. For Becker (1963: 155–56), and for sociologists and criminologists generally, the ultimate consequences of such moral enterprise were no small matter either, since as he said, "the most obvious consequence of a successful crusade is the creation of a new set of rules," and "the final outcome of the moral crusade is a police force." Here Coyle's scholarship offers a lovely explication of Becker's original insights by exploring the particular linguistic mechanisms by which moral entrepreneurs disseminate and insinuate their agendas. It offers something else, too, and of perhaps even greater importance: the understanding that successful moral crusades result not only in rule sets and police forces, but in residues of language and conversation that seep into the taken-for-granted conventions of everyday life, and so continue to shape them even when rule enforcers and police forces are absent. In this way Coyle's work likewise sharpens our understanding of the labeling process that Becker, Tannen-baum, Lemert, and others first explored. To the extent that crime and deviance are constructed less from individual actions than from others' reactions to them—from others' labeling and categorization of them—then Michael Coyle's analysis itself becomes an essential archaeology of the origins of such categories and labels.

In these and other ways Coyle's work also contributes directly to contemporary cultural criminology, and to its ongoing evolution. From the first, cultural criminologists have argued for attentiveness to the cultural processes by which meaning is constructed around issues of crime and crime control, and have found that these processes are animated by the immediacy of everyday interaction, certainly, but also by the shared symbolism of mediated discourse and the contested politics of public inter-pretation. Perhaps more to the point, cultural criminologists have attempted to bridge these various dimensions of meaning by investigating, for example, the ways in which legal control and resistance to it come to be encoded in the environments of everyday life (Ferrell, Hayward, and Young 2008). With his carefully situated ethnographies of criminal justice language, Michael Coyle builds this bridge across a variety of locations—the everyday language of politicians and criminal justice practitioners, the pre-meditated language of press conference and public reports, the perceptions proffered through public discourse—and so pushes ahead the project of cultural criminology. With his willingness to engage criminal justice language across the political spectrum, he also suggests a new direction in cultural criminology's interrogation of meaning: an attentiveness to words not spoken and meanings not constructed. After all, to critically understand what is said is also to hear what is not said, and to imagine what else might be.

Back in the 1930s the music of labor organizers and itinerant radicals provided a sort of popular sociology of people's troubles. Songs like Woody Guthrie's "Talking Dust Bowl Blues" (1936–37) created a new language of compassion and critique, and a new way of confronting the layered inequities of the Great Depression; as "Talking Dust Bowl Blues" laid out in poetic detail, the breakdowns of that difficult time were both economic and emotional, and automotive to boot. With *Talking Criminal Justice*, Michael Coyle offers another sort of linguistic confrontation. For any criminology concerned with crime and its cultural construction—concerned, that is, with the little nuances of linguistic interaction and the overwhelming power of linguistic obfuscation—*Talking Criminal Justice* is a song well worth singing.

References

Becker, Howard S. 1963. *Outsiders: Studies in the Sociology of Deviance*. New York: Free Press.

Ferrell, Jeff, Keith Hayward, and Jock Young. 2008. *Cultural Criminology: An Invitation*. London: Sage.

Guthrie, Woody. 1960 [c. 1936–37]. "Talking Dust Bowl Blues." New York: Woody Guthrie Publications, Inc., and TRO-Ludlow Music, Inc.

Preface

This book is a venture into a research field I call *Language of Justice*, or the study of the words we use when we talk about justice.

My interest in *Language of Justice* research arises from a lifelong awareness of and attraction to the power of language, and its usefulness in interpreting myself and other people. I began to read language critically in religious studies where I encountered the crisis of representation that still affects the social sciences and humanities. I studied the work of Ken Morrison and his predecessors and learned how insufficient attention to language masks and endorses conceptual misinterpretations in Native American religious studies. Their scholarship highlights how language choices create discourses that view Native peoples as "primitive" and their traditions as "supernaturalistic" (Morrison 2002).

My interest in language has deepened as I have shifted my research focus to how we select and define those to be excluded, controlled and punished. I closely follow David Altheide's "tracking discourse" methodology, which transforms media documents into evidence for the social construction of everyday life (2000). As an example, Altheide uses media records to underscore how fear and social crisis are daily assembled (1997 and 2002).

In my *Language of Justice* research I point to language choices to argue about their great impact. I work to accentuate how language choices affect not only how we conceive of and reproduce justice, but also how we act in everyday life to create a just community. I find that the study of justice-related phrases, such as "innocent victim" or "tough on crime," reveals the ways in which our language choices sometimes reflect our claim that we value justice and at other times they do not. In scrutinizing how we talk about justice-related matters, I also find that the words we use have implications about how we think about justice and ultimately how we work to achieve justice. Finally, I see that while sometimes our justice-related actions are clearly acknowledged, at other times attempts are made to conceal them in language.

In *Language of Justice* research, I highlight how the words we use to discuss justice reveals how we act to control others. I expose that unacknowledged justice commitments are hidden in our word choices, and in the contexts in which we use these words. These justice commitments have enormous consequences, as they form and inform public policy, and especially affect the least powerful who disproportionately bear the costs: the so-called "deviant," the excluded, the underclass and the numerous groups created by a deep fear of difference (racial/ethnic minorities and more). Throughout this work, I will use the terms justice speech, justice discourse and justice language to refer to ways of using language that have both implicit and explicit ramifications for the systems of justice we enact.

I examine our justice discourse as a means of understanding how we interpret justice. I underscore that when we do not pay attention to how we talk about justice we often surrender ourselves to a justice system already determined by the rhetoric of moral entrepreneurs (public discourse leaders), whose language can conceal justice agendas that vary from the regressive to the progressive. I argue that unexamined justice discourse is dangerous whether it comes from conservatives or from liberals. There is as much danger in a conservative discourse of "longer prison sentences," which leads directly to a policy of life imprisonment for a person who has shoplifted $300 worth of property, as there was in the liberal Quaker reformist discourse that led to the invention of the penitentiary.

In this book I study justice speech and draw close attention to the use of such language in order to outline how justice discourses develop and change. I scrutinize justice speech in two ways: I examine justice language that pervades our discourse (without regard to a speaker's politics), and I analyze the language of interviews with speakers (both conservative and liberal) who are moral entrepreneurs in justice matters.

My research purpose is to demonstrate the power, importance and impact that language choices have in constructing justice discourse, justice policy, and, consequently, justice outcomes. I work with the hope that the more conscious and intentional we can be about our justice language choices, the more we will be able to design justice policy that aligns with our claimed justice ideals, such as having an equitable society with justice for all (The United States Department of Justice 2012). I do not argue for one particular justice schema or another, but rather alert the reader to the fact that language choices impact the building of any justice schema.

After a brief prologue that aims to illustrate the power and impact of justice language (Introduction), I place my research in its conceptual lineage and lay out the logic and main arguments of *Language of Justice* research (Chapter 1 – The sociology of *Language of Justice*). Next, I situate my work in relation to previous studies of justice language in order to highlight how *Language of Justice* research differs from and contributes to them (Chapter 2 – A history of *Language of Justice* research). I then conduct three language studies on the phrases "tough on crime" (Chapter 3 – The meaning of "tough on crime"), "innocent victim" (Chapter 4 – An ethnography of "innocent victim" language), and "evil" as it relates to "crime" (Chapter 5 – Delineating the "evil," "criminal" other). I also explore justice language by analyzing the word choices in interviews with social and "criminal" justice moral entrepreneurs (Chapter 6 – Talking justice: interviews with justice workers). Finally, I summarize my most important findings and place *Language of Justice* research in the context of critical criminology (Chapter 7 – *Language of Justice* as critical criminology).

My act of placing justice-related words in quotation marks throughout this work is something I have thought deeply about. I argue that all words pertaining to justice should be read within quotation marks to draw attention to their use; we often use justice words from habit and without cognizance of their profound impact. Even though my discussion focuses on what we refer to as the "criminal justice system," in this work I will use the phrase "social and criminal justice." I do this because I consider it hollow to discuss "criminal justice" without discussing "social justice" at the same time. This is a primary argument, position, and assumption of critical criminology, a perspective that I claim.

Knowing that our speech affects reality makes it possible to assess the degree to which we actually create social policies parallel to our justice claims. I will demonstrate that we must care about language because words have a profound impact on the quality of justice we actually achieve. If we are to be just, we must keep asking two questions: "Does our justice discourse reflect our claimed justice principles?" and "Do the actions rising from our justice discourse reflect our claimed justice principles?" The answer to these questions is in great part what *Language of Justice* research reaches for.

Acknowledgments

My mother, Sallie Coyle, taught me that the purpose of life is to recognize and eliminate injustice. When as a young boy I refused to join my school for Sunday church services in order to protest an injustice, she came to my defense without hesitation. My eldest sister was seen holding hands with a boy and was judged by our deeply conservative community to be disrespectful to God. The hypocrisy of this evaluation in the face of others' far more serious, but ignored, trespasses stung me deeply. I announced to my mother that if they were right, if God did not approve of people holding hands, then I was not interested in God. In the words of a child, I told her how I felt the pressure to attend church was merely a tool to control and negatively label children, especially those who, for entirely different reasons, had been chosen for censure. My mother stood by me in the storm of contempt and trouble that followed – a significant event on a forty-square-mile island of 3,000 people. She also made sure to draw to my attention that, while we acted for a just cause, there was little to celebrate: we could not ignore the negative effect our actions had on others. In these ways, my mother fostered a deep sense of justice and taught me to act responsibly in the face of injustice. As this story illustrates, she also taught me about the inherent tension between self-expression and the work of maintaining community. My *Language of Justice* research, my efforts to examine social and "criminal" justice language to highlight the process of social control, is yet another context for working out my mother's lessons about justice and the inherent tension between self and community.

This work exists because of the generous contributions of many colleagues. I owe much to David Altheide, John Johnson and Ken Morrison who viewed early drafts and provided insights and questions that dramatically improved this work. My time with Marc Mauer at The Sentencing Project in Washington, D.C. has been seminal, as has been my earlier work toward basic human rights for people in prison. After meeting with hundreds of imprisoned people, the injustices that wholly determine their lives, as well as those of their loved ones, still shock me.

No other person deserves more credit for anything worthwhile in this work than my partner, Anne Seiler, who has been an endless source of personal support and intellectual encouragement, a conversation partner and a sounding board for developing ideas.

I am deeply conscious of how much I owe to all those people who have deeply sustained me in the years I have worked on this research. All my work is done because of and with others in Greece, the US and elsewhere. I thank them all: family, friends, colleagues, students and more.

Finally, I would like to thank Wolf Legal Publishers for granting permission for the research in Chapter 5 ("Delineating the 'evil,' 'criminal' other"), which appeared in their 2010, *Transnational Criminology Manual*, edited by Martine Herzog-Evans.

All errors in this work, whether conceptual, argumentative or other, are mine alone.

Introduction

My aim in this section is to briefly illustrate the power and impact of justice language. I draw on two brief examples of justice discourse to set a context for the next two chapters, which detail the logic and arguments of *Language of Justice* work, while tracing the conceptual lineage and history of justice language research.

Both examples of justice discourse are taken from moral entrepreneurs[1] who speak on "criminal" justice matters, and who represent opposite ends of the political spectrum. I specifically draw on these two to highlight that the purpose of *Language of Justice* research is not to build support for a particular set of political commitments in our justice discourse, but for underscoring how – regardless of political color – our justice discourse:

1　is built on language choices that impact how we think about and produce justice;
2　can be analyzed to show what actions it promotes (commonly exclusion, social control and punishment); and
3　if unchallenged leaves us in the hands of moral entrepreneurs with differing and sometimes concealed agendas (that vary from the regressive to the progressive), instead of free to build justice schemas that parallel our expressed justice values and commitments.

Ashcroft and Soros: twenty-first-century moral entrepreneurs of justice

In February 2005, departing Attorney General John Ashcroft delivered a farewell lecture at the Heritage Foundation (for the full, prepared text, see Ashcroft 2005; the quotes that follow are from the speech Ashcroft actually delivered, see Serrano 2005). Ashcroft took the opportunity to reflect on the four years that he led the US Department of Justice, an office charged "to ensure fair and impartial administration of justice for all Americans." As the nation's highest law enforcement officer, he called for Congress "to enact tougher federal sentencing guidelines." Ashcroft referenced the positive difference such past legislation had made a few months prior in "the quick arrest of the woman charged with killing Bobbie Jo Stinnett and stealing Stinnett's baby" (an infant removed with a kitchen knife from the strangled mother's womb). Ashcroft described the arrest as "a final act of grace in a sad, savage drama." He also criticized what he considered an unfavorable Supreme Court ruling on sentencing guidelines as "a retreat from justice that may put the public's safety in jeopardy," and said that "this decision could lead to more lenient treatment of violent offenders." Disagreeing with the high court's decision to give judges greater discretion with punishment severity, he reminded his audience that "in all, 35 million Americans have been spared the pain of violent crime in the past decade – in no small part because the criminals who would have victimized them were serving tough sentences" (Serrano 2005).

In October 2010, more than five years after Ashcroft's departing speech, George Soros, the well-known philanthropist of liberal "criminal" justice reform efforts, wrote a column for *The Wall Street Journal* titled "Why I Support Legal Marijuana" (Soros 2010). Soros called for the electoral support of California's (ultimately unsuccessful) Proposition 19, which sought to legalize the recreational use and small-scale cultivation of marijuana. Soros claimed marijuana laws were "clearly doing more harm than good" and were resulting in "extensive costs and negative consequences." He labeled marijuana laws as an "unenforceable prohibition," and claimed that the police should "focus on serious crime instead." Soros also pointed to the "racial inequities that are part and parcel of marijuana enforcement policies," and discussed the early twentieth-century use of marijuana by Mexican migrants to argue that "racial prejudice also helps explain the origins of marijuana prohibition." He then argued that keeping marijuana illegal produces "easy profits" for "major criminal organizations" that "would rapidly lose their competitive advantage if marijuana were a legal commodity." Lending authority to his claim, Soros then cited three former presidents of Brazil, Colombia and Mexico who have called for "marijuana decriminalization." He also expressed worry "about young people getting into trouble with marijuana and other drugs," and advocated that the best solution "is honest and effective drug education." Soros wrote, "I'd much rather invest in effective education than ineffective arrest and incarceration."

On first inspection, Ashcroft's and Soros' speeches appear to be polar opposites. In their theses, for example, the first calls for increased sentencing and the second for decreased sentencing. However, a close reading of their language choices highlights how more than any differences they both have a predisposition to define complex issues in simplistic, digestible notions. As I will show, many of these notions are common to both of them.

Questions for moral entrepreneurs of justice

According to the popular polarization of public opinion along conservative and liberal lines, Ashcroft and Soros occupy opposite political positions within our justice discourse. But seeing them this way displaces a vital series of questions that should be at the center of our attention.

For example, Ashcroft's speech raises some important questions: how does selecting infanticide as an example of "crime" in general impact how we construct and define "criminal" justice policy? Who is served and who loses when such "crime" choices are made for the discussion? How do we understand the invocation of imaginary categories, such as "savage drama" and "monster," to interpret "crimes" or the persons accused of them? How are phrases such as "a retreat from justice" and "the jeopardy of public safety" used? Who uses them? What are they used for? Against whom are they directed? Does their use have an impact? Does "tough on crime" have a constant definition? Do time and setting shift its meaning? Does the distinction between "tough sentences" and "lenient treatment" refer only to the degree of punishment, or does a choice demarcate who is deemed suspicious, punishable or redeemable?

Soros' speech equally demands a series of important questions: what is the impact of using "financial cost" arguments to critique "criminal" justice policy? How do economic arguments about "easy profits" and "competitive advantage" emphasize current perceptions of political realism at the cost of formulating justice outcomes that correspond to declared justice values? Who is served and who is losing when justice discourse develops from a consideration of "extensive costs"? Can we understand why "crime" typologies and categories, such as "serious crime," are constructed and what purposes they serve? Who is served and who is harmed by these various typologies, especially in the context of the ubiquity of "crime" and the likelihood that the vast majority of people will participate in all such typologies of "crime" in their lifetime (no matter how categorized)? In the context of a racialized "criminal" justice system, when do we emphasize "racial inequities" or "racial prejudice," and when do we deemphasize them? How are phrases such as "criminal organizations" and "young people getting into trouble" used? Who uses them? What are they used for? Against whom are they directed? Does their use have an impact? When do we speak of law "doing more harm than good" or of its "negative consequences," and when do we applaud law and look the other way? When facing a prison population almost half of which is without a high school diploma or its equivalent, which "crimes" do we respond to with "honest and effective education," which ones do we not, and why the difference? In the context of recidivism rates well above the thirtieth percentile in most states, when do we see incarceration as effective and when as ineffective? How do moral entrepreneurs reorganize their justice discourse when negotiating a public shift from a "war on drugs" paradigm to one of "decriminalization"?

There are many questions that can be asked of both speeches. For example, what happens to the meaning of the phrase "fair and impartial administration of justice for all Americans" when justice agencies acknowledge that such a practice is not always achieved? Who are these lesser Americans who do not experience fair and impartial justice? How are their persons and circumstances described when this ideal justice principle is not realized? How is selective injustice rationalized? How do language choices legitimize and delegitimize "criminal" justice institutions, such as law and policing (marijuana laws as "unenforceable prohibition" and police that should "focus on serious crime instead")? In constructing different "crime" contexts, how do language choices reveal who we think of as an "innocent victim" and who we think of as a "victim" bearing responsibility for their victim status? Does the "criminal" justice system respond differently to each of these situations? Why do we use polarizing labels such as "criminals" and "victims"? What does their use demonstrate?

Talking justice

The words in Ashcroft's and Soros' speeches are in no way unique. Any speaker, whether discussing "criminal" justice policy, particular "crimes," human motives around justice, or opinions about justice in social life, has access to numerous justice words to choose from. Any speaker also enjoys relative freedom to create new linguistic combinations to discuss matters around justice.

The study of justice words and the contexts in which they arise is the center of activity in my *Language of Justice* research. Justice words are encountered daily in the nation's media whether the context is liberal, centrist or conservative commentary. Most justice words are used widely and repeatedly. Sometimes liberal reformers use them to introduce significant changes in how law enforcement resources will be used, to describe how prisons will operate, or to discuss how justice will be done or be imagined. At other times, conservative reformers use such justice words to argue for expanding the "criminal" justice system response to "crime" (e.g. increasing the length of prison sentences). Frequently, liberal and conservative speakers share justice words. For example, most call for "fair and impartial administration of justice for all Americans," claim to be "tough on crime," are against a "retreat from justice," shore up "public safety" and are opposed to "criminals" while supporting "victims." Speakers also use justice words in disparate ways. Differences vary from the extreme ("savage and evil criminals" versus "those whom we must protect ourselves from") to the subtle ("avoid the lenient treatment of criminals" versus "protect ourselves while not increasing harms").

Actors use justice words daily to construct, maintain and renew the operating meanings of the US social and "criminal" justice system. Such meanings affect our perceptions, experience and imagination, and determine how justice in everyday life is constructed and practiced. These words and their meanings are popularly internalized, subsequently used from intention and habit, and form the distinctions that drive policy. Thus, my *Language of Justice* work is significant because by studying the contexts of justice words I can interpret and evaluate the construction of justice meanings and justice policy.

Moral entrepreneurs use justice words (meanings) to build phrases that, in turn, generate justice-related images and metaphors, such as "unenforceable prohibition" or "savage drama." Frequently, such phrases are combined in complex ways to create what can only be called recipes for achieving social and "criminal" justice. One example is how, in his 2005 speech, Ashcroft combines the key ingredients: "criminals who victimize" with "savage," the "public's safety in jeopardy" with "a retreat from justice," and "punishment severity" with "lenient treatment of violent offenders," to construct a recipe for justice that requires "tougher sentencing guidelines" (Serrano 2005). Another example is how in his 2010 text, Soros combines the ingredients "laws clearly doing more harm than good" with "extensive costs and negative consequences," "unenforceable prohibition" with "police should focus on serious crime instead," and "racial inequities that are part and parcel of marijuana enforcement policies" with "I would much rather invest in effective education than ineffective arrest and incarceration" to construct a justice recipe that calls for the electoral support of California's attempt to "decriminalize marijuana" (Soros 2010).

Combining justice language into a justice recipe is a complex process because a justice recipe is more than its ingredients. Frequently, a justice recipe can hide complex meanings. Such meanings can and frequently do take on an existence and social life all their own, and may appear to be separate from recipe-making acts. In other words, the author or *authoring* of a justice notion may seem to disappear, leaving the notion to appear true, objective, undisputed – and importantly without consequence. Thus, a justice recipe can come to define the ways things are and ought to be in the "criminal" justice system. For example, consider the ubiquity and seemingly authorless construction "crimes are acts by offenders against victims." Alternative constructions, such as "parties in conflict can harm each other," are rarely encountered. Pointing to these processes and the meanings chosen (or avoided) is the deconstructive work of *Language of Justice* research.

Appropriately manipulated, language can hide actors, their agendas, and sometimes their attempt to convince us that they speak for us. One example is the popular ingredient "tough on crime," which may be used in vastly different ways to create and communicate vastly different justice recipes. One justice speaker may use "tough on crime" to call for "a greater rate of incarceration and the building of more prisons," while another may use "tough on crime" for an opposite rationale, calling for "the use of alternatives to incarceration that are more demanding on the offender." A third justice speaker may use "tough on crime" in a way that traverses the first two, or that introduces a third element, such as "smart on crime" (Altheide and Coyle 2006).

It is rarely recognized that justice language is created in complex social interactions. Justice language is even less frequently acknowledged as a moral entrepreneur's product, that is, as originating from actors who construct justice meanings, viewpoints and recipes that they wish to see more widely accepted. These speakers share a common language (justice words) and a desire to define justice situations or obtain justice goals in everyday life. Moral entrepreneurs' work may or may not be aligned with broadly accepted justice definitions and goals and is always susceptible to their individual politics, agendas and worldviews.

Conclusion

As a researcher and moral entrepreneur, my agenda is first to identify moral entrepreneurs as intentional actors producing rules around justice. Second, I seek to distinguish methodologies (language studies) for uncovering moral entrepreneuring around justice and for analyzing justice speech acts. Third, I work to articulate that the words and recipes commonly used today to "describe" justice, which seem to be obvious and authorless, actually permit and encourage very particular constructions of situations and people. For example, the justice language that is encountered daily in the media, naturalizes "social control," "punishment" and "criminals," and validates how we decide who is legitimate or illegitimate, and whether a person is "good" or "bad." These constructions serve to exclude certain people from our common spaces and from our social life.

In sum, in *Language of Justice* research I study the words, phrases and *lingua franca* of modern justice discourse to unpack how justice meanings and justice recipes are created and modified in everyday life. I track how these meanings and recipes are produced and changed under the influence of moral entrepreneurs, and how they become established in bureaucracies and institutions (such as the "criminal" justice system). I track justice discourse through media documents and interviews with justice workers, and in the process also examine (1) how news media create and reflect change, and (2) how media formats and news routines shape and establish justice language and justice recipes for wider publics.

Thus, my research includes a theory and a methodology to capture empirical materials that can be followed over time to show how social meanings around justice change, and to demonstrate the consequences of opting for one justice meaning over another. While my work borrows and benefits from previous scholarly efforts, I take justice language analysis a step further by employing a social science discourse to empirically examine justice meanings and how they shift. I also connect moral entrepreneuring in justice speech to what is being practiced and communicated through policy. Ultimately, I am distinguishing how justice discourse as a whole is created and transformed.

The next two chapters continue to present the logic and arguments of *Language of Justice* research by tracing the conceptual lineage and history of language research. They also serve, similarly to this section, as preparation for the chapters that follow. In these latter chapters I conduct four language studies: three are on justice language phrases ("tough on crime," "innocent victim" and "evil" as it relates to "crime"), and one is an analysis of the justice language speech of interviewed moral entrepreneurs.

1 The sociology of *Language of Justice*

It is in this connection that a moral code arises, which is a set of rules or behavior norms, regulating the expression of the wishes, and which is built up by successive definitions of the situation. In practice the abuse arises first and the rule is made to prevent its recurrence. Morality is thus the generally accepted definition of the situation, whether expressed in public opinion and the unwritten law, in a formal legal code, or in religious commandments and prohibitions.

William I. Thomas
The Unadjusted Girl

Introduction

I have two purposes in this chapter. My first purpose is to define the conceptual background for *Language of Justice* research and to place my work within the social sciences. Although my research relates intimately to many disciplines, my focus on the process and products of human interaction situates it squarely in the social sciences. More specifically, my research belongs to the discipline of justice studies because I study the social and "criminal" justice of everyday life. My second purpose is to demonstrate the logic and arguments of *Language of Justice* work. To clearly illustrate this I deconstruct the justice language of two more moral entrepreneurs of justice: Joe Arpaio and Michael Hennessey.

In *Language of Justice* work I examine language as a means of studying the sociology of justice. I read everyday language (media documents, moral entrepreneurs' speech) to interpret how humans act to invent, develop and organize justice in everyday life. I do this by scrutinizing how people converse about justice. My research tracks language closely, and while it may contribute to other scholarly disciplines with a central concern for language, it does not belong to linguistics, sociolinguistics or any of those intellectual traditions that place language at their analytic core. In my work, the central concern is the interactional production of justice. Studying language is seminal; however, my main purpose is to contribute to that inquiry that concerns itself with justice in everyday life, or justice studies.

I study justice language to access and interpret justice discourse. I study justice discourse in turn to demonstrate how justice norms are created and modified, and to interpret how moral entrepreneurs employ such discourse in order to accomplish various goals, such as social control.

As with all sociological research, *Language of Justice* work rests on a body of assumptions about human action and social life. In this chapter I consider the conceptual paradigms that are foundational to my work. First, I examine the argument that all situations of social life are defined. Second, I explore the argument that all situations of social life are constructed. Third, I use these two lines of thinking as an entry point to the broader paradigm of sociology I use to interpret social life, symbolic interactionism. Finally, I consider a broad array of theoretical approaches that *Language of Justice* research draws from, stands in importance difference to, and contributes to: content analysis, structuralism, post-structuralism, pragmatics, semiotics, sociolinguistics, critical theory and discourse analysis.

Defining the situation

Introduction

I derive a central premise, that social situations are defined, from the work of William Thomas (1923). I am interested in Thomas' idea that "situations are defined," because I want to demonstrate how "justice situations are defined." I am also interested in tracking how moral entrepreneurs work to define justice situations, and how their tools are language choices that produce such definitions.

In the epigraph that introduces this chapter, Thomas suggests that morality rises from a generally accepted definition of the situation. The idea is straightforward enough to seem simplistic. For example, although killing one's partner during an argument and killing an enemy soldier in wartime are both acts of killing, the first is broadly seen as objectionable and the second as suitable. The definitions of these two situations as respectively abhorrent and heroic are generally accepted. Much in the way that Thomas establishes how we develop a sense of what is moral, I will demonstrate that we develop a sense of what is just – a sense we use to explain, support and legitimize sets of justice rules, justice norms and justice laws – by defining justice situations. Simply put, as with morality, so with justice: what is seen as just is the generally accepted definition of the situation.

In his 1923 work, *The Unadjusted Girl*, Thomas demonstrates that people enter social situations that are already defined. In other words, human beings are born into communities that have already defined the vast majority of situations that any individual will encounter. To bolster his argument Thomas cites numerous interview and observation examples from his fieldwork in small communities in Poland and Russia. He uses the criminal code as an example to demonstrate how an individual's definition of a situation may differ from the broader social definition: one may wish to define the situation of taking food to feed one's starving child as an innocent or appropriate act, but the situation is clearly defined by the criminal code as a criminal act of theft, and no amount of insistence will shift this definition of the situation. Thomas establishes that social situations are so well defined that the individual "has not the slightest chance of making his definitions and following his wishes without interference" (1923: 42). For example, theft is a clearly defined action in social life, and in most cases no amount of individual interference can redefine the situation. The example of theft also demonstrates Thomas' point that situations are defined before actors step into them, e.g. before actors take food that is not theirs, this act is defined as theft.

Historical shifts in "defining the situation"

Thomas' work shows how social situations are, more than ever before, susceptible to being redefined. In his fieldwork in the small communities of Eastern Europe, Thomas observes that the family and community are the primary definers of situations. When he turns his analytic gaze to the West he distinguishes that family and community lack a similar power to define situations; oppositely, he finds them weak and continually declining. Thomas demonstrates that in the West,

> ... by a process, an evolution connected with mechanical inventions, facilitated communication, the diffusion of print, the growth of cities, business organization, the capitalistic system, specialized occupations, scientific research, doctrines of freedom, the evolutionary view of life, etc., the family and community influences have been weakened and the world in general has been profoundly changed in content, ideals, and organization. Young people leave home for larger opportunities, to seek new experience, and from necessity. Detachment from family and community, wandering, travel, "vagabondage" have assumed the character of normality. Relationships are casualized and specialized. Men meet professionally, as promoters of enterprises, not as members of families, communities, churches. Girls leave home to work in factories, stores, offices, and studios. Even when families are not separated they leave home for their work.
>
> (Thomas 1923: 70–71)

For Thomas, history and progress have meant a decline in the ability of powerful social institutions to define situations of everyday life. He finds that by the early twentieth century, the ability of social institutions to define situations has markedly fallen, partly due to changes in how we work and socialize, partly due to the pervasive ramifications of technology on our lives, and partly due to how all these changes have fundamentally altered human relationships. As he says:

> The world has become large, alluring, and confusing. Social evolution has been so rapid that no agency has been developed in the larger community of the state for regulating behavior which would replace the failing influence of the community and correspond completely with present activities. There is no universally accepted body of doctrines or practices.
>
> (Thomas 1923: 78)

Thomas associates the waning of family and community influence in defining situations with a rise in individualism. He defines individualism as directly opposed to situations being defined by the community. As he says, individualism is "the personal schematization of life, making one's own definitions of the situation and determining one's own behavior norms" (Thomas 1923: 86). Thomas highlights how the social changes of modern life where new inventions, new friends from diverse backgrounds and exposure to new environments have resulted in a world where it is now possible to constantly redefine a situation, or to knowingly introduce changes that will eventually redefine situations for individuals, a community or of the whole world (1923: 71).

Moral entrepreneurs *"defining the situation"*

Thomas' work lays a foundation for my argument that moral entrepreneurs can redefine the situations of social and "criminal" justice. He argues that in time individuals can introduce definitions of situations and can influence communities to assume attitudes toward values other than those conventionally accepted – even ones that can de-legitimate plans of action or rearrange existing norms (Thomas 1923: 234). He identifies how a problem of modern Western social life is the presence of multiple discourses that compete to "define the situation." He recognizes that competition among leaders of public discourse (moral entrepreneurs) to define situations is intense: "The churchman, for example, and the scientist, educator, or radical leaders are so far apart that they cannot talk together. They are, as the Greeks expressed it, in different 'universes of discourse'" (Thomas 1923: 78). Thomas also recognizes the impact of this competition. As an example, he discusses a Johns Hopkins University study, which aimed to produce the consensus of the medical community in order to address problems in sex education; however, finding no agreement, the situation of sex education was left undefined (Thomas 1923: 79).

Thomas' elucidation of the "definition of the situation" highlights the importance of the moral entrepreneur in modern social life. With the collapse of consensus among previous organizing powers, such as the family, the church, science or education, situations are more open to redefinition. Alternative definitions of the situation are possible, at times frequent, and moral entrepreneurs now compete for who will define the situation. It is interesting to note how Thomas' discussion reflects the stress of modern life: the need to define situations in ways that are congruent with one's immediate environment while not conflicting too harshly with the definitions of those older institutions that have by no means disappeared (the family, the community groups one participates in, etc.).

Thomas demonstrates that the problem of "the definition of the situation" is so critical that it is felt by every individual. He characterizes the rise of individualism as a shift between living in a world where situations are defined by the community to a world where, as he says, one makes "one's own definitions of the situation and determine(s) one's own behavior norms" (Thomas 1923: 86). In other words, the world has become a place where one must choose which, or rather *whose*, definitions of the situation one will accept. The implication of Thomas' argument is that individuals must draw on imagery, values or other meanings in their environment to construct their definitions of situations. The question of which moral entrepreneur will provide such influence or ready-made meanings, becomes one of deep importance.

Thomas highlights the powerful rise of the moral entrepreneur above and beyond the influence of the churchman, scientist, educator or radical leader. Though he never uses the term "moral entrepreneurs" to discuss the influence of individuals or organizations, he clearly distinguishes their role as brokers of influence who work to define situations. As he writes: "There are in society organized sources of influence, institutions, and social agencies, including the family, the school, the community, the reformatory, the penitentiary, the newspaper, the moving picture. These are sources of mass influence … " (Thomas 1923: 249).

The multiplicity of sources of mass influence generates stiff competition for defining the situation. Thomas uses a plethora of examples to demonstrate that while in the Russian Mir or "in the American rural community of fifty years ago nothing was left vague, all was defined," in the modern West "[t]he definition of the situation is equivalent to the determination of the vague" (1923: 81). As he outlines:

> But in the general world movement to which I have referred, connected with free communication in space and free communication of thought, not only particular situations but the most general situations have become vague … There are rival definitions of the situation, and none of them is binding.
>
> (Thomas 1923: 81–82)

Thomas demonstrates that in modern social life innumerable moral entrepreneurs exist, and they use their influence – however acquired – to compete for the definition of the situations of everyday life. The centrality of this cannot be underestimated, for as discussed at the very beginning of this section, one must have already defined a situation in order to be able to act in it. Thus, modern social life entails a flurry of activity to define situations, and a flurry of moral entrepreneurs weighing in with their influence. As Thomas writes, we are "met at every turn with definitions of the situation" and with ongoing attempts to influence the definitions of situations (1923: 62). The point is this: we are often acting within situations already defined by moral entrepreneurs.

Thomas' argument about the numerous influences available for the definition of a situation raises an important question for each of us: "What definitions of situations am I operating out of?" This question is in many ways the heart of *Language of Justice* work: when we act to achieve justice (build law, judge in the courtroom, etc.), what definitions of justice situations are we operating out of? Thomas proves how important and necessary moral entrepreneurs have become and how key their influence is to how we think and act in the justice situations of everyday life. Moral entrepreneurs are central, for as Thomas discovered in his fieldwork, "[t]he measurement of the influence is the definition of the situation" (1923: 249).

Joe Arpaio, moral entrepreneur

To demonstrate the strength and usefulness of Thomas' argument regarding the "definition of the situation," I present a case study of one moral entrepreneur, Sheriff Joe Arpaio, and his efforts to define "crime" and justice situations.

Arpaio has been Sheriff of Maricopa County, Arizona since 1993. As the highest ranked law enforcement officer of the fourth most populous county in the US, Arpaio's approach to his work has earned him local, national and international attention. Frequently, his methods are reviewed in the world media and he is variously applauded, criticized or ridiculed as "America's toughest sheriff." One highly critical appraisal appeared in *The Economist* under the title "Joe Arpaio – Tyrant of the Desert," and judged that "Mr. Arpaio styles himself America's Toughest Sheriff, and seems determined to ensure that the honor is never snatched away from him" ("Joe Arpaio" 1999). Arpaio is profiled as a man who has "decided to do away with country club jails," who houses inmates in army tents (including during the long desert summers when temperatures exceed 115° F), who has banned cigarettes along with coffee and hot meals, who has resurrected chain-gangs, and who requires all males in jail to wear pink underwear and striped prison clothing ("Joe Arpaio" 1999).

Arpaio consistently goes to great lengths to characterize the distinctiveness of his correctional approach. As the Sheriff's Office webpage declares: "Arpaio has done many unique things as Sheriff," including instituting the "world's first ever female chain gang" (Maricopa County Sheriff's

Office 2006). Arpaio expresses pride that he budgets more money per day to feed a canine unit dog than the 20 cents a day he budgets for feeding a person imprisoned in a county jail. He boldly claims to subject persons in jails to undesirable, physically tormenting and psychologically humiliating lives (Maricopa County Sheriff's Office 2006 and Arpaio 2004).

Arpaio's justice recipe combines the ingredients of "pink underwear," "chain-gangs," "115 degree heat desert tent-living," "banned cigarettes, coffee and hot meals," and "eating less well than a dog" to define the "jail situation" as one that should not "coddle criminals" or be "country club," but one that produces generally undesirable, physically tormenting and psychologically humiliating experiences. Consequently (according to his logic), those who come to his jails will not want to come back, and therefore (again, according to his thinking) will not come back (Arpaio 2004, "Joe Arpaio" 1999 and Maricopa County Sheriff's Office 2006).

Arpaio's claims are buttressed by results, however. The prize of all correctional policy, reduced recidivism rates, has eluded him; a study commissioned by Arpaio's own office found that his "tough" policies had virtually no effect on whether people leaving his prisons would return again (Hepburn and Griffin 1998). His unorthodox policies have cost taxpayers more than 50 million dollars in lawsuits (Rangell and Tomasch 2011), and in 2012 the US Department of Justice filed a civil rights violations lawsuit claiming racial profiling, abuses in county jails and harassment of critics.

Arpaio has been enormously successful as a politician despite these serious problems. In his first reelection bid as sheriff he ran unopposed, and he has not stopped being sheriff since his initial election in 1992. His approval ratings are consistently high and have been reported to reach 90 percent (Joe Arpaio 1999). As his winning relationship with the electorate demonstrates, Arpaio enduringly defines "crime" and imprisonment for voters in Maricopa County. He defines and fulfills his job as sheriff in a manner that speaks to the public's voting expectations. Despite reputable and eloquent opponents, unorthodox policies and systematic failures, there is little question that for the vast majority of voters in Maricopa County, Arpaio has succeeded in defining the situation for the proper management of jails and of persons convicted of "crimes."

Near the end of *The Unadjusted Girl*, Thomas writes that in determining the situation, "[e]ven fictitious representations are significant" (1923: 250). The power of fictitious definitions is clearly demonstrated in *The Economist* article cited above. The article is interesting not only for its portrayal of Arpaio's moral entrepreneuring, but also for the following sentence: "[Arpaio] decided to do away with country club jails housing inmates in Korean-war army tents in the Sonoran Desert." Language such as "country club jails" points to the success of "tough on crime" moral entrepreneuring; how else could the words "country club" become associated with "jails"? Logically, associating the country-club image with incarceration is absurd: jail life has never included Sunday brunches, tennis or mimosas.

But *the jail situation* defined as a *country-club situation* by a moral entrepreneur of the "tough on crime" variety evokes images of free TV and free meals while obliterating images of physical, mental or psychological suffering. The inclusion of this phrase in *The Economist* article is significant because it demonstrates that elements of the definition of "jail life" as a "country club life" have been so successful, that it is employed even in an article as critical of the "tough on crime" rhetoric as one titled "Joe Arpaio – Tyrant of the Desert."

Though important, the issue in the Arpaio example is not whether he defines the situation of "tough on crime" or "tough management of persons convicted of crimes" for the electorate, or whether the electorate has defined a situation which Arpaio has merely been successful in recognizing and fulfilling. What matters is that Arpaio continuously develops and deepens the definitions of the "tough on crime," "incarceration as country club" and "crime actor" situations. In fact, he is the means by which these definitions gain ground, strength and life in public exchange. His role in defining justice situations in Maricopa County as sheriff and administrator of one of the largest justice institutions in the US has more impact, significance and consequently more power, than the vast majority of individuals. As such, Arpaio is a powerful moral entrepreneur.

Conclusion

Thomas' work deftly draws a connection between moral entrepreneurs as meaning brokers and as definers of the situations of justice in everyday life. Arpaio's success in Maricopa County seamlessly illustrates how a moral entrepreneur can impact the definition of a situation. Arpaio is successful as a moral entrepreneur because he defines the situations of "crime," "crime actor" and "punishment" in a way that speaks to the vast majority of voting residents in Maricopa County.

As Thomas understands, the power wielded by moral entrepreneurs is immense and, as he identifies, these sources of influence must "naturally be the main objects of study" (1923: 249). Thus, in studying the character of our justice discourse, the way moral entrepreneurs define justice situations is critical. Whenever a person, in ordinary life, encounters a justice situation, that situation has already been defined but its construction is seldom clear or obvious, and its character – no matter how seemingly certain – is never stable. Justice situations, though defined at any given moment in time, are continuously contested by moral entrepreneurs with a range of ideological commitments, who assert their influence, hoping either to reinforce or alter the definitions of justice situations. Thus, in *Language of Justice* work I hope to produce a theory of encounter with everyday justice situations, and by consequence a theory of encounter with moral entrepreneurs of justice.

Moral entrepreneurs act intentionally to form public opinion on what is just and to fashion a sense of justice that functions as (written or unwritten) law. Ultimately, then, to understand how justice situations are defined, we must closely track and deconstruct the word choices in these moral entrepreneurs' justice discourse.

My work builds on that of Thomas in that I identify moral entrepreneurs as providing those definitions of justice that predominate in everyday life. Thomas distinguishes that a "society is more or less successful to the degree that it makes its definitions of situations valid" (1923: 233). He also identifies that "[t]he problem is to define situations in such ways as to produce attitudes which direct the action exclusively toward fields yielding positive social values" (Thomas 1923: 243). An important aspect of my work is that I locate the directions and the social values toward which moral entrepreneurs direct social justice, "criminal" justice and consequently much of everyday life. I aim to locate their work by tracking their language and how they use their language to construct definitions of situations in ways that elicit certain responses over others.

What I am after in *Language of Justice* work is a method and a theory to engage moral entrepreneurs working to define justice situations. I am not in search of a method to critique the work of conservative moral entrepreneurs. Nor am I in search of a theory to critique liberal moral entrepreneurs. I am in search of a method and a theory to encounter all moral entrepreneurs – regardless of their politics or ideology – that will allow us to assess whether their definitions of justice situations are aligned with the demands of our professed and documented values, such as "equal justice for all."

Constructing the situation

Introduction

In *Language of Justice* research I encounter moral entrepreneurs of justice by studying their everyday words. Everyday words of justice are the ones we use to talk about our justice ideas, justice practices and hopes about creating a just communal life.

My research interests are deeply connected to the ideas of everyday life (everyday actions that define situations and construct social life), moral entrepreneurs, social control as well as "crime" and justice. So far in this chapter I have highlighted (1) how powerful moral entrepreneurs can be in defining justice situations, and (2) how examining the language used to define a justice situation can demonstrate the influence of moral entrepreneurs. In this section I will examine how the idea of social construction demonstrates the process by which actors define, challenge and shift justice situations.

Language as human action and meaning making

Any systematic study of language is a study of human action because language is always a human activity that either creates meanings or reflects adopted meanings (Shotter 1993). My research examines justice language as an expression of human attention and commitment to justice as features of social life. As a study of human action, *Language of Justice* research is part of the tradition of the human sciences that studies living, acting human beings. I study human action from a perspective that views people as acting toward other people and things based on the meanings those people and things have for them (Blumer 1962 and 1969). This perspective, known more widely as symbolic interactionism, argues that meanings in human life are socially derived and socially constructed.

In the proposition, "meanings in human life are socially derived and socially constructed" the keyword is "socially." The word "socially" points to the fact that meaning in human life is arrived at through the interaction of individuals. Consequently, how any situation is defined (what a situation comes to mean), will depend on the shared meanings that individuals give it. This again draws attention to the central role of moral entrepreneurs who use language to create, communicate and define justice situations.

My purpose is to trace the words used by moral entrepreneurs to define justice situations, and to show how our ongoing interactions with these words lead to justice meanings that we accept and eventually recognize as our own. Another way of saying this is that I deconstruct justice discourse to demonstrate how our justice situations and justice meanings are constructed. In my language studies (Chapters 3, 4, 5 and 6), I show that shifts in definitions (and uses) of words coincide with changes in social situations and the actions of moral entrepreneurs. Frequently, my studies point to social meanings that though ubiquitous have gone largely unrecognized. At other times, my research points to moral entrepreneurs' encoded rule-making and rule-enforcing activities that have also widely gone unrecognized.

The sociology of knowledge: human thought as social

As work that assumes meaning is created in human interaction, my research contributes to the work of sociologists whose purview is the social (interactive) construction of reality. Another central premise of my work, then, is that of social construction, particularly as elaborated within symbolic interactionism and critical criminology, the primary frames that I employ to think about human action around justice. In this section I introduce the underpinnings of social construction theory and use them to demonstrate the logic and arguments of *Language of Justice* research.

Social constructionists interpret all propositions about social life, "crime," "deviancy," etc., as social meanings that are created, maintained and changed by interacting individuals. The social constructionist asks, "How exactly are meanings achieved by interactive action?" The social constructionist also asks, "How can we say meanings are created in human interaction when it appears perfectly clear that meanings exist outside of, or independent of, our acting or agreement?"

Beginnings

I use four seminal social constructionists to build my *Language of Justice* theory: Max Weber, Karl Mannheim, Alfred Schutz and C.W. Mills.

I begin from a Weberian acknowledgement that *Language of Justice* research is inherently one of interpreting the actions of persons and not merely that of, for example, measuring the frequency of word occurrence. I argue that to understand how the dominant "tough on crime" meanings impact our social life it will never suffice to provide a description of the variety of phenomena that constitute its existence. To interpret human actions around such meaning making I instead build on Schutz's theory of social constructions and his method of tracing such constructions as developed in time by others. In *Language of Justice* research I also argue for the need to continuously consider Mannheim's call for context. For example, it makes no sense to consider the meaning of "tough on crime" without also considering whether it is spoken by political actors seeking reelection, or by "criminal" justice reformists protesting that one in three African-American males born today are destined to be incarcerated at some point in their life (Mauer 2006: 130).

Mannheim is a seminal figure in the sociology of knowledge. In *Ideology and Utopia* (1936), he argues that the concept "ideology" has historically been employed in a totalitarian sense (as by Karl Marx). Mannheim's complaint is that broad conceptions of persons and their actions, such as the structural conceptions of "society" and "ideology," displace the way in which each person constructs ideological convictions (1936). He argues that the study of human acts must therefore always consider the context in which they emerge because there is an inherent relationship between human thoughts on existence and conditions of existence (Mannheim 1936).

Like Mannheim, Max Weber reacts against abstract, non-person-centered sociology. Along with Ferdinand Tonnies and Wilhelm Dilthey, Weber brakes from the sociology of Emile Durkheim and his followers who seek to describe social phenomena without attributing action to individuals (Durkheim 1964). In distancing himself from Durkheim's "social facts," Weber (1949) argues that social action can be said to be social only insofar as it accounts for behavior between persons. With his theory of *Versthehen*, Weber is the first to point out that, in contrast with the physical sciences, which rely on a methodology of positivistic measurement, the social sciences depend on an "interpretive" stance (Weber 1949). Weber points out that to understand human phenomena we cannot simply claim to describe them; we are forced to "interpret" the actions of persons to make any sense or analysis of them (1949).

Schutz builds on Weber and, relying on a deeply phenomenological approach, argues that to interpret human action one must trace how actors understand other actors' motives (1964). In other words, Schutz sees interpretation as an action of observing and making sense of others' constructions (Schutz 1967). While both Weber and Schutz are heavily influenced by positivist theoretical and methodological pressures to measure human action in categories or types (e.g. Weber's "ideal types" or Schutz's "constructs"), they nonetheless lay the foundation for a theory of social construction that is phenomenological and person-centered.

My *Language of Justice* research is also informed by Mills, who argues that sociology must connect individual experiences and social relationships. Mills reasons that to do sociology means to imagine how the sociological problem one considers (1) comes into existence in the first place (history), (2) is related to the people for whom it is a phenomenon (biography), and (3) is related to institutions and other dominant power structures (social structure) (2000). Mills has a concern for doing sociology that examines the construction of experience and social context, but he also wants to look at social structure, i.e. Marxian issues of power, class, alienation and domination (2000). Like Mills, I proceed by analyzing the speech and contexts of individuals to comment on the impact of moral entrepreneurs who frequently speak as representatives of powerful structures, e.g. John Ashcroft and George Soros.

Building everyday life: the social construction of reality

In *Language of Justice* research I build on the assumption that everyday life is socially constructed. Peter Berger and Thomas Luckmann defined the social construction of reality perspective to be the identification of the processes in which social constructions occur (1966). Essentially, they remind us that we are the ones who create knowledge and reality. Berger and Luckmann argue that, while to the unstudied mind "reality" appears self-evident, to the sociologist, that different peoples operate according to different realities as equally self-evident. As they see it, the human role is one of constantly creating the world.

Berger and Luckmann argue that while we shape reality through our interactions (externalizing), these same interactions also shape us through our participation (internalizing). This constant "dialectic process" eventually generates a structure of meanings, definitions, propositions and institutions that most people accept as "objectively" true (Berger and Luckmann 1966). By this "objectification" process we orient how we see our existence and our purpose in this world, including our ongoing relationships with others. We call this complex web of objectifications "society." As the authors point out, society is maintained only as long as we take for granted that it provides true and valid definitions of our reality. According to Berger and Luckmann we not only construct society, but we also maintain it. Of note here is the implication that we are also those who change society, i.e. we are the ones who shift the definitions, meanings, propositions and institutions of what gets called "our reality" or, to remember Thomas, our definitions of situations.

Berger and Luckmann argue that objectification means that society appears to be "real" in the sense that it occurs as something other than the creation of human interactions. Thus, to unstudied minds, born and raised in a society already established, the definitions, meanings and institutions that surround them appear to be real and exist outside their participation. While this society can seem true momentarily, it collapses when we consider that if everyone ceased to cooperate in maintaining any specific meaning it would cease to exist.

Social constructionists see all meanings as created, defined and supported by human interaction. In *Language of Justice* research I argue, along with Berger and Luckmann, that our participation in human interactions (agreement, disagreement, negotiation, etc.) impacts both the meanings and definitions of justice and their content (what Berger and Luckmann call externalization). These meanings and definitions of justice in turn impact our interactions and their content (what Berger and Luckmann call internalization). For example, imagine a person beginning to interact with local political and community leaders, media and voters and imagine her declaring homeless persons as "the persons we have abandoned and have responsibility toward." Imagine she carries her views to churches and community groups, and then begins to convince others to the point that she successfully runs for an elected office where she has an even greater impact on how the homeless are discussed in human interactions. In all this work, this moral entrepreneuring work, she redefines homeless persons for many other people, and she reframes the previous definition of them as "a public nuisance damaging businesses" to "persons we have abandoned and have responsibility toward." Building on the success of her interactions she impacts the definition of a situation (homelessness), and has begun a new cycle of internalizations, that is, a cycle of interactions in which homeless persons are no longer considered "a nuisance," but are seen as "the abandoned." For many, the definition of the homeless as "the abandoned" will be internalized, that is, until other successful externalizations by other moral entrepreneurs occurs (if it occurs), which again shift the definition of the "homeless situation."

Language of Justice research draws on Berger and Luckmann's "dialectic process" to point out how justice meanings are created – and how we use these to build propositions, definitions and institutions of justice. I argue that justice meanings and definitions of justice situations are only maintained as "real" so long as, in our interactions, we take for granted that such definitions are true and valid. By implication, my research highlights how, as creators and maintainers of "the real" within our interactions, intentional actors are also those who change society, i.e. are the ones who shift the definitions, meanings and propositions of what is justice (reality). These intentional actors are moral entrepreneurs who enjoy success when people accept their definitions and constructions of justice.

There is much room here to argue about the degree of alienation occurring in everyday life, and the degree to which we operate in what Karl Marx would call false consciousness and Jean Paul Sartre bad faith: a failure to recognize that the definitions and constructions of meanings are our own despite the fact that we unthinkingly adopt the views of moral entrepreneurs and then view them as imposed upon us, as objectively true or as "real" beyond our will. However, the justice meanings that moral entrepreneurs create or define are "real" only in the sense that we maintain them by accepting them as valid in our interactions in everyday life.

Reality, as the old adage goes, is what we all agree is real. Similarly, justice is what we all agree is just.

Recent work in the sociology of knowledge

My *Language of Justice* research also draws from subsequent developments in social construction theory. I use Stanley Fish's (1980) argument regarding how claims about meanings are produced to highlight that both justice language and the interpretive actions of moral entrepreneurs are constructions. I also use Anthony Giddens' work to argue, for example, that while "tough on crime" can only be the product of human action it also takes hold as a structure that legitimizes incarceration norms, organizes social control and functions as the state's tool for dominating populations defined as "deviant" (1984).

In his work on "interpretive communities," Fish moves our focus from the constructed nature of meaning to the context within which interpretation occurs. For instance, in the previous example of "tough on crime," where classical constructionists such as Mannheim would argue that the phrase means what a speaker makes it mean (e.g. "public safety" for a politician, or "racism" for a "criminal" justice reformist), Fish would add that, not only will actors construct "tough on crime" differently, but these actors themselves will be constructed in a variety of ways. Fish's argument elaborates how claims about meaning are produced. The relevance to *Language of Justice* research is significant because Fish contextualizes not only all justice language as constructions, but he also contextualizes the interpretive actions of moral entrepreneurs as constructions (I carefully consider this below).

In my above discussion of Weber, Mannheim and the early social constructionists, I showed how sociology developed within a debate about the importance of human action and structural forces. Giddens deepens the attempt to reconcile the impact of agency and structure on interpretations of social life with his theory of structuration, which balances the importance of agency and structure by arguing that actors are produced through human interaction and that structure is produced by their repetitive acts (1984). Giddens' theory of structure avoids Weber's "ideal types" and Schutz's "constructs" by demonstrating that structural forces are the products of human action (1979). Using Giddens, I argue it is equally true to say, (1) that "tough on crime" is a meaning created by political moral entrepreneurs (agency), as it is to say (2) that the discourse of "tough on crime" is already in place (structure). The implication is that any political moral entrepreneur wishing to succeed (agent) must place herself within an existing discourse (structure).

Numerous thinkers seek to reconcile the interpretive split ascribing agency to humans (the view that human actors shape institutions and norms) or to social structure (the view that institutions and norms shape actors). While at times theorists argue over the importance of agency versus structure, at other times they spotlight integrative solutions (Archer 1995, Mouzelis 1995 and Ritzer 2000). I will examine these debates in greater depth later, in my discussion of structuralism and poststructuralism.

Michael Hennessey, moral entrepreneur

To demonstrate the strength and usefulness of social construction in *Language of Justice* research, in this section I spotlight the efforts of another moral entrepreneur, Michael Hennessey.

Michael Hennessey, sheriff of the county and city of San Francisco, retired in 2012 as the longest-serving elected official in the history of San Francisco. In a city known for leading the nation in liberal politics, Hennessey distinguished himself as a reformist advocating for education in the jails and the legalization of marijuana in the streets. He took these views long before they were popular – even with progressives – and has been a leading liberal voice throughout his career. In his first campaign he sought the closure of the main county jail on the grounds that it violated the Eighth Amendment's prohibition against cruel and unusual punishment. Once elected, he established the distribution of condoms in jails, and he openly advocated against the death penalty (Gordon 2012). It is important to note that Hennessey took these views and developed these policies in the context of deep "law and order" sensibilities that defined the times of his tenure, and which typically also define his profession. Throughout, Hennessey, much like Sheriff Joe Arpaio of Phoenix, AZ, has been variably applauded, criticized or ridiculed as "the most progressive sheriff in America."

Hennessey was an enormously successful sheriff. When he retired in 2012 he had held his office without interruption for 32 years. Though not as famous as Arpaio, Hennessey is a powerful and nationally recognized moral entrepreneur whose influence is broadly recognized for shepherding rehabilitative programming that has been duplicated in other states, such as New York and Illinois (Kransky 2011). Debra J. Saunders, a nationally syndicated *San Francisco Chronicle* columnist and blogger, dubbed

Hennessey as "Sheriff Joe Arpaio's polar opposite" (Saunders 2010). Hennessey has also been commonly referred to as "the anti-Joe Arpaio" (e.g. Kransky 2011).

Neither Arpaio nor Hennessey have ever shied from controversy, but how they have been constructed in media is markedly different. Arpaio is often caricatured by international media as an extreme representative of the "tough on crime" conservative viewpoint, and Hennessey is frequently portrayed in San Francisco and other media as a liberal hero forwarding the progressive agenda. Arpaio is known for building citizen-based posses to seek out undocumented immigrants for prosecution, while Hennessey is known for working to protect undocumented immigrants in his jails from prosecution by the Immigration and Customs Enforcement. While Arpaio has been policed and sued by the Justice Department for overly aggressive law enforcement, Hennessey has resisted the Justice Department's attempts to link county arrest records to their databases.

Media constructions of Arpaio and Hennessey suggest that one would be hard pressed to find two moral entrepreneurs working in "criminal" justice systems who are less alike. However, an analysis of transcripts of an interview with Hennessey conducted on the occasion of his retirement reveals something different (Kransky 2011).

Sheriff Hennessey's speech enables me to highlight the value of a *Language of Justice* analysis by demonstrating the impact of language choices on the administration of justice. Hennessey's discourse also allows me to show the usefulness of the social construction concept in understanding how actors define, challenge and shift justice situations. Finally, the similarities between Hennessey's language habits and those of his "polar opposite" Joe Arpaio show that (1) despite the seemingly drastic differences in terms of justice discourse, policy and outcomes, these moral entrepreneurs share far more than they do not, and (2) both lead us to the same confusion about justice matters, both are deeply disconnected from the ideology of "equal justice for all", and both fate us to the political agendas of their brand of moral entrepreneuring.

The importance of Hennessey's discourse is apparent in the very first topic of conversation in the Kransky–Hennessey interview: the jail population. When Kransky asks directly about "what kind of people go to jail," and suggests that it is "the rabble," or "drunks and homeless," "petty criminals" and "petty thieves," Hennessey is quick to agree. Hennessey also adds that "40 percent of people in jails are there for drugs," "25 percent are in for a violent crime" and "a smaller percentage for public nuisance." He then invokes the influence of his friend, the late sociologist and convict criminologist John Irwin, who argued that "county jails keep the undesirables out of the view of the public eye." While he finds this claim to be "to some degree true," he emphasizes that jails are "also a place where people who are charged with very serious violent crimes await disposition of their case; society fears violent criminals more, and rightly so." As the interview continues he applauds religion in the jail as it can "get people the values they need to avoid future criminal activity." As I will show, all of this is important.

When the conversation turns to race, the discussion about who is in prison takes a new turn. Hennessey is asked to comment on the fact that while African Americans constitute only 5 percent of the general population, they constitute 55 percent of the jail population. He declares that the imbalance "is one of the most troubling issues that I have had to deal with and had to look at during my entire 32 years as sheriff" and plainly names it "just scandalous" and "a real tragedy." His explanation is that "it comes down to a lot of social factors such as unemployment and unemployment leading to people going to the underground economy to make a living selling drugs" and "many African American families having had generations of people incarcerated and therefore it sort of seems inevitable." He concludes: "It is something that I've brought to the public's attention many times but [it] does not seem to be abating."

When the interview turns to "jail rehabilitation" and "programs," Hennessey declares that "people can change their worldview" and that "people can change," "rehabilitate themselves" and "become productive members of society." As Kransky congratulates him for all his efforts in this area, Hennessey says: "I do think San Francisco is a compassionate city, and will continue to support programs that help ex-offenders get back on their feet." Hennessey also calls for "giving people in custody education," for "getting the riskier population ... counselors and therapists," for helping "these men to first recreate their own life and what has caused them to commit violence." Finally, although Hennessey may see problems in his jails, on the whole he likes them. As he says, "people can also learn while they are in jail and essentially take advantage of the time they have to change their lives for the better."

Hennessey's speech about "what kind of people go to jail" is so familiar that most would be hard pressed to recognize its profound inaccuracies. He identifies the people who go to jail as "criminals," drug addicts and those committing very serious violent "crimes." Yet research tells us otherwise. The first problem is that the complete population of "criminals," drug addicts and those committing very serious violent crimes would include the vast majority of Americans. Research shows that most people habitually violate the law (committing a variety of both non-violent and violent "crimes" in their lifespan, see Gabor 1994), a large proportion of people experiment with or regularly use illegal drugs (more than one-third of all Americans have tried an illicit drug [Office of National Drug Control Policy 1997] and 22.6 million Americans are currently illicit drug users [Substance Abuse and Mental Health Services Administration 2012]) and high numbers of people commit very serious violent crimes (for instance, one out of four college women in the US is sexually assaulted – usually by someone they know personally – and one in six women in the US will be sexually assaulted in their lifetime, see Fisher et al. 2000 and Tjaden and Thoennes 1998).

A second problem with Hennessey's construction of "what kind of people go to jail," and with the accompanying constructions of "crime," "criminals" and "criminal justice," is that he never acknowledges that the majority of economic damage, violent harms and death derive from white-collar "crimes," environmental "crimes" and corporate or state "crimes." By consequence, he fails to recognize that instead of being in his jails, these perpetrators are massively under-policed, rarely counted and infrequently arrested, prosecuted or incarcerated. Research shows that the annual cost of white-collar "crime" is more than 80 times that of the total amount stolen in all thefts (Reiman and Leighton 2010). Similarly, the annual cost of antitrust and trade violations has been reported as more than 60 times that of the total amounts in all thefts (Cullen et al. 1987). Although the sum of a year's worth of robberies, burglaries, larcenies and motor vehicle thefts will represent only a fraction of the cost of a single corporate crime (e.g. Enron), most harms committed by corporations will go as unstudied as they are unprosecuted (in its first and last study of the kind, the Justice Department found that approximately two-thirds of large corporations violated the law, see Clinard and Yeager 1987). Finally, while the annual U.S. murder rate, according to the FBI, is about 16,000 people, more than 70,000 die in the same time period from product-related accidents (Friedrichs 2009); these numbers do not include the thousands of annual deaths connected to corporate pollution, such as the more than 11,000 who die annually from industrial pollution alone (Steingraber 1997).

In more ways than one, as it turns out, the only accurate way to speak about "what kind of people go to jail" is to ask "what kind of people are selected for jail?"

Hennessey's construction – and for that matter the constructions of the other moral entrepreneurs I have already discussed – not only fails to recognize the mythology of "the criminal" but in fact perpetuates it. Hennessey does this when he speaks about the need for religion in jail to "get people the values they need to avoid future criminal activity," for "getting the riskier population ... counselors and therapists," for helping "these men to recreate their own life and what has caused them to commit violence," or the need for "rehabilitation," "giving people in custody education" and "programs" where "people can change," where "people can change their worldview," "rehabilitate themselves" and "become productive members of society." Yet the meaninglessness of his construction in the face of the ubiquity of serious and non-serious "crimes," and the targeting of only some for participation in the "criminal" justice system appear to escape him.

When asked about race and incarceration rates in his jails, Hennessey finds the reality that African Americans constitute only 5 percent of the general population, yet constitute 55 percent of the jail population "just scandalous" and "a real tragedy." But instead of recognizing the selection process, his explanation blames the "victims" (they are "unemployed," "sell drugs," "come from families with incarceration history"). Blind to the selection process (see Coyle 2010b), he sees no opportunity to take responsibility, admits to being confounded by the persistence of imbalanced numbers, concludes that inequity is inevitable and comforts himself by assuring us that he has done his job by "bringing it to the public's attention many times."

The words that Hennessey uses to talk about the people living in his jails and the images that they evoke are all cliché. In Thomas' terms, our society has been extraordinarily consistent in "defining the situation" of "what kind of people go to jail." In social construction terms, this formation has been so successful that moral entrepreneurs on either side of our political spectrum employ the same language. Regardless of politics or agenda, the base construction remains the same: for Ashcroft it is about focusing on "criminals who victimize," for Soros it is about placing the "police off marijuana and on serious crime," for Arpaio about "not coddling criminals," and for Hennessey it is about "the rabble and those charged with very serious violent crimes." While on the face of it these moral entrepreneurs have real differences in terms of the policies and outcomes they pursue, they ultimately share a set of language terms that leads them to think and construct policy in ways that are deeply disconnected from the principles of "equal justice for all," that leads the general public to a deep confusion about justice matters, and fates us all to the politics and agendas of their brand of moral entrepreneuring.

The above analysis of Hennessey's speech demonstrates how attention to language (1) highlights how we select those to be excluded, controlled and punished, (2) shows that we both value justice ideals and accept achieving far less and (3) underscores how our justice-related actions are expressed and hidden in language. In later chapters I will conduct in-depth language studies to demonstrate these arguments further. For now the important point I make is this: in our everyday life, despite evidence to the contrary, the "criminal justice" situation is well defined and the "criminal justice" construction is well in place. As Thomas tells us, these justice situations are the reflection of the influence of moral entrepreneurs, and as Berger and Luckmann tell us, these justice constructions are maintained as "real" because we continue to use them and assume that they are valid and "objectively" true. Thus, we arrive at the inter-subjective, the place where justice meanings are created and used to build the propositions and institutions of justice.

Symbolic interactionism

Language of Justice studies aim to examine justice-related language in the context of everyday life. They do so in order to distinguish a set of justice meanings and to argue that these meanings are embedded in the everyday language we use. Thus, whether "crime" acts are defined as "morally reprehensible choices," as "evil partaking in the metaphysical," or as something else, will be the result of a discursive construction.

For positivists, knowledge is the certainty that phenomena are real and have an existence beyond a subject's agreement. Berger and Luckmann offer another worldview for consideration, namely that the definitions, meanings and institutions of everyday life may seem real outside of an individual's cooperation (objective), but actually they are constructed through ongoing individual (subjective) cooperation. Symbolic interactionists take this insight to develop the intersubjective, where they argue that reality, everyday knowledge and meanings are created between acting persons (Prus 1996). In the interactionist view, social life is based on the interactions of people who attach meaning to behavior, and whose identity and sense of self is itself an interactional product. Thus, propositions about social life ("crime," "deviancy," etc.), are understood to be created from meanings built in human interaction. For interactionists, in the deepest of senses, communication between persons creates social reality. From this vantage, the problems to solve are the roles of individuals in interaction, their reference groups and perspectives, their definitions of situations and selves, and the process through which all these lead to actions, reactions and interpretations.

Symbolic interactionism has become known largely through Herbert Blumer and Erving Goffman. Their work draws on both social psychology and the classical works of Charles Cooley, George Herbert Mead and the philosophy of pragmatism (especially Charles Pearce and William James). At the heart of the interactive–interpretive dimension of Symbolic Interactionism is Mead's concept of the "generalized other" (1934). This central tenet not only launches "The Chicago School" (where symbolic interactionism came to maturity) but also establishes ethnography as the key method of the perspective. Blumer extends the commitment to reflectively taking the role of the other and further distinguishes that individuals act towards objects on the basis of the meanings that they have for them and that these meanings are arrived at through social interactions (1969).

Symbolic interactionists emphasize process and view the individual as a dynamic actor who is in a constant state of becoming, unfolding and changing, simultaneously defining and being defined through interaction (Charon 1979: 30). According to the interactionist view, even an individual's self and mind are the result of interactional processes. However, as one scholar points out:

> The person does not possess a mind so much as a minding process, meaning an ability to converse with self, an ability to pull out stimuli selectively from the environment, assess their significance, interpret the situation, judge the action of others and self, and so on. All of this

means an active, dynamic conversation is taking place within the organism in interaction with others.

(Charon 1979: 30)

Interactionists take from Mead an emphasis on the human capacity to use symbols. Indeed, to this tradition symbols are at the center of the entire perspective, for the individual depends on symbols recognized in interactions with the other to understand self and identity (Cooley 1983). The reverse is also true, for as Charon puts it: "Society makes us, but we, in turn, make society" (1979: 36).

Symbols, which importantly include language, are critical for our perception of reality. Indeed it could be said that one is not possible without the other. While others debate whether there is an objective reality "out there," for symbolic interactionists the important point is that even if a reality "out there" does exist, it can only be interpreted symbolically. As Blumer points out, regardless of whether we accept a tree as "out there," as a symbol, its reality will be entirely different to lumber workers, to poets and to botanists (1969). Howard Becker perfectly demonstrates the power of social definition in his study of marijuana users; he shows that even *the effect of how a drug feels* to a user is a process of social construction and education (1963). Thus, objects (trees) and even experiences (getting high) are defined through interactions.

From this viewpoint, we can see language as a set of symbols, which are open to being defined and used differently. As in the above discussion about reality being "out there," symbols (such as language) for symbolic interactionists are both signs (Charon 1979) and are strictly emergent from interaction (Gergen 1997). However, even if we see language as signs, they can only be understood (interpreted) by actors symbolically within interactions.

Symbolic Interactionism offers a paradigm through which to view language as a set of symbols arrived at through social interaction. To put it another way, meanings are socially arrived at, negotiated and changed. The keyword "socially" points to the fact that meaning in human life derives from the interaction of individuals. Consequently, how any situation is defined (what a situation comes to mean), or how it is constructed (what it will look like) will depend on the shared meanings that interacting individuals give to it.

In *Language of Justice* research I look beyond the customary meanings of words to shed light on the contexts in which they appear. I assert that context is critical because language does not have static meaning (simply being passed on from one generation to the next), but is contextual, process based and continuously redefined. As I will show in Chapters 3, 4, 5 and 6, the meanings of linguistic symbols are constantly shifting – as one would expect given that the content and context of human interactions also change in time.

Symbolic interactionism contributes to *Language of Justice* research the concept that social life and its products are the result of making and interpreting meaning within human interactions. *Language of Justice* research is based on the assumption that justice speech is the result of a complex and ceaseless layering of meaning making and meaning interpreting.

Language of Justice as critical theory

Social constructions are created, maintained and changed within language. However, language is also created, maintained and changed within the parameters of construction. In *Language of Justice* research I argue that through our participation in human interactions (agreement, disagreement, negotiation, etc.) we both impact the meanings and definitions of our language and the language content itself. In such a fashion, justice meanings, words, phrases, etc. are created and used to build propositions, definitions and institutions of justice. Thus, *Language of Justice* research is about identifying the social construction process of justice language. In order to situate this theoretical contribution of my research, in this final section I elucidate how *Language of Justice* research draws on, stands in important difference to and contributes to several important methodological and theoretical approaches to language: content analysis, structuralism, post-structuralism, pragmatics, semiotics, sociolinguistics, critical theory and discourse analysis.

Content analysis

Content analysis (CA) is a technique for systematically studying texts to make educated interpretations of the uses and meanings of both texts and language. Because CA examines recorded communications it is ideally suited to *Language of Justice* studies, in which I examine media articles and interview transcripts to analyze the content of justice speech.

Traditionally, CA has been used to measure the occurrence of words or concepts within a specific text (Holsti 1969 and Krippendorf 2004). Harold Lasswell (1950) is credited with establishing the key questions of content analysis: who says what, to whom, why, to what extent and with what effect? As these questions indicate, CA emerges from communication studies (Berelson 1952 and Pool 1959) and is centrally concerned with both the content of communication and the circumstances that generate and impact communication. Such concerns have made CA a useful tool in the study of media messages (Riffe, Lacy and Fico 2005), human behavior (Gottschalk 1995), speech (Carley 1990) and more.

CA is methodologically useful in *Language of Justice* research because it enables me to track the presence of meanings, the relationships between meanings and the multiple interpretations that exist about how meanings are created for, and delivered to, disparate audiences. As with the collection of any body of data, the textual analysis that emerges in CA is a result of interpretations made and organized under the assumptions of a theoretical framework. In other words, CA draws on prior theoretical commitments in selecting data for analysis; this very selection informs the interpretation the data will receive. Although such theoretical commitments are inherent to all research, they are especially evident in CA, which consciously selects some data and ignores other data. David Robertson calls this a priori commitment the "coding frame" of CA; he argues that the decision of what to look for already begins the coding process (1976). Though I examine this methodological implication more closely in Chapter 3, here it is useful to note that CA's demand for a coding frame reveals the symbolic interactionism and critical criminology theoretical commitments of *Language of Justice* studies.

Differences between CA and *Language of Justice* research are significant. While CA traditionally focuses on the examination of directly mentioned words and explicitly stated concepts, in *Language of Justice* research I focus on relationships between words and underlying ideas: I am in search of assumed connections, indirectly expressed meanings and how all these together construct justice-related meanings and eventually justice recipes. In *Language of Justice* work I explore the relationships of different words/ concepts within a text to discover meaningful relationships. There is an important difference because CA is interested in meanings and their retrieval from in-text relationships, whereas *Language of Justice* studies seek to uncover the meaning relationships that social interaction and moral entrepreneurs have created and the implications they have for the quality of justice we create.

An important difference between CA and *Language of Justice* research is captured precisely in Peter Manning's and Betsy Cullum-Swan's criticism of CA as "unable to capture the *context* within which a written text has meaning" (1998: 272). The criticism is in some ways inappropriate as some CA work has concerned itself with context. For example, narrative content analysis examines narratives in search of the role of "form" in communicating meaning (Jameson 1972), or the role of a "humanistic rationale" in medical patients' narratives about their healing (Mishler 1984). However, the criticism has validity because even narrative content analysis examines context as an element of research, not as the purpose of research. Here is where *Language of Justice* research departs strongly: the very center of my research is to highlight how context is a powerful determinant of justice discourse. In *Language of Justice* research I argue that the very words, distinctions and justice recipes we construct are more frequently than not the result of the contexts in which they are produced and hence it is contexts that we should be looking at. For example, as I have already begun to show, "tough on crime" speech is the product of a justice context and not the result of some arbitrary or undeterminable linguistic choices. Thus, while differences are important, I am interested in CA as a research tool and method for accessing communication content, but more importantly as a framework that provides theoretical propositions to organize my research.

Structuralism and poststructuralism

The problem of agency in relation to structure is one that I have already briefly examined, but is one that requires much deeper analysis. The question whether human actors shape institutions or whether institutions shape actors is deeply important in *Language of Justice* research because language figures centrally in the work of both actors and institutions.

The argument that human behavior is determined by various structures, such as "society," is the basis of structuralism (Levi-Strauss 1969a). According to this view, people are born into a social life that exists independently of them and which significantly determines their behavior. For structuralists, individuals act according to the "institutions," "values" and "culture" of the society in which they live (Levi-Strauss 1963). Therefore, in order to analyze social interactions, a structuralist will look at "social structures" and how they determine behavior.

For a structuralist, meanings are necessarily always produced within a "culture." Levi-Strauss, the founder of structuralism, argues that the human mind has structures that predetermine all practices of social life (Levi-Strauss 1963, 1966 and 1969b). In other words, for a structuralist there is such a thing as a "society," which predates individuals, and not the other way around as an interactionist argues. For a structuralist, for example, language is the product of the grammatical structure of opposites (cold/warm, peace/war, male/female etc.) and a Saussurean system of signs whose logic can be uncovered by studying the biological and social structures that produce it.

A structuralist's fundamental assumption is that all content is determined by structure, and that all meaning is a result of relationships between structures or networks of structures. Structuralists have sought this kind of grammar of structure in everything. Claude Levi-Strauss found it in kinship structures and myths (1963), Jacques Lacan in the unconscious (1968) and Roland Barthes in narratives (1986). Thus, to a structuralist, all phenomena are organized around systems of signs, i.e. they are languages that are given by deep structures. Thus, analysis can be said to be structuralist when an object's meaning is assumed to be dependent on the arrangement of its parts (Descombe 1980).

For structuralists, phenomena are explained in terms of "underlying rules, principles, or conventions that produce surface meanings" (Denzin and Lincoln 1998: 254–55). The focus is toward structure and away from human action. This has been interpreted by some scholars as dehumanizing. As Charles Lemert describes it: "It rejects the 'homocentric' subjectivism and metaphysic of theories such as existentialism and pragmatism: persons are not seen as bundles of sentiments or investigated with reference to inner subjective and cultural meanings" (1979: 944). Indeed, one can see how under this paradigm a person is really

> ... the "speaking object," a user of codes and symbols who selects among pre-reconstituted options, voices, and programs. Structures exist as the organizing centers of social action; persons are in every sense not only the creations of such structures, but manifestations of elements and rules created by social structures.
>
> (Denzin and Lincoln 1998: 255)

For structuralists, the study of texts and speech becomes research on how structures show up in discourse. The study of language is either the study of a sign system or the location to identify what is normally the unobservable social structures that underlie all phenomena. Meaning is produced by persons, not because they arrive here alone, nor because they create them in context or interaction, but because they are guided to meanings by the larger structures and networks of structures. According to structuralists, though meanings can organize experience, meanings are always products of structures and not intentional individuals. Thus, while the practices of social life can produce meanings, the practices themselves are produced by deeper structures that exist within our own minds (Levi-Strauss 1963).

These basic structuralist assumptions are heavily reconsidered in the 1960s and beyond by Michel Foucault and others who begin to suspect that human nature and behavior are too complex to be simply a product of structural forces (1973). The problem that emerges is also a methodological one; namely that despite what structuralism suggests, one cannot so neatly step outside of discourse to "objectively" assess matters. Drawing from the philosophies of Martin Heidegger and Friedrich Nietzsche, and armed with Jacques Derrida's "deconstructive" method, poststructuralists emerge with a new paradigm built on the inherent ambiguity of texts and the impossibility of final or complete interpretations (1976).

Though almost all those labeled as poststructuralists at one point or another deny such membership, we can locate the work of intellectuals working to modify structuralist conclusions. The works of Barthes, Derrida, Foucault, Lacan and Julia Kristeva, alternately posited as postmodernist, reject the foundationalist and essentialist nature of the "structures" of structuralism. These authors also reject enlightenment ideas about human nature as sacred, separate and timeless. Instead, persons are seen as constructed within interaction and, importantly, within discourse. A person is seen as a collection of roles depending on environment, location and time, and is seen as living in different discourses that are produced, reproduced and shifted in interaction (Barthes 1972).

Consequently, poststructuralists emerge with the view that attention to context and discourse is primary, especially over any concern with structure (Barthes 1975). For poststructuralists, language becomes the primary concern as it is no longer simply the product of structure as it was in structuralism, but is now the site where meaning is created and which gives birth to experience (Barthes 1972). Meaning becomes a result of a particular context, a particular discourse or a particular "text" (the word *text* hereon comes to mean a context with a complete set of assumed rules and relationships).

For the poststructuralist, meaning is perceptible only from the angle of a particular text: "objective" and "subjective" in the structuralist sense become an impossibility, and an intersubjective understanding of meaning remains the only thing possible (Derrida 1976). Reading meanings or texts can only occur within the experience of reading meanings or texts together (and by this I mean both multiple texts and multiple readers). My use of "experience" in the previous sentence is problematic for poststructuralists, as it implies the possibility of an objective reality, such as history. The poststructuralist replaces history with "historicity" in order to indicate the tentativeness of meaning agreement, the innate multiplicity of meanings any single text offers and the centrality of the "reader" or interpreter (Foucault 1973). Interpretation always occurs within discourse, because what we know, analyze and conclude is accomplished through discourse and within a text – neither of which we can step out of (Barthes 1975). For poststructuralists, texts are only what they are read as, because reading only occurs within and through discourses that are innumerable even within a single linguistic tradition. Simply put: we cannot step outside of our hermeneutic.

With poststructuralism the "there-ness" of meaning is replaced by the insight that texts have no inherent meanings, only shifting and unstable ones (Lacan 1968). Languages or discourses cannot deliver us to the "True" interpretation because a language or a discourse itself derives its meaning by contrast with other languages and discourses (Derrida 1976). Meanings cannot exist in the logocentric sense of Plato; there is no beauty, truth or right/wrong way, but only beauties, truths and right/wrong ways.

Like structuralism, poststructuralism is a study of how knowledge is produced. Unsurprisingly, poststructuralists advise extreme caution in the interpretation of texts as such acts frequently favor dominant interpretive models, values or influential authors/thinkers, and frequently ignore the marginal (Kristeva 1980). Derrida's deconstructive method is a process that allows us to take apart the ways in which meanings are designed and put into operation (1976). In this fashion poststructuralism draws our attention to the fact that what we usually "see" and "hear" is the dominant discourse (Foucault 2003) and the dominant codes that frame or "educate" us on how to "see" and "hear" other interpretations (Barthes 1975).

In the end, the debate between structuralism and poststructuralism has resulted in shifting our attention in the social and human sciences from "facts" and "data" to the implications of language, discourse and text. While scholars seize the opportunity to rethink various aspects of knowledge and social life, e.g. ontology and epistemology (Tyler 1987), genres (Geertz 1988), the senses (Stoller 1992) and the disappearance of individual speakers into the patterns of discourse (Moerman 1988), in *Language of Justice* research I find that the weightiest implications are elsewhere: what is our justice discourse? What does its deconstruction demonstrate? What does our discourse posit as beautiful justice, true justice and the right/wrong way? What meanings is our justice discourse privileging? What meanings is our justice discourse marginalizing? Which persons do such meanings privilege or marginalize? Who are the agents (moral entrepreneurs) of the dominant discourse? What are the Foucauldian "subjugated knowledges" which are not apparent in our public discourse of justice (Foucault 2003)? In other words, what are the justice knowledges that are confined, given no place or driven underground? What are marginalized agents declaring about justice meanings? Who in our discourse is defined as "fighting for" and "fighting against" justice? How do all these claim to speak for us?

Pragmatics

Scholars interested in pragmatics respond critically to structuralists' assumptions that meanings exist in "objective signs" (such as language), and provide evidence for poststructuralists' criticism that varying contexts introduce varying interpretations (Blakemore 1990 and Cole 1978).

Pragmaticians study how context impacts interpretation. Of relevance to my *Language of Justice* research, pragmaticians explore the myriad effects context can have on the production and consumption of interpretation. They study performative meanings that are created by a speaker's voice fluctuations, hinting techniques or word choices whose combinations express attitudes (Austin 1962 and Searle 1969); implicit or indirect meanings or other determinants of speech such as contributions that keep speech flowing (Grice 1975), politeness (Brown and Levinson 1978) and attempts to accomplish relevancy (Sperber and Wilson 1986); the effects of social distance, social status, social and cultural knowledge (Kasper and Blum-Kulka 1993) and more.

Pragmaticians are also interested in utterances. In pragmatics, an utterance is viewed as an immensely complex act and a powerful way to acknowledge that new meanings are created by "merely" uttering them (Carston 2002). Another way to say this is that much happens beyond "simply saying." For example, where is a speech act made? When is it made? Who is it made by? Whom is it made to? Is there a conscious or an unconscious intention in the speech? Is the speaker or audience related to some but not to other communities? What language is being used or ignored? For the pragmatician, such questions make a simple "utterance" far more complex than for the Saussurean or structural linguist who thinks of signs as independent carriers of abstract and objective meaning.

All these questions are central to *Language of Justice* research. To ask how such questions about justice language relate to justice situations in particular is what my work is about.

Semiotics

Like *Language of Justice* research, semiotics is the study of how meaning is constructed and interpreted. Charles Peirce is credited as a primary influence in semiotics because of his reinterpretation of the Saussurean "linguistic sign" (Chandler 2002). Peirce extended Saussure's definition of linguistic signs to include anything that, for someone, could stand for something, e.g. a thought (Peirce 1960). Thus, semiotics is defined as the study of signs, where "signs" is understood to mean not just linguistic signs, but the kind of signs we refer to when we speak of photographs, sounds, menus, etc. (Eco 1976). As Barthes, one of Semiotics' greatest proponents argues:

> Semiotics aims to take in any system of signs, whatever their substance and limits; images, gestures, musical sounds, objects, and the complex associations of all of these, which form the content of ritual, convention or public entertainment: these constitute, if not *languages*, at least systems of signification.
>
> (Barthes 1964: 67)

Barthes argues that these new complex signs are not independent in the Saussurean sense, but are actually part of larger systems of signification. As Daniel Chandler has argued, the result is that semioticians do not study isolated signs, but systems of signs, or the creation of meanings in entire "texts" (2002).

In the introduction to this work I argued that *Language of Justice* research matters because by studying justice words in their context I can observe and analyze webs of justice meanings that interrelate in complex ways and that have important consequences in the construction of ideas about justice and justice policy. I look at the justice text of modern social life. I have argued, much like a semiotician would, that justice words, metaphors and images are important beyond the word level because actors daily use them to construct, shift and renew the meanings operating in the social and "criminal" justice text of our social life. I gave examples of the complexity of this text in the introduction when I argued that meanings, images and metaphors are combined in intricate ways to create what are best called recipes for achieving justice. In one example I gave, Ashcroft combines the ingredients "criminals who victimize" with "savage," the "public's safety in jeopardy" with "a retreat from justice" and "punishment severity" with "lenient treatment of violent offenders," to construct a recipe for justice that requires "tougher sentencing guidelines" (Serrano 2005).

Semioticians examine texts – not as an opportunity to quantitatively account for sign content – but as locations where meanings above the single word-sign level can be identified. For example, much like I do in *Language of Justice* research, in examining media texts, semioticians look at discourse-level meanings beyond a specific news article (Sturrock 1986). In a way that is reminiscent of the earlier discussion of social construction, semioticians also ask the reader to consider the constructed-ness of meanings and social life (Eco 1984). Semioticians see discourses from a post-structuralist angle, that is, as possessing no "reality" and as the creations of interpreting readers. Through semiotics we come to see that meaning is not part of a simple container–contained metaphor (Lakoff and Johnson 1980), is not something that can be directly transmitted to us, but is something that we create within a network of codes and signs. The word "meaning" is no longer a noun, but a verb signifying action: we are always meaning creatures. As Robert Hodge and Gunther Kress have shown, the promise of semiotics is not just a theory, but a method that will take us beyond the study of single instances of communication, and into the systematic and comprehensive study of communications phenomena as they arise in a complete environment (1988). My aim in *Language of Justice* research is similarly to read the justice text of our social life and to expose the environment of our communication phenomena regarding justice. I do this by conducting studies on what semioticians understand as the complex signage of our social life.

Chandler clearly demonstrates that semiotics converges on the argument that all sign work is actually ideology work (2002). As he points out, we only know signs through the mediation of other signs, and all signs are related to their signifieds by conventions produced in social interaction. These conventions become familiar to the extent that we begin to view them as "natural," "obvious" and "true." Once we forget their constructed nature and come to see them as unmediated and transparent, we use them to build what can only be an illusion of an "objective reality" (Chandler 2002). We further view this reality as something that is communicable again and again outside of the inherently constructed nature of signs – an implausible proposition. For semioticians, this view is immensely problematic as it conceals the presence of ideology. As Burgin argues, an ideology is the sum total of the perceived objective, real and taken-for-granted meanings (1982). Another way of saying this is that in defining realities, signs inherently attend to ideological functions.

Semioticians remind us that although things may exist outside of signs, we can only know them through the signs that mediate them (Chandler 2002). Indeed, if signs are constructions, the idea of a neutral set of signs is impossible. Where there is a sign, there is an ideology (Voloshinov 1973). The unavoidable semiotic conclusion is that where there is thought or speech (in other words, where there is text or discourse), there is ideology. Despite the apparent "reality" of media presentations, these presentations are fictions – not in the sense of lies or misrepresentations – but rather as constructions and ideology. Although sign systems take on the appearance of "the ways things are," or appear to be free of ideological commitments, it is not possible for there to be an ideologically neutral sign system (Chandler 2002).

This semiotic argument is critical to *Language of Justice* research that seeks to read moral entrepreneurs as actors who intentionally and unintentionally present ideology as "naturalized signs" (Culler 1985). In this sense, what I claimed at the beginning of this work is now apparent: *Language of Justice* work is not about locating better or preferred justice speech (progressive, conservative, etc.), but is about locating all justice speech as (1) a text that is never neutral, objective or real, and as (2) organized around an ideology. While I may interpret that our justice language is committed to an ideology of social control and punishment, this interpretation should not obscure the main point: while it appears that daily our justice discourse takes place in an ideologically neutral sign system, this is patently false. In *Language of Justice* work I want to "denaturalize" justice speech, justice texts, and the justice sign system of our everyday life.

Semioticians demonstrate that discourse analysis will always be the analysis of ideology. This is so because if signs do not so much represent reality as construct it, then whoever controls the sign systems will control the social construction of reality (Chandler 2002). Semioticians like Barthes, Baudrillard, Foucault and Eco teach us that (1) life is experienced and communicated inside of sign systems, and that (2) it is only through learning how to read sign systems that we can denaturalize them and what they present. In *Language of Justice* work, these sign systems would be the "facts" of the social and "criminal" justice system: "crime," "criminals," "victims," etc.

I want to argue through *Language of Justice* research that we cannot assess the justice we produce or fail to produce in our social life without first coming to terms with the assumptions, costs and consequences of our ideology. Similarly, we must assess who are the dominating/dominated, or the privileged/suppressed within the ideology created by our justice signs, sign systems, discourses and texts.

Sociolinguistics

The *Language of Justice* focus on how language, as a social activity (e.g. the public activities of moral entrepreneurs), impacts the social construction of reality and the individual experiences of those involved with the "criminal" justice system, brings me to the study of sociolinguistics.

Sociolinguistics, as the term indicates, is both the study of language in the contexts of social life and the study of social life in the contexts of language (Coupland and Jaworski 1997). Defined in this way sociolinguistics is a vast interdisciplinary field centered on language as social behavior. William Labov is often described as the grandparent of this discipline. His studies launched the field, albeit in a methodologically quantitative direction from which many sociolinguists have since departed from (Labov 1972a, 1972b, 1994 and 2001). As the study of language in social life, sociolinguistics examines language in the external world, and can thus be differentiated from studies of language in the abstract (Wardhaugh 1992).

Sociolinguists consider a vast territory, including the variety of dialects across a geographical region, the variety of cultural communities that use a particular dialect or the plethora of "speech communities" (Labov 1972a). A speech community describes a group of persons who tend to use a particular language in a way that is unique to them (Wardhaugh 1992). We are familiar with such groups developing special languages in our daily life, as in the slang of a particular family or the jargon of a profession. Similarly, we are familiar with "discourse communities," that is, language patterns that a person owns by virtue of participating in a community. In *Language of Justice* research I am interested in identifying the varying discourse communities of moral entrepreneurs as a method for tracing and exposing their influence on the public discourse of social and "criminal" justice.

Sociolinguists who are interested in speech communities and discourse communities ask a series of questions that are of profound importance to *Language of Justice* research: what variety of speech communities is there for moral entrepreneurs involved in our public discourse on justice? Which discourse communities are privileged and which are suppressed in public justice discourse? What networks of social power do various justice speech communities give rise to, and who benefits or loses from their presence?

Sociolinguists are also deeply interested in the issue of context in language, including contexts of geography, class, race/ethnicity, gender, age, religion and the like (Labov 1972a). For example, sociolinguists' studies of gender demonstrate that a "women's register" maintains women in an inferior role in social life (Lakoff 1975), indicates a power difference between men and women (McConnell-Ginet and Borker 1980), demon-strates gender differences in communication styles (Tannen 1991) and is tied to a host of gender differentiations: turn-taking, change of conversation topic, verbal aggression and many more (Trudgill 1995). In *Language of Justice* research I have all these concerns about justice discourse.

Finally, sociolinguists study the way language is used in social life. Much like them, in *Language of Justice* research I am interested in the ethnography of language, especially that of justice language. I work to discern the perspective and claimed values of our justice discourse, but unlike sociolinguists I am not interested in explaining either behavior or social organization. I am, however, interested in discerning the process of social control, i.e. the process of dominating and subjugating others by virtue of how our discourse promotes certain definitions of justice and injustice over others.

Critical theory

Critical theory draws its origins from Marxist scholars working in the intellectual tradition known as the Frankfurt School. Max Horkheimer, the grandparent of critical theory, distinguished it from other theories by its purpose: to liberate people from the situations that enslave them (1993). Critical theory reflects a continuation of the Enlightenment project and an effort to rescue it from the hegemony of the modern state, from the inequities produced by capitalism and globalism, and from any and all forms of expression in social life that dominate or subjugate others (Held 1980). Horkheimer's idea of a "critical theory" (1993) organizes the perspective of many theorists and paradigms unsympathetic to social organization that limits individual liberty. In time, critical theory has become an umbrella term through which we see scholars critiquing subjugation (e.g. the works of Pierre Bourdieu and Michel Foucault). It is also an umbrella term through which we see modes of social inquiry as critical theories centered on critiquing domination, e.g. feminism, postcolonialism and cultural studies (Kellner 1989).

As the term suggests, critical theory begins with the assumption that there is a critique of a liberating sort to proffer. Implicit in critical theory is the assumption that there is an action to be taken (Ingram 1990). Critical theorists see their work as producing critiques that increase human freedom (Habermas 1979). For example, feminist theory is a critical theory as it seeks to liberate women from sexist oppression.

Critical theories begin by asking what thwarts the realization of ideals, such as gender equality. In critical theory work, the obvious quickly becomes a site for discovery. As discussed above, what appears to be "obviously apparent" in social life is, more frequently than not, expressing a dominant view, which in turn subjugates other views or knowledges. For example, as a critical theory of gender, feminism argues that women's ways of knowing, speaking and being have been subjugated. Critical theories work to disclose the processes through which such subjugation occurs, whether they be intellectual, emotional, historical, spatial, political or within personal relationships, behavior or situations and events, or other (Held 1980).

As deconstructive work, critical theory is intimately related to ideas of social construction, and to the constructive processes of social interaction and communication. William James famously pointed out that in the everyday we rarely worry about how all our theories (about how things work in social life) fit together (1975). Critical theorists add that we also fail to consider whether our various theories are critical or not, i.e. whether the judgments we have come to hold as part of our cognitive maps sustain an equitable and just world or not (Ingram 1990).

Cultural studies is a critical theory that applies poststructuralist tools to analyze politically charged representations. The term "cultural studies" was coined by Stuart Hall (1980 and 1992) to indicate a scholarship that asks which representations are deemed to be significant in social life and what their historical and political legacies are (Grossberg et al. 1992). For example, researchers in this tradition assess film, fashion and what we call popular culture to ask how these endeavors create, reproduce or shift the ownership of economic or social capital, how they privilege differing socioeconomic classes, how they subjugate differing groups by race/ethnicity or gender, and the like (During 2003).

My *Language of Justice* research is a critical theory of justice in social life. In this work I argue that analysis of our justice language demonstrates that our social control practices are used in order to subjugate and dominate particular chosen others. Insofar as I argue that our constructions of justice have privileged some and suppressed others, like critical theory, my research offers a critique in the service of liberation. In *Language of Justice* research I also look at that which our language presents as "obviously apparent" about justice in our social life. By examining our justice discourse I unpack the "obvious" justice meanings within which we operate. I show their constructed nature and demonstrate that they are not outside of ideology or authorship. I look at how prevailing justice phrases like "tough on crime" demonstrate the dominant linguistic, cognitive and organizational distinctions used to define social and "criminal" justice in everyday life. I highlight how our language exposes the social construction of certain people as "evil," others as "innocent victims" and still others as "criminals" in ways that (1) privilege some and subjugate others along lines of class, race/ethnicity, gender and other, and that consequently (2) do not match our stated value commitment of "equal justice for all."

Discourse analysis

Discourse analysis is commonly defined as analysis of language above the sentence level (Johnstone 2002). Scholars in this field are interested in "reading" texts or written communication as units in order to comment on what they can teach us about social contexts (Brown 1998). As a critical theory, discourse analysis explores how language is used in social situation "performances" to display social identity, social struggle, power and more (Schiffrin, Tannen and Hamilton 2001). Though the work of discourse analysis researchers is intimately related to that of researchers in sociolinguistics, semiotics, pragmatics and others working in a variety of critical theories examining or using language, discourse analysis scholars differ in how they closely examine entire linguistic narratives, including as texts or political debates (Johnstone 2002). Frequently, scholars perform such analysis to gain knowledge about rhetoric, about conversation dynamics or to study the ethnography of communication (Brown 1998).

Discourse analysis researchers seek to problematize more than to solve. For example, in examining a text a researcher might locate a series of assumptions, motivations or arguments that were not necessarily evident or obvious (Gee 2005). The process is intimately related to Derrida's deconstructive method (1976). Much like deconstruction, discourse analysis is not so much a set of theoretical propositions about the world as it is a way of looking at the world that promises to show whether things a researcher is interested in finding are actually there or not (Gee 2005).

As a tool that excels in locating problems, researchers use discourse analysis to study what we have seen is poststructuralists' favorite target: the seemingly obvious. Thus, scholars examine texts for hidden meanings in locations that would seem most impervious, such as political speeches (Jorgensen and Phillips 2002). Researchers have also examined verbal interactions in judicial settings (Atkinson and Drew 1979), law school texts (Mertz 1996), urban African-American peer speech (Goodwin 1990), medical discourse (Foucault 1975), institutional conversations (Heritage 1998 and Baynham and Slembrouck 1999) and much more. Such research is done to uncover privilege, expressions of political power and the like.

Ultimately, discourse analysis is a tool for dismantling discourses, and for exposing what lies behind the curtain. I do not mean to suggest that researchers using discourse analysis purport to discover "reality." Most discourse analysis scholars are poststructuralists resigned to the impossibility of a single reading or a single reality, and are committed to the existence of multiple discourses or multiple realities. Rather, I use the expression "behind the curtain," to point to scholars' desire to locate assumptions, intentions and problems in what they study.

Discourse analysis points to the ways in which in *Language of Justice* research I look to see behind the curtain of our language discourse. I do not seek "final" or "real" meanings about justice, nor do I attempt to offer foundationalist interpretations of our justice discourse. My aim is to encounter the "obvious" terrain of our social and "criminal" justice discourse and by examining some of the most common justice words, metaphors and phrasing that we employ, to enquire about the justice results we claim to achieve.

Critical discourse analysis (CDA), which emerges from discourse analysis, is defined by a body of researchers who assume an explicit sociopolitical analysis with a focus on dominance as produced by institutions and elite groups (van Dijk 1993). CDA scholars study discourse to locate the role of power and ideology in the contexts of gender (Lazar 2005), social change (Fairclough 1992), elite discourse (van Dijk 1994), education (Rogers 2003), class (Slembrouck 2005) and more. They also work to establish that discourses are tightly controlled by institutions, i.e. that language is itself a location of struggle (Fairclough and Chouliaraki 1999).

Much like CDA researchers, in *Language of Justice* research I am interested in locating the impact of power and ideology on justice discourse.

My work, like CDA scholarship, examines texts in order to discover how our justice discourse is textually reproduced, institutionally controlled and dominated by moral entrepreneurs with varying agendas. In other words, as a CDA researcher, I aim to study language as a site of struggle for the accomplishment of justice.

Conclusion

Empirical investigations do not take place in a theoretical void. Theoretical commitments are inherent in all research and take place early in the research process. Long before researchers consider a body of data about the world they have made up their mind in various ways about what the world is like and consequently what is worth observing. In this chapter I hope to have clarified my working assumptions about the world and how it operates, so that my later assessments of data are seen to be driven by that which they are indeed driven.

My purposes in this chapter were dual. The first was to define the conceptual background and theoretical basis for *Language of Justice* research and to place my work within the social sciences. The second was to use the conceptual background along with an analysis of the speech of two moral entrepreneurs to demonstrate the logic and arguments of *Language of Justice* work. In the next chapter I will analyze the work of scholars who have closely considered justice language in a variety of ways to identify how my efforts relate to and differ from theirs, as well as to further elucidate *Language of Justice* research.

2   A history of *Language of Justice* research

Introduction

In this chapter I situate *Language of Justice* research in relation to previous studies of justice language. My major goal is to highlight how *Language of Justice* work differs from and adds to previous scholarship.

In this chapter I explore other scholars' justice language research to identify seven things. First, what issues in justice language they focus on. Second, what lines of reasoning (paradigms) they use to approach their data. Third, what theory they use to interpret their data. Fourth, what methodology they use to study their data. Fifth, what theoretical and substantive conclusions they reach. Sixth, how their work differs from my *Language of Justice* research, and seventh, what their work contributes to how I think about and do my justice language research.

I organize the presentation of previous literature first by introducing the study of language as part of social life. I then move on to work that has looked at language critically and work that has looked at language as part of broader discourses. Next, I present how scholars contributing to justice studies have used the idea of justice discourse as a way to make arguments about the social and "criminal" justice we do and do not achieve. Finally, I present the research that has come closest to my *Language of Justice* work, that is scholarship which examines justice words to ask critical questions about modern social and "criminal" justice discourse.

Language and everyday life

The study of language has become so advanced that no discipline can be uncritical of the language it employs. In any modern intellectual enterprise, to take language for granted, as representational, or to proceed as if it plays anything less than a dominant role, is no longer possible. In this section I look at how the study of language has developed into a critical examination of social life, and more specifically, how learning to "read" language has become a domain of great importance to scholars in justice studies.

Although the study of language is an ancient preoccupation, the modern formal study of it is commonly traced to Ferdinand de Saussure (Cobley and Jansz 1998). While advanced knowledge of linguistic theory is not essential for critical language studies, Saussure contributes several distinctions that are helpful in conceptualizing *Language of Justice* studies.

Saussure distinguishes two aspects of language: parole and langue (2006). He defines parole as an individual act of speech, and langue as a common storehouse of signs that can be used in any single construct of parole (speech). The notions of speech acts and a storehouse of language are useful to *Language of Justice* research in a particular way. As my data studies show (Chapters 3, 4, 5 and 6), my research is deeply concerned with how individual speech acts are created, propagated and deposited in a storehouse of language that then enables and encourages their ongoing use.

Saussure's notion of a "pool" of language has come to be seen in linguistics as the product of an abstract, oversimplified and positivist interpretation of language (Cobley and Jansz 1998). Scholars in the second half of the twentieth century have generated a far more complex view of language, especially in terms of the role of structure and agency. However, Saussure remains important not just for instigating the modern study of language, but also for inspiring the empirical investigation of the life of signs (language) in social life.

One of the first to take on Saussure's call to study language in social life is Louis Hjelmslev. He proposed that study of language ought to focus on how (1) signs cannot be interpreted independently of context, and (2) language is created and shifted in the context of social life (Hjelmslev 1961). My purpose in *Language of Justice* work is to investigate those justice speech acts that are being used in our social life, and used widely enough to dominate the storehouse of language (langue) that we choose from when we discuss matters of social and "criminal" justice. I am interested in the justice language choices (signs, speech acts, etc.) made by moral entrepreneurs because they create, sustain and shift the dominant everyday justice discourse (as well as alternative justice discourses).

In *Language of Justice* research I study language both in a historical sense (diachronic linguistics, which points to change over time within a language) and as a snapshot of a given point in time (synchronic linguistics). My interest in diachronic linguistics leads me to trace (1) how the phrase "victim" or "tough on crime" has been used differently in time, (2) how various meanings of a word develop ("innocent victim" or "smart on crime"), (3) how definitional shifts of "victim" or "tough on crime" occur and (4) how such shifts impact the larger social and "criminal" justice discourse. My concerns are also deeply synchronic as I investigate current justice language to interpret contemporary justice discourse as a whole.

Thinking critically about language

Language of Justice studies build on the Sapir-Whorf hypothesis, which posits that language influences perception (Sapir 1921 and Whorf 1956).

The meaning of this theory is that language embodies theories of reality, i.e. that merely by using the language we do, we determine whatever we seek to describe. Whorf compares English and Hopi languages and shows that the language of either is incapable of conveying the world and reality of the other (Whorf 1956). In other words, he finds that for an English speaker, Hopi worldview can be properly grasped only by understanding how Hopi language defines the parameters of Hopi thought and reality. According to Whorf, the very language we use determines how we think.

Scholars in linguistics hotly debate the Sapir-Whorf hypothesis, especially along the lines of structure versus agency: these theorists explore whether language origins and usage are determined by structural linguistic programming mechanisms (Chomsky 1975) or agents (Sapir 1921 and Whorf 1956). In my *Language of Justice* research I assume the second is necessarily true because I interpret moral entrepreneurs who actively attempt and frequently succeed in impacting justice discourse – and through this social and individual life. However, I also assume the first because I interpret that language used and promoted by moral entrepreneurs becomes structurally hegemonic and colonizes justice discourse, which can make the success of opposing moral entrepreneuring difficult or unlikely. As my concerns in the rest of this chapter show, I am interested in the role of both agency and structure in the play of language in social life.

Ironically, the most compelling argument for centering both agency and structure in the immediacy of justice language comes not from a linguist, but from a journalist, George Orwell. In his fiction and essays, Orwell has made a deep impact on the study of language (Bosmajian 1983). In his essay "Politics and the English Language" Orwell argues that language is a powerful tool frequently used (and abused) by powerful moral entrepreneurs (2000). Orwell is especially interested in political moral entrepreneurs, and his analysis of their language demonstrates how the public is deceived with clever uses of metaphor, filler language, pretentious diction and meaningless words (see the Orwell epigraph to this book). He argues that political language is highly obfuscating and that it is created and promoted by moral entrepreneurs ("big brother") to dominate public discourse with their agendas. As examples consider the "war is peace" language of his *1984* novel, or the "all animals are equal, but some animals are more equal than others" language of his *Animal Farm* novel (Orwell 1981 and 1946).

In *Language of Justice* research, I follow Orwell's lead to argue that moral entrepreneurs frequently develop language in order to promote a discourse of social control about social and "criminal" justice matters. I argue that such language enters our pool of language and, with use and reuse comes to dominate and suppress other languages or discourses of justice.

Orwell's body of work on language and social life has impacted many scholars, some of whom see their work as an extension of his. For example, in *Language and Control*, Roger Fowler and his co-authors write:

Orwell's … work, predominantly *1984*, is a monument to a number of definitive premises about language and society. He saw clearly that the social structure acts on every aspect of personal behavior, affecting active and passive linguistic experience … In all these beliefs Orwell seems to us to have been essentially correct. Such things need saying now as much as they did when he wrote.

(Fowler et al. 1979: 24)

Fowler and his co-authors convincingly argue that given how people belong to different social groups that use different varieties of language, discourse is inseparable from social and economic factors (1979). Consider, for example, how non-incarcerated persons speak of "jails" and "prisons," while incarcerated persons speak of "the can," "the frying pan" and "the butcher's shop." The first are detached, neutral descriptions of institutional buildings. The second viscerally convey an experience of dehumanized horror. These authors, who embrace the Sapir-Whorf hypothesis about language and social reality, consider a variety of case studies (texts) to demonstrate the connection between language and ideology, e.g. rules of behavior as found at a public swimming pool and at a university, the interview language of a middle manager, the disparate coverage of identical social issues in different media, and legal documents that register births and birth notices (Fowler et al. 1979).

Fowler and his co-authors use these case studies to demonstrate that certain varieties of language and discourses, e.g. the managerial or the legal, have a greater impact on social life than others. As they describe it, "[d]ifferent forms of language should not be regarded as cognitively equivalent. They are not 'merely stylistic' in effect, but affect the potential expression of concepts, and thus the availability of concepts, too" (Fowler et al. 1979: 195). The authors go on to argue that power in social life and power in language are significantly connected; they further qualify that an important relationship exists between powerful or dominant discourses and social inequalities. As they point out, "[l]anguage not only encodes power differences but it is also instrumental in enforcing them" (Fowler et al. 1979: 195).

The role of dominant discourse that Fowler and his co-authors argue for is taken up by Frank Burton and Pat Carlen in a study of "Official Discourse" (1977). These authors analyze two English government reports: one on a debate about the wrongful imprisonment of two men and another on complaints about police response to 1969 events in Northern Ireland. Burton and Carlen find that, although the reports are issued to address an audience challenging the legitimacy of the issuing agency, for a broader audience, the reports succeed in legitimating government actions. Burton and Carlen's arguments about politics and legitimacy are less relevant to my *Language of Justice* research. More to the point is their observation that moral entrepreneurs in powerful bureaucracies deliberately attempt to define situations for a group and frequently succeed in creating dominant discourses. In this example, the documents reflect a politician's statements used as discourse to build legitimacy. As the power of the state is significant, the implications of this argument are clear: some discourses have greater impact on social life as they are owned and propagated by parties with disproportionate power to owners of other discourses on the same topic. Burton and Carlen demonstrate that "official discourse" is a dominant discourse.

Adrian Blackledge and Aneta Pavlenko point out how language ideologies are produced and reproduced in multilingual contexts (2001). These editors amass a body of papers that demonstrate how language ideologies take form and dominance in discourse processes occurring at both micro and macro levels that "come into being in the context of power relations at local, national, state and global levels" (Blackledge and Pavlenko 2001: 243). Yet another example is Justin Evans' study of the hurdles indigenous peoples face in Australian courts (2002). As he says, "[i]n the case that the social and economic problems can be overcome, they face problems related to the intellectual structures of the court and the language and philosophical beliefs that the court systems are based on" (Evans 2002: 127). Evans is pointing to how the dominance of Australian (Euro-centric) justice discourse in the courts makes it difficult if not impossible for a non-European people to get anything resembling meaningful legal justice. In the US, the debate about the constitutionality of peyote use between federal courts and some Native-American communities is a similar issue (Pohlman 2004). The dominant justice discourse, whether in Australia or the US, prevents indigenous people from reaching the possibility of a just solution in debates they enter, as the social and "criminal" justice system they encounter is constructed on the ontology and epistemology of the Australians and Americans. Their justice discourse differs, and because it is subordinate it is suppressed.

Fowler and his co-authors argue that the use of language in social life perpetuates the dominant discourse. As they write:

> The structure of discourse of texts reflects and expresses the purposes and roles of its participants, these in turn being products of the prevailing forms of economic and social organization. But communication (thus language) is not just a *reflex* of social processes and structures. In the expression of these processes and structures they are affirmed, and so contribute instrumentally to the consolidation of existing social structures and material conditions.
>
> (Fowler et al. 1979: 195–96)

In other words, prevailing discourse is always oppressive discourse. Their solution for this problem is to call for a critical linguistics – or the study of dominant language and discourse – to unmask hegemony, colonization and suppression. Critical linguistics becomes the authors' call to interpret texts as a means of making explicit what power and habit have made implicit: the social inequality hidden in everyday language. The call for a critical linguistics by Fowler and his co-authors is illuminated by Foucault's argument that the powerful have the ability to dominate and control discourses (Crampton and Elden 2007), and by David Mumby's argument that narratives develop their meanings within specific social contexts that, simultaneously, help to construct that very context (1993).

Fowler, his co-authors and Burton and Carlen, as well as the others who follow such reasoning, are deeply related in theory and substance to *Language of Justice* research. Like these authors, I begin from the hypothesis that language impacts reality (justice language impacts what and how we think about and do justice) and like them I hold a critical sense of language (power and domination over others is inherent to justice language and justice discourse). Like these authors, I argue that some varieties of justice language have greater impact than others on what becomes the justice discourse of our social life. Specifically, I argue that control language, commonly propagated by moral entrepreneurs, dominates other justice language options and comes to define our social and "criminal" justice discourse. Moral entrepreneurs by definition have the power not only to encode their language in discourse but also to replicate the language and enforce its content. Like these authors, in *Language of Justice* research I argue that not all justice language is equivalent, and that differences are not merely stylistic. In fact, differences in justice language determine justice discourse parameters, i.e. determine the potential expression of justice concepts and thus the availability of justice concepts for debates about social and "criminal" justice. Thus, we arrive at how one form of language (control language) has greater impact and dominates social and "criminal" justice discourse.

There is, however, a fundamental difference between my project and the one of Fowler et al. and the others discussed here. These authors look at language to argue that in any number of environments one can observe how a single kind of discourse can control other alternative discourses. I look at language to argue that in the environment of our social and "criminal" justice system, a control language dominates our discourse that is additionally produced, reproduced and shifted by moral entrepreneurs. As these authors identify, not all forms of language share equal opportunity in public space, and consequently not all forms of language are equally available for public consumption and debate. Fowler and his co-authors present how moral entrepreneurs actually work: as their justice concepts come to dominate the available set of justice concepts, other concepts remain largely unknown or disappear without ever being widely heard. For example, the debate about prisons in the US ranges from a conservative discourse (build more of them) to a progressive one (stop the building and create reform programs). Widely unheard are calls to close prisons on a massive scale or to use entirely different paradigms for facing issues of social and "criminal" justice and injustice. Given that prisons disproportionately warehouse minorities, the poor and the undereducated, moral entrepreneurs of our public justice discourse, wittingly or not, create, maintain and perpetuate a social reality defined by immense inequality.

Other researchers are responding to the call by Fowler and his co-authors for a critical linguistics (1979). Paul Chilton's study, *Language and the Nuclear Arms Debate: Nukespeak Today* is one example (1985). Faithful to Fowler and his co-authors, Chilton looks at news magazines, television and films, and asks what kinds of ideologies are created and maintained through "nukespeak" language and what class or group of persons is served by the ideology found to dominate nuclear arms discourse. Similarly, I argue that *Language of Justice* research is a critical linguistics. I look at dominant justice language to make a point about our dominant justice discourse: that it operates hegemonically, that it colonizes and suppresses other justice language and alternative justice discourse, and that it perpetuates social control formats and frames.

Language as discourse

In this section I demonstrate how scholars have used the idea of language choices as building a discourse. Specifically, I show how they deconstruct discourse in order to make important arguments about their fields, for example in political science, in economics, environmental studies, social work and feminist studies. Along the way I will show how their labors relate to the work I do to deconstruct our social and "criminal" justice discourse.

George Lakoff and Frank Luntz, two researchers of political discourse, represent two sides of the same coin. The first seeks to educate liberals how to construct public discourse to their political advantage, while the second attempts exactly the same, only with conservatives. In his aptly subtitled, *Don't Think of an Elephant!: Know Your Values and Frame The Debate*, Lakoff details a path for progressives to win American minds: that of using language choices to build a discourse that will frame political debates to their advantage (2004). He recommends that liberals construct their own key language terms (e.g. countering the conservative military budget calls for a "strong defense" with a call for investment diversity for "a stronger America"), and build other discourse control mechanisms (such as promoting values over programs). Luntz's equally Machiavellian title, *Words that Work: It's Not What You Say, It's What People Hear*, argues for the use of language that will control public discourse for conservatives' advantage (2007). For example, he recommends using "personalization" instead of "privatization," "death tax" instead of "estate tax," and to avoid the word "outsourcing," by explaining job losses as "caused by taxation and regulation." Both Lakoff and Luntz acknowledge that clever language choice is more effective than rational argument and propagate controlling discourse through language control.

Just how far the intentional use and abuse of political discourse can carry motivated parties is demonstrated by Victor Klemperer in his work, *The Language of the Third Reich* (2006). Klemperer details how the Nazi party in the Second World War used language as a political tool to hide their motives and intentions. He cites, for example, their use of "special treatment" for murder and "final solution" for genocide. Klemperer shows how with the right language, perpetrators can construct a national discourse that abstracts mass murder and renders even the most violent political ideology and public policy rational and palatable.

In *Language of Justice* work, taking the lead from Lakoff, Luntz and Klemperer, I argue that our modern social and "criminal" justice discourse is constituted by both intentional and habitual language efforts to shape discourse and frame debates. While as yet no "take control of the discourse" books have been written for opposing viewpoints in the social and "criminal" justice debates, this hardly means that moral entrepreneuring, language construction/destruction, and strong efforts to control the discourse are not occurring. Reading and interpreting such language and discourse manipulations is the work of *Language of Justice*.

The use of language strategies to control political discourse is also the focus of Samuel Obeng's work, "Language and Politics: indirectness in political discourse" (1997). Obeng highlights how politicians use conversational strategies, such as indirectness, to avoid politically risky topics. Like I do, Obeng demonstrates how moral entrepreneurs use linguistic strategies to achieve goals, gain advantage, deceive, hide and misdirect.

In *Economics as Discourse: an analysis of the language of economics*, Warren Samuels examines the language of economics in much the same way I do the language of justice: with an eye for interpretation, rhetoric, metaphor and ultimately ideology (1990). In his introduction to this edited collection of essays, Samuels argues that phrases thought to be ironclad in economics, such as "economic data" or "economic reality," are empty without the commitments to an array of paradigm-specific assumptions that systematically go unacknowledged and are instead accepted as self-evident. My purpose in *Language of Justice* research is remarkably similar to Samuels' work. Like him, I argue that our justice discourse includes linguistic categories ("tough on crime," "criminals," etc.) that are void of meaning unless an entire paradigm of assumptions, interpretations and ideology are accepted about human nature, human action and the meaning of social and "criminal" justice. Like Samuels, I argue that our everyday justice discourse takes place within a body of interpretations, rhetoric, metaphors and ultimately ideology that are rarely acknowledged and are instead accepted as self-evident. In my research I also go further to explore how justice language choices connect to social control, permit political action (such as suppressing others with imprisonment) and relate to the work of moral entrepreneurs.

The power of deconstructing discourse is demonstrated by Karen Powers Stubbs in *The Nature of Language: Rhetorics of Environmental (In)justice* (2000). She examines how rhetorical, political and other overlapping discourses construct ideas about "nature" and "environment." Powers Stubbs uses her analysis to disrupt what she finds in her discipline to be a disturbing trend to see our environmental past as occurring within a seamless and homogeneous discourse. Specifically, she outlines non-dominant narratives about the "environment," such as that of women and people of color, to show that they have neither been heard nor reflected in our collective discourse. Much like Powers Stubbs, in *Language of Justice* research I work to disrupt what I find is the disturbing trend in our justice discourse to uncritically accept a supposedly seamless and homogeneous language that defines social and "criminal" justice as the domain of social control: "criminals" are "offenders" to be "treated tough" by being "imprisoned." The dominance of this language supports a discourse that ignores or suppresses non-dominant narratives such as those of critical criminologies.

In their study, *Language and the Shaping of Social Work*, the change in disciplinary discourse is taken up by Marilyn Gregory and Margaret Holloway (2005). They analyze social work education texts used in the UK between the 1950s and the 1990s to distinguish shifts in the dominant discourse of social work identity. They conclude that over time language has reflected and determined the direction of social work's identity alternately as a moral enterprise, as a therapeutic enterprise and as a managerial enterprise. The authors trace socio-politico-economic contours in larger social life as providing a framework for the changing discourses: the moral mode is abandoned for a clinical mode as a result of post-Second World War optimism, which is then abandoned for the managerial mode in the face of growing pessimism regarding clinical successes. Similar findings on social workers' use of the language of social justice were published in the same journal four years earlier (Hawkins et al. 2001). Linette Hawkins and her co-authors examine social workers' interview transcripts to find that not only is social justice terminology absent in discussions of their work, but also that the preference for a language that is clinical and professional expresses ambivalence about social justice and social action. As the authors conclude: "Individuals, their families (and less commonly, their situations) are 'interviewed,' 'assessed,' 'treated' and 'intervened in/with' using a variety of 'strategies.' Social workers' language use appears to be quite incongruent with our stated mission of social justice" (Hawkins et al. 2001: 10). Much like Hawkins et al., Gregory and Holloway find that the language currently dominating social work is not the language of social justice, but rather is oriented to the language of punishment, risk-behavior management and consumerism.

Like these social work scholars, I examine documents and interview transcripts to interpret discourse. While Gregory and Holloway are interested in historical periods and linguistic shifts, in *Language of Justice* studies I mostly follow synchronic uses of justice language, although I also consider how phrases such as "tough on crime" have changed in meaning over time. Much as I argue in Chapter 1 about justice, Gregory and Holloway conclude that social work is a socially constructed activity that is both created and replicated in a process of language use. These scholars discuss the construction of their discipline by pointing to a wider context within which and out of which their discourse develops. This is an important point of difference because in my work I argue that justice discourse is at least in part the result of powerful moral entrepreneurs who both intentionally language justice discourse and habitually replicate the dominant justice discourse already in place. Finally, it is worth noting that these scholars all conclude that their discipline of social work, self-defined as a social justice enterprise, is currently deeply entrenched in the language of assessment and control.

The relationship of discourse to disciplinary concerns is also studied by Margaret Beetham, a scholar of women's studies (2002). Beetham acknowledges class and gender differences between various justice discourses but seeks to hold on to "the dream of a common language" (2002: 175). On the one hand, Beetham claims a desire to follow Donna Haraway's call for a "feminist infidel heteroglossia" (a direct challenge to the "imperialist" desire for a common language). On the other hand, she expresses a desire to hold on to the promise of dialogue and translation. As she says, "I return to the utopian idea of the just society and the dream of a common language aware of these critical debates ... If we want a future just society we need ... to address ... crucial questions of language and of translation" because "the problem of how to speak to each other and therefore the problem of translation is at the heart of the (im)possible idea of the just society" (Beetham 2002: 176–77).

In her work to locate how we can remain faithful to our own identities while sharing a single justice discourse, Beetham draws on Derrida, who asserts that the problem of translation is central to achieving justice in a multi-discourse world. In this view, justice is nearly impossible to achieve because classical European justice theory requires justice to be the same in every circumstance (Beetham 2002: 178). Beetham wants justice discourse to recognize a world made up of "others" who are very different. As she says, "[a]n ethics and a commitment to social justice which does not recognize that the other may be unlike me is always in danger of becoming paternalistic or even oppressive and therefore unjust" (Beetham 2002: 178).

Beetham recognizes that a common vision of justice entails a common justice discourse. As a reader of oppressed justice discourses prevalent in her own discipline of women's studies, the author views language as carrying both the promise of equality and the reality of oppression. The problems encountered by indigenous people in search of justice in Western law come to mind again. As Beetham is pointing out, getting justice in someone else's language can be difficult.

Much like Beetham, in *Language of Justice* research I argue that a dominant justice discourse exists within fields that consider social and "criminal" justice matters. I find, like Beetham, that the dominant "justice by social control" discourse suppresses other justice discourses considering social and "criminal" justice matters with different eyes. Beetham argues that if we are to achieve a just society we must both stay faithful to our identities and find a way to translate to each other our justice discourses. In my research I empirically argue that moral entrepreneurs in the dominant justice discourse have no such concerns and in fact operate as if oppressed justice discourses either do not exist or have no legitimacy.

Justice as discourse

In the previous section I demonstrate how scholars have used the idea that language choices build a discourse to make important arguments about their disciplines. In this section I show how scholars contributing to the justice studies discipline have used the idea of justice discourse as a way to make arguments about the social and "criminal" justice we do and do not achieve in our social life. I examine how scholars have looked at pre-print era "visual" justice discourse, legislative justice discourse, judicial discourse, medico-legal justice discourse, restorative justice discourse, political "crime control" justice discourse as well as law enforcement justice discourse, to argue for the success or failure of accomplishing justice in our social life. Along the way I will show how their efforts relate to the work I do in *Language of Justice* research to assess our social and "criminal" justice discourse and the justice that we are and are not achieving.

In her essay "Symbols of Culpability and the Universal Language of Justice: the ritual of public executions in late medieval Europe," Esther Cohen looks at social control and punishment in the Middle Ages (1989). Cohen theorizes that public executions communicated a justice discourse from political authorities to the public; that only the state had the authority to administer justice. She argues that public executions were used as a key feature, not so much to avenge transgressions, but "as a visual enactment of implemental authority, displaying the full power of the law to all observers" (Cohen 1989: 408). Her analysis, though reminiscent of Foucault's (1977) historical examination of discipline and punishment, is unique because it considers the justice discourse of a pre-print era. Her argument is that symbols of justice in the Middle Ages are primarily non-linguistic, visual and theatrical: the heavily ritualized – and hence symbolic – public execution of convicted persons.

Cohen's argument that justice discourse was successfully transmitted visually by public executions, does not differ substantially from assessments made by many other scholars, including myself, about the transmission of justice discourse through print. Her analysis invites us to consider how our modern life, dominated as it is by visual images, continues to produce and disseminate a justice discourse visually; however, I am interested in a different aspect of her argument. In common with my goals for *Language of Justice* research, Cohen makes the argument that justice discourse is intentionally produced by powerful moral entrepreneurs with specific social control goals in mind. As she theorizes, the King, the church and others she leaves undistinguished as "authorities" use public executions as a symbolic production of their legitimacy and as proof of the legitimacy of the justice discourse that the executions themselves produce.

In *Linguistic Aspects of Legislative Expression*, Frederick Bowers considers the language of written English law (1989). Bowers is primarily focused on grammatical and syntactical analysis, though he occasionally explores the contextual and situational meanings of the language he encounters. He presents his work as a contribution to the discipline of linguistics, to lawyers and those whose interest in law would lead them to consider his linguistic analysis (Bowers 1989: 7). Bowers' defining interests in lexical decomposition, precision of term definition, structural and semantic constraints, lexical style, reliability, tense and the like, constitute a disparate concern from those I have in *Language of Justice* research. However, his analysis of legislative language is highly relevant to the study of justice discourse and sheds light on how certain legal problems, including peyote use and political trials, fundamentally occur within an established body of written law that fails to consider how our justice discourse ignores the reality of dominant discourse, powerful moral entrepreneurs and silenced others.

An example of such legal justice discourse work is *Feminism and the Power of Law*, Carol Smart's analysis of how law and legal language is used to control women, not on their terms, but in the terms of socially proscribed gender roles (1989). Smart examines the legal discourse of pornography, rape trials and abortion legislation to outline how they not only disqualify other forms of knowledge but also silence perspectives and issues significant to the women's movement and contemporary feminist theorizing. For example, she highlights how law ends up regulating women's bodies. Like Smart, in *Language of Justice* work I trace how the way that social and "criminal" justice discourse takes shape leads to the silencing of alternative justice theories, perspectives and practices. Smart examines legal discourse and delineates that law which sets out to accomplish one thing for women frequently accomplishes something different. Similarly, I examine dominant justice discourse and delineate that moral entrepreneuring that appears to be working to produce one thing (justice) frequently produces something different (e.g. perpetuating social inequities).

Within legal discourse, the language of judicial opinions has been taken up by both Lawrence Solan and Susan Phillips. In *The Language of Judges*,

Solan examines the language of judicial opinions in order to comment on judges' work, law and judicial process (1993). His focus, unlike mine, is on the semantics of law, philosophical analysis and legal discourse. Closer to my research, although also different, is Phillips' study, *Ideology In the Language of Judges* (1998). Her work appears under the Oxford Studies in Anthropological Linguistics series, and examines the intersection of judges as law workers and political workers. Her interest in judges' ideology approaches my interest in moral entrepreneurs as ideological laborers working to define public justice discourse. Phillips focuses on judicial discourse, especially as it relates to the speech of judges. Her work points to my identification of the need to examine all law-related language – including that of all "law" participants, i.e. not just judges, but also prosecutors, defense attorneys, witnesses and so forth.

Language in the legal process is explored in *Just Words: Law, Language, and Power,* by John M. Conley and William M. O'Barr, who examine how power and ideology pervade the legal process (2005). As their title suggests, and as I argue about justice discourse, there are no words that are simply "just words." Rather, as the authors show, the work of law is done through careful and intelligent manipulation of language to the distinct advantage of some, and to the loss of others. In one example, the authors detail the use of language in court by a lawyer constructing a rape "victim" as being "interested" in her attacker, and in another how the language work resulted in the advantageous positioning for one party in a divorce mediation.

Legal discourse is joined with medical discourse in a powerful essay by Bruce Arrigo, "Transcarceration: a constitutive ethnography of mentally ill 'offenders'." Arrigo examines the impact of discourse on the lives of persons characterized as mentally ill offenders (MIO) (2001). Through an ethnography of the lives of three MIO, Arrigo powerfully demonstrates the impact of medico-legal discourse by showing their entrapment in either "mad" or "bad" identity categories and their subsequent transcarceration (being shuffled between the mental health and "criminal" justice systems).

Arrigo demonstrates how the prescribed language of both medical and legal professionals define MIO identity, make alternate identities impossible, and can ultimately lead MIO to social ruin and/or premature death. Arrigo examines the impact that the words and expressions used to define MIO ("dangerous," "diseased," "criminally insane") have on their lives and their options for change. He concludes that medico-legal language "speaks" the person, i.e. creates the person. Arrigo shows how language operates as a stand-in for the subject who can no longer define either self or a route to recovery that will produce a socially functioning individual. He finds that "[d]iscourse is pivotal to how agents recover from their historically mediated, discursively constituted, and structurally situated existences" (Arrigo 2001: 166).

Arrigo's work neatly ties together social construction, social control, social repression, punishment and postmodern criminological theory to explore the results of moral entrepreneuring within the medico-legal establishment. He examines the language used to classify MIO and persuasively deconstructs both the process of their confinement and, more importantly, the process of their social control. Much in the way that I discuss dominant discourses, Arrigo finds that medico-legal discourse not only defines MIO's selves, but also prohibits "replacement discourses" (or what I have been calling alternative and suppressed discourses), and thereby limits their own capacity to construct identity and reality.

In sum, Arrigo argues that powerful agents (medico-legal professionals) choose language (labels such as "dangerous" or "insane") that construct discourses (medical, legal) with immense power to define persons (MIO). Similarly, though in reverse order, in *Language of Justice* research I argue that what we recognize as social and "criminal" justice situations and what we recognize as definitions of persons involved with the social and "criminal" justice system are constructs of a discourse (on social control), which is built through language choices ("criminals," "tough on crime") that are promoted by powerful agents (moral entrepreneurs). Consequently, Arrigo's work is deeply relevant to my *Language of Justice* argument about moral entrepreneuring, social construction and social control.

In other research, Arrigo, this time along with Robert C. Schehr, again demonstrate how the analysis of justice discourse can point to success or failure in accomplishing justice (1998). In "Restoring Justice for Juveniles: a critical analysis of victim–offender mediation," Arrigo and Schehr examine transcripts of juvenile mediations and find that the justice discourse present in "victim–offender" mediations advertently or inadvertently marginalizes juveniles. The authors demonstrate, therefore, that these mediations fail to achieve justice results worthy of the restorative justice label.

The power of legal discourse to define behavior is explored by Tamar Liebes-Plesner in "Rhetoric on the Service of Justice: the sociolinguistic construction of stereotypes in an Israeli rape trial" (1984). While Arrigo shows how existing discourse can shape perceptions of identity, Liebes-Plesner shows how moral entrepreneurs can construct others' identity by shaping discourse. The author deconstructs the sociolinguistic techniques that opposing lawyers in a rape trial use to create a discourse that defines the plaintiff as a "good" or "bad" person. She concludes that the manipulation of language and discourse is in service of the opposing sides at battle, and not for establishing justice. Her point, much like Arrigo's and mine, is that language choices and discourse go a long way to define justice.

Justice discourse in political speech has also been examined as a way to make arguments about the social and "criminal" justice we do and do not achieve. For example, in *Beyond Public Speech and Symbols: explorations in the rhetoric of politicians and the media*, Christ'l De Landtsheer and Ofer Feldman collect works examining political rhetoric in Western and Eastern countries to study citizenship and the connections between political behavior and its consumption (2000). In these essays, various authors study political communication in a discourse analysis project of political rhetoric in the media. The editors point to the promise of public speech as a liberation and education tool when used to bridge the gap between political elites and citizens. Ultimately, this collection contributes both to discourses (those of political speech and public speech) and disciplines (including communication, linguistics, psychology and political science) that seemingly bear little relation to the justice discourse and justice studies discipline that are the central focus of *Language of Justice* research. However, De Landtsheer's and Feldman's work points to how the study of discourse contributes significantly to substantive and disciplinary understandings of *how* we construct and *what* we construct through politics, economics, law enforcement, legislative writing, judicial opining and, of course, administering justice.

Our justice discourse is frequently studied by researchers with specific purposes in mind. For example, in their *Crime Control in the 2000 Presidential Election*, Nancy Marion and Rick Farmer complete a content analysis study of Al Gore's and George Bush's statements regarding crime issues during the 2000 US presidential campaign (2003). The authors examine how the candidates use crime issues to frame their campaigns by analyzing how crime issues appear in candidate television advertisements, debates and interviews, as well as in *The New York Times, The Washington Post* and *The Los Angeles Times*. Marion and Farmer find evidence to argue that both candidates (1) use symbolic language to acknowledge that they share public perceptions of crime and public safety, and (2) fail to address specific crime problems.

I consider work such as Marion's and Farmer's to be very similar to my *Language of Justice* studies. Much as I do, they study the language of our justice discourse to answer questions about the quality of justice we are achieving. In this research the authors trace the language of two leading moral entrepreneurs to assess the quality of justice discourse, and disappointingly find only rhetoric. In *Language of Justice* work I similarly trace justice language, but with a concern for the emergent dominant discourse, and not that of particular moral entrepreneurs.

The discourse of law enforcement is powerfully explored in a fantastic study titled, *Creating Language Crimes: how law enforcement uses (and misuses) language*, by Roger Shuy (2005). Shuy demonstrates that powerful conversational strategies used by law enforcement in undercover operations are best described as "crimes." Shuy, who spent 25 years working with attorneys on criminal and civil cases, has previously discussed such "language crimes" (1993) and the language of confession, interrogation and deception (1998).

Shuy analyzes undercover law enforcement documentations (such as tape recordings) to trace how law enforcement workers, in an effort to accomplish their law enforcement work, often commit language "crimes," such as creating misleading impressions to cause targets to say something or agree to something that leads to their imprisonment (2005). Shuy's work does not seek to vilify law enforcement, but rather study the consequences of their language actions. He demonstrates that sometimes their focus to "get" a target leads them to employ conversational strategies that make targets look guilty whether or not any evidence suggests they are. His analysis of documentation shows conversational strategies that include: overlapping language, creating ambiguity, interrupting, lying, not taking "no" for an answer, characterizing illegality differently to separate targets in a single case, scripting, restating inaccurately, blocking the target's words, speaking on behalf of the target and more. Shuy argues that while law enforcement workers tend to view such actions as appropriate language strategies to "get" the target, such strategies actually lead to serious "crimes," e.g. a case where law enforcement workers use conversational strategies to make a target appear to be soliciting murder and then use that as evidence to convict him of attempted murder (2005).

Shuy describes his research as belonging to forensic linguistics (a subdiscipline of applied linguistics that examines the meeting of language, law and "crime"). His work, much like *Language of Justice* research, employs a content analysis framework to study the consequences of language action. However, he is fundamentally interested in how language is used to commit illegal acts, and his purpose is to delineate the use of language to commit "crimes" in work by law enforcement. My work seeks to delineate our justice discourse as a whole, and to argue that it is intimately connected to social control. From the perspective of my research, Shuy's work is an applied *Language of Justice* project, which demonstrates that social control is accomplished through the manipulation of language.

Forensic linguistics is a field with an enormous body of literature. It is the study of the application of linguistics in any legal or "criminal" justice context, as well as the study of any and all language that could be considered relevant in a legal or "criminal" justice context, e.g. a parking citation or a judge's statements in a trial (Olsson 2008). The topics in this field are far reaching and while most often concerned with matters not related to my work (e.g. language as evidence in trials), at times scholars in this field point to issues deeply relevant to *Language of Justice* research. For example, *Language in the Legal Process* (a collection of essays edited by Janet Cotterill) examines the language of the courtroom, i.e. the language of judges, juries, police, etc., to show the importance of language for all these in understanding, accepting and shifting justice contexts and practices (2004). In *Speaking of Crime: the language of criminal justice*, Lawrence M. Solan and Peter M. Tiersma demonstrate how spoken language, such as witness testimonies, impacts the application of law (2004). These works, along with many others, though primarily concerned with language and its impact on the assessing and punishing processes of the "criminal" justice system, often point to the central importance of justice language and justice discourse in defining what is and is not just.

The justice discourse of a major Australian government drug policy summit is examined by Therese Burton, Brian Dollery and Joe Wallis in "A Note on the Rhetorical Patterns at the 1999 New South Wales Drug Summit" (2000). They highlight how moral entrepreneurs actually accomplish the intentions identified by Shuy and Obeng. The authors follow the development of summit discourse as participants consider current drug policy, suggested reforms and counter proposals. They note that the discourse follows distinct rhetorical patterns. In one such pattern, a suggested reform (drug law liberalization) elicits the perversity thesis (as in "the relaxed criminal prosecution of drug users will result in an increase of illicit drug use"). Reformers counter with the desperate predicament response ("we have no room left in our prisons and no money to build new ones, we have to change policy"). This counter is challenged with the futility thesis (which holds that the suggested drug reforms will have no effect, e.g. "such risk as changing drug policy is unnecessary as drugs are here to stay, there's no getting rid of them"). The futility thesis is rebutted by reformers with the futility of resistance thesis (which holds that it is pointless to resist, e.g. "much of drug law will inevitably go the way of prohibition anyway"). This in turn is counter-responded to with the jeopardy thesis (which asserts that though perhaps desirable, the suggested reforms, e.g. non-incarceration of drug offenders, will have unacceptable consequences, e.g. the collapse of moral society). Finally, the reformers reply with the imminent danger thesis (which highlights the danger of inaction, e.g. "all youth will soon be in prison for doing drugs").

Though complex, the authors' analysis neatly portrays at least four things. First, they prove that justice discourse is a product and not a given, regardless of how simple, obvious and "there" justice discourse appears in everyday life. Second, the authors show that justice discourse is at least in part the product of moral entrepreneuring (concerned, vocal and active persons participating to control discourse). Third, the authors make obvious that justice discourse (on illicit drugs) is the result of various parties' *efforts* to produce commonly accepted definitions of situations, more than the result of any such definitions themselves. Fourth, such discourse analysis both tracks the competition to define events and actions (including "criminal" acts), and importantly deconstructs the fashion by which meaning is asserted, debated and attributed to human action and interaction.

The emphasis on discourse from Burton and her co-authors draws attention to Alasdair MacIntyre's insight on the problem of justice and rationality: every conception of justice rests on a conception of rationality, and there is no rationality that is not a rationality of some discourse (1998). When MacIntyre points out that the Gordian knot of justice is tied with the threads of discourse he distinguishes the central role of language.

Prison discourse is carefully analyzed in three in-depth studies. In *Captured by the Media: prison discourse in popular culture*, edited by Paul Mason, the authors highlight how the media engage in moral entrepreneuring work by constructing a particular discourse on prisons and punishment (2006). The authors demonstrate that the collective performance of media culture constructs punitive public attitudes that, in turn, encourage punitive constructions of "offenders," punitive public policy and ultimately the greater use of increasingly punitive prisons. John Sloop's *The Cultural Prison: discourse, prisoners, and punishment*, pursues similar themes of cultural discourse on prisons and punishment by carefully tracing media discourse from the perspective of rhetorical studies (1996). In a 50-year study of US media coverage, he theorizes four distinct periods of imagining people in prison as either redeemable or "criminal": in the 1950s the person in prison is characterized as an essentially "good" white male facing challenging life circumstances, in the 1960s as an angry black male, in the 1970s this black person in prison is "unmasked" as trapped between his violent nature and an unfairly racially charged society, and in the 1980s he is seen as an incorrigible "bad" person whose behavior justifies a "tough on crime" attitude. Finally, Andrea Mayr's study, *Prison Discourse*, contributes a critical discourse analysis of prison talk (2004). Mayr examines the writings and conversations of prison life and finds that power relations in prison translate into strikingly different discourses. She tracks an emphasis on control by those who work in prisons, and a contrasting emphasis on resistance by those living in prisons.

Much like the work of these and the other scholars discussed in this section, in *Language of Justice* studies I trace the successes and failures of justice rhetoric to make assessments about the justice we are succeeding or failing to produce. Their work, much like mine, views the construction of justice discourse as a competition between moral entrepreneurs. In this section I have given evidence for the ways that scholars contributing to the justice studies discipline have used justice discourse to make arguments about the social and criminal justice we do and do not achieve in our social life.

Studies of justice language

In this final chapter section I review research that has come the closest to my *Language of Justice* research. The scholars of this work examine justice words to ask critical questions about modern social and "criminal" justice discourse as a whole, its relationship to social control and moral entrepreneuring and the quality of justice we are achieving.

The study of justice words has a long history. One reason for this is the frequent use of language to define others as illegitimate, and therefore, eligible for punishment, moral disapproval and the like. Historically, much important work has been done in this direction (see Becker 1963, Cavender and Mulcahy 1998, Ericson 1987, Erikson 1966, Goffman 1959 and 1971, Matza 1969, Pfuhl and Henry 1993, to mention only a few). In more contemporary work, Turner Royce studied the transcripts of the British House of Commons and discovered that almost without exception when parliamentarians discuss the Rom (commonly known as Gypsies) they discuss them as dishonest, "criminal" and dirty (2002).

The use of language to construct others as deviant and therefore justify their control is a common focus of both my *Language of Justice* work and Haig Bosmajian's work on language and oppression. The history of the use and abuse of justice words in our social life makes my *Language of Justice* research in some sense a deviance language theory, i.e. a study of how we use language to create both "deviant" behavior as well as "deviants." An example of the power of language to define situations, construct social reality and deeply impact human lives is demonstrated in Bosmajian's dissertation on the use of metaphors to redefine Jews as "vermin," "parasites" and "plague" (1960). He continues this research with his award-winning *The Language of Oppression* in which he examines again the power of language to label, construct and suppress people by metaphorizing them: Native Americans as "uncivilized barbarians," African Americans as "beasts" or "nonpersons," along with similar implications for persons through the language of sexism and the language of war (Bosmajian 1983). Finally, in his *Metaphor and Reason in Judicial Opinions*, Bosmajian questions whether language that is used to define people into submission deserves protection under the First Amendment (1992).

Throughout his work, Bosmajian demonstrates that language choices in naming and defining people are enormously consequential. His work is concerned with studying communication records to identify language acts and their consequences, as is centrally the case with *Language of Justice* studies. Bosmanjian and I both argue that language defines and constructs situations, provides a context for social interactions and ultimately forms powerful social structures such as institutions and habits of language and culture. Above all, we care to show how language can be used to justify human action, such as suppressing others. In my research I show that in our social and "criminal" justice discourse, language choices have considerable ramification. For example, when we define others as "evil," as "innocent victims" or as "criminals," we justify the liberal application of social control upon selected others in our community, i.e. we allow ourselves to liberally suppress others. Ultimately, both Bosmajian and I point to social control through language choices, but we differ in focus. He is interested in how language choices permit and encourage one human group to suppress another human group, as in Aryans of Jews, whites of blacks, males of females. I am interested in how our social organization has evolved to allow for moral entrepreneurs who use language to control others through a social and "criminal" justice discourse, and how both the behavior and its consequences are a dominant feature of modern life.

The use of research in media documents to investigate the meaning of single words is an approach I share with Jeanne Flavin. In "(Mis)representing Risk: headline accounts of hiv-related assaults," Flavin examines newspaper articles to survey media descriptions of nonsexual HIV-related assaults (2000). Much as I have been arguing, she begins from a theoretical position that posits ideas of social control and social construction as central. Flavin finds that assault descriptions rely on sensational language, and negative stereotyping of those making the assaults, and generally exaggerate the public threat from HIV+ persons. She argues that HIV+ related assault accounts are characterized in media stories by highlighting a perceived danger in a headline, by using sensational or emotionally charged language and by identifying some negative quality of the perpetrator and/or some positive attribute of the "victim." Additionally, Flavin notes accounts tend to highlight assaults against "criminal" justice workers, particularly police officers, and rely on "neutral and objective" court actions, while simultaneously downplaying any legal challenges.

Flavin concludes that media coverage of HIV+ related assaults is consistent with the creation of a moral panic, and communicates an image of HIV+ persons as drug addicts, as likely to be incarcerated or mentally ill, and as prone to spitting, biting or violent behaviors. Thus, Flavin connects social order, social construction, "crime"/"deviancy" and media studies.

Several articles pursue studies of situations where language is used by individuals to accomplish specific purposes. Two articles identify how language is used to mitigate sexual assaults. In "Is it Sex or Assault? erotic versus violent language in sexual assault trial judgments," Janet Bavelas and Linda Coates examine the language used to describe sexual offenses in British Columbia trial judgments, and find that they are more frequently likely to employ sexual (erotic or affectionate) language than to employ language that demonstrates violence or force (2001). The authors argue that such sexualized descriptions hide both the violence of sexual assault and the experience of "victims." In "Convicted Rapists' Vocabulary of Motive: excuses and justifications," Diana Scully and Joseph Marolla beautifully demonstrate how the careful analysis of speech can highlight the use actors make of language to achieve their own purposes (1984). Scully and Marolla highlight how convicted rapists acknowledge rape as a wrongful act while simultaneously using language to justify it by portraying women as meaning "yes" when they say "no," enjoying the "sex," and ultimately committing "minor harm."

The same work of language control is demonstrated in Brenda Danet's "'Baby' or 'Fetus'? language and the construction of reality in a manslaughter trial" (1980). Danet highlights how words do not describe, so much as they construct, facts and intentions. In the trial of a doctor who had performed a late-term abortion, she details how opposing lawyers created two differing realities through word choice. Depending on the intent to prosecute or defend, the lawyers used either "baby," "child," "the deceased" and "person," or "fetus," "embryo" and "products of conception" language.

The next example reviews a study where language is institutionally used to achieve specific objectives. In "Indigenous Young Australians, Criminal Justice and Offensive Language," Rob White explores how "offensive language" is socially constructed in ways that serve to "criminalize" the street activities of young indigenous people in Australia (2002). He looks at swearing, and specifically how using words such as "fuck" comes to disproportionately involve Aboriginal youth in the Australian "criminal" justice system. White's convincing argument is that state power is used (in the policing and regulating legacy of colonialism) against certain groups of people in ways that "criminalize" and further marginalize these groups. In this example, the focus on "bad language" both legitimates systematic intrusion into the lives of less powerful Aboriginal persons, and contributes to their eventual "criminalization" and marginalization on an exceptionally disproportionate scale.

White acknowledges racial bias, cultural factors and conflict with colonial authority, as causes for the over-representation of Aboriginal youth in the "criminal" justice system. However, he also suggests that a significant cause is the perception of Aboriginal youth as a "problem" to be dealt with by the larger society and the police. White draws attention to how policing is associated with defining and regulating what is normal and habitual versus what is deviant, and thus cultural activity and social space are heavily regulated by a power of which police are but the representatives. The logic of police intervention builds on this.

White argues that the "offensive language" charges brought against Aboriginal youth demonstrate the failure to recognize two things: differential language use by another (Aboriginal) culture, and language as resistance to oppression. He argues that "language offenses" are offenses against a notion of civility, and that this civility code may or may not be shared and may or may not be symptomatic of an oppressive experience. If the latter, one might naturally expect it to be resisted and possibly experienced as an instrument of an unbalanced, unjust and offensive social control mechanism. Aboriginal youth are controlled, defined and kept in place by the use of law that defines specific uses of language as "illegal," "uncivil" and "inappropriate." White reveals the relevance, power and impact of language on issues of social and "criminal" justice.

How language ideologies influence legal outcomes is also the focus of John B. Haviland's "Ideologies of Language: some reflections on language and US law." In this study he exposes how, in the US, actors using a language other than English are interpreted as inherently offensive and dangerous (2003). Both these authors' work is an excellent demonstration of how language is used to do social control.

Conclusion

In this chapter I have placed *Language of Justice* research in relation to previous efforts to engage justice language and justice discourse. In important part I have done this work so that along the way I could highlight the logic and arguments of *Language of Justice* work.

3   The meaning of "tough on crime"

Positivist history of culture thus sees language as gradually shaping itself
around the contours of the physical world. Romantic history of culture sees
language as gradually bringing Spirit to self-consciousness. Nietzschean history of culture, and Davidsonian philosophy of language, see language as we
now see evolution, as new forms of life constantly killing off old forms – not
to accomplish a higher purpose, but blindly.

Richard Rorty
Contingency, Irony and Solidarity

Introduction

In *Language of Justice* research I point to the language of our social and
"criminal" justice discourse to argue about its great impact. I work to
establish that language choices affect not only how we interpret what is just,
but also how we act in everyday life to create a just community. I find
that studying justice words and phrases, such as "tough on crime," and the
contexts in which they are used, is deeply edifying in at least four ways.
First, I find that while at times our speech acts reflect our justice claims (e.g.
"equal justice for all"), at other times they do not. Second, I see that while
sometimes our justice actions are clearly acknowledged in language, e.g.
our concept of "criminals" as "bad people," at other times attempts are
made to conceal them in language. Third, in scrutinizing our justice
discourse I discover that the words we use often impact how we think about
justice and frequently promote social control and punishment. Fourth,
I locate that what we come to consider "our" social and "criminal"
justice discourse is in part formed and altered by moral entrepreneurs who
intentionally construct justice recipes that they wish to see more widely
accepted.

In the next four chapters I conduct a series of language studies: "tough on
crime" (this chapter), "innocent victim" (Chapter 4), "evil" in the context
of "crime" (Chapter 5) and the justice discourse from interviews of four
powerful moral entrepreneurs (Chapter 6). In these studies I provide
empirical evidence to argue that failure to consider our justice speech leads

to (1) a confusion regarding our justice commitments and (2) the experience of injustice for some of the most vulnerable members of our community. I find that our word choices, and the contexts in which we commonly use them, often obscure justice commitments that lie beyond our conscious actions. These unacknowledged commitments have enormous consequence because they form and inform public policy, which especially affects the least powerful among us: the so-called "deviant," the excluded, the underclass, women and various minorities (racial/ethnic, sexual orientation, etc.), that disproportionately bear the costs of our blinders.

In the next four chapters my aim is to read social and criminal justice discourse to ask several questions. First, how does the language we use reflect and create the justice/injustice we accomplish? Second, how do our words reflect and define the roles and actions of persons according to race/ethnicity/class/gender, especially in their interactions with the social and "criminal" justice system? Finally, what do the words we use reveal about our justice ideologies?

As I have already shown, examining our justice discourse is an opportunity to interpret how we actually understand and do justice. Importantly, if we do not carefully choose our justice speech we are fated to a social and "criminal" justice system created by moral entrepreneurs who cover the spectrum of political and moral opinion and who may (or may not) lead from the commonly embraced justice values and principles. These public discourse leaders include legislators, government administrators, law-enforcement representatives, judicial and legal actors, and public voices ranging from the Sunday preacher, to the national or local journalist, the activist and many more. These speakers share both a common language (a "pool" of justice words that they use in different ways) and the desire to define justice situations or achieve justice goals. I am interested in their justice rhetoric because of its influence and its capacity to conceal agendas ranging from the regressive to the progressive.

Many terms could be studied to argue that our justice language reflects the social construction of human meanings around issues of justice or to ask critical questions about everyday social and "criminal" justice discourse as a whole and its relationship to social control and moral entrepreneuring. There are a plethora of terms that could serve my purposes (e.g. "right versus obligation," "criminal character," "fault," etc.). The *Language of Justice* project is so deeply underexplored that I could begin in numerous places. As analysis of my interviews with justice-concerned moral entrepreneurs makes clear (Chapter 6), the need and potential for future research work in this domain are vast. The choice to study "tough on crime," "innocent victim" and "evil" in the context of "crime" reflect my decision to examine terms that are central to social and "criminal" justice discourse.

I suspect that almost all justice language is worthy of a *Language of Justice* study; the more time I spend with justice words the more potential I see. Only by thinking critically about those justice words, whose ubiquity makes them appear authorless, can we develop the possibility of seeing their authorship. Only by making ourselves strangers to the most common justice language do we see that all justice terms are authored, are chosen over other options, and deliver a distinct impact. This process of estrangement may be triggered by experiencing an initial odd feeling about a word or a phrase, or perhaps by a momentary striking encounter. For example, I was first struck by "innocent victim" while reading a news story about the Twin Towers. The story included an author's (or editor's) decision to characterize the people who were killed by the airplanes flying into their office windows as "innocent victims." At the time I thought: "why on earth do they have to be qualified as innocent? Is it not obvious that people sitting at their desks who are killed by airplanes flying through their windows are innocent?" Similarly, I initiated my research on "evil" as it relates to "crime" after noticing that "crime" acts or actors are sometimes described in metaphysical language (such as "diabolical plan" or "evil criminal"). This made me wonder about when and why theological language is chosen to modify "crime" and "criminal." This, in turn, made me wonder when and why in our justice discourse we choose theological language over other languages, such as medical ("insane") or sociological ("poor").

Above all, I want to alert the reader to how language choices impact the building of a justice schema, regardless of its content. Knowing that speech reflects and creates reality matters because it makes it possible to see whether we are actually creating just social policies. As I discussed in the Introduction, if we are to be just, we must keep asking two questions. First, "does our justice discourse reflect our claimed justice principles?" and second, "do the actions rising from our justice discourse reflect our claimed justice principles?" The answer to these questions is in great part what *Language of Justice* research reaches for. The work in the next four chapters is completed with the hope that the more intentional and conscious we are about our justice language choices, the more we will design justice policy in alignment with our claimed justice ideals, such as having an equitable society with justice for all.

Justice situations as constructed

In his analysis of how young girls are socially constructed as maladjusted or deviant, Thomas writes that any attitude toward any subject "means that some attitude (tendency to action) among the other attitudes has come to the front and subordinated the other attitudes" (1923: 241–42). Thomas argues that (1) all dominant attitudes are ultimately constructed by subordinating other attitudes, (2) construction of dominant values subordinates other values and (3) the representation of dominant attitudes and values in law subordinates other attitudes and values that might have, but never did, become law. Such attitudes, values and laws are justice schemes that subordinate the existence or application of other justice schemes.

Thomas argues that to control the evolution of such schemes, i.e. to control definitions of situations by characterizing certain populations as maladjusted or deviant, is "to control the evolution of society and to determine an ideal organization of culture" (1923: 254–55). In a fascinating turn, Thomas then wonders whether the problem of abnormality, i.e. "crime" and "deviancy," forces us to deal with something unexpected. As he asks, "[h]ow far is abnormality the unavoidable manifestation of inborn tendencies of the individual, and how far is it a matter of deficient social organization – the failure of institutional influences?" (Thomas 1923: 255).

As I read Thomas here, he has made at least the following four points. One, if we accept that when human communities choose one body of attitudes, values and laws we do so by subordinating another body of such options, then we are forced to accept that our justice schemes will define situations and construct reality. Two, if we accept that it is we who define justice situations or justice schemes then we are forced to accept that it is we who define the situations of social control. Three, even if we define social control as a means toward the noble goal of organizing an ideal social life, when we accept that we define these schemes then we are forced to accept that it is we who single out certain populations as maladjusted or deviant. Lastly, and most importantly, if we accept that it is only our choices and definitions that determine the abnormal ("crime," etc.), then to what extent can abnormality be the result of deficient individuals and to what extent the failure of deficient social organization? When it comes to the question of defining and managing the so-called "crime problem," how one answers this question will be significantly determined by ideological commitments: is the individual responsible to the society, is the society responsible to the individual or is it somewhere between these two?

In *Language of Justice* research I am not interested in demonstrating a particular ideological vision. I am interested in highlighting that our definition and construction of justice schemes target the parties they do because these are the parties we target, and not because (as is frequently argued) external reality so threatens our very existence that severe actions are required ("tough on crime"), nor because some people are particularly horrible ("evil"), nor because others are so exceptional that we must protect them ("innocent victims"). Instead, we construct a world that demands "tough on crime" responses, we interpret "crime" as "evil," and we identify some people as "not innocent victims" to make more palatable a sanctioning choice we are unwilling to accept as just that: a choice.

The "tough on crime" scheme

We encounter liberal and conservative justice discourse daily in the media. Moral entrepreneurs of both stripes call for "fair and impartial administration of justice for all Americans," claim to be "tough on crime," object to a "retreat from justice," shore up "public safety," are opposed to "criminals" and support "victims." However, as my studies in justice language demonstrate, speakers also use justice words in exceedingly disparate ways. Differences vary from the extreme ("savage and evil criminals" versus "those whom we must protect ourselves from") to the subtle ("avoid the lenient treatment of offenders" versus "protect ourselves while not increasing harms").

Moral entrepreneurs conjure up justice-related images and metaphors by combining the elements of justice words into phrases such as "criminals who victimize" or "savage criminals." Frequently, such phrases are combined in complex ways to create what I earlier called recipes for achieving justice. For example, in the Introduction I demonstrated how Ashcroft combines the ingredients "criminals who victimize" with "savage," the "public's safety in jeopardy" with "a retreat from justice," and "punishment severity" with "lenient treatment of violent offenders," to construct a recipe for justice that requires "tougher sentencing guidelines" (Serrano 2005).

A justice recipe is more than its ingredients. Frequently, a justice recipe can hide complex meanings. Such meanings can and eventually do take on an existence and social life all their own, and can appear to be independent of recipe-making acts. In other words, the author or *authoring* of a justice notion may disappear leaving the notion to appear true, objective and self-evident. One example is "tough on crime," which is not only a recipe, but also an ingredient used in vastly different ways to create and communicate new justice recipes. One justice speaker may use "tough on crime" to call for "a greater rate of incarceration and the building of more prisons," while another may use it to call for "the use of alternatives to incarceration that are more demanding on the offender." Yet a third may use "tough on crime" in a way that traverses the first two, or that introduces a third element, such as being "smart on crime" (Altheide and Coyle 2006).

For many decades, the call for being "tough on crime" has been a phrase used to indicate a supposed leniency toward convicted "crime" actors, and importantly to endorse a solution of strong incarceration policies. Traditionally, the impact of incarceration policies is assessed by asking to what extent incarceration can be demonstrated to have had an impact on crime rates (Spierenburg 1984, Colvin 1997 and Rusche and Kirchheimer 1968). Assessing this relationship turns out to be more complicated than one might assume because, as with any social science observation, a variety of factors impacting "crime" rates (and potentially sentencing rates) may be occurring simultaneously. Different explanations have included environmental criminology (Newman and Franck 1980, Cisneros 1995 and Holzman et al. 1996), broken-windows theory (Kelling and Coles 1997), and spatial behavior crime analysis (Goldsmith 2000). Other research has reflected concerns with drugs, gangs and policing (Knox 1995), and has brought to light a variety of factors to explain "crime" and high sentencing results (Newman and Franck 1980, Burney 1999 and Goldsmith 2000). Another line of argument questions this connection and looks to larger social structures such as poverty and social inequality for explanations (e.g., Caulkins 1997, Christie 2000, Gainsborough and Mauer 2000, Mauer 1999, Simon 1993 and Spelman 2000 to name only a few).

For decades, political trends have favored "tough on crime," "one strike and you're out" and "zero tolerance policing" approaches to crime (Dekeseredy et al. 2003). Policymakers have argued that the success of incarceration policies is evinced in the declining crime rates of the 1990s (Mauer and Coyle 2004). During the seven-year period 1991–98, for example, the rate of incarceration rose by 47 percent and "crime" rates declined by 22 percent (Beck et al. 2002). Such numbers can easily seem to imply a simple cause and effect relationship between rising incarceration rates and declining "crime" rates.

However, the relationship turns out to be far more complex (for this discussion, see Mauer 1999). One complication is the prior seven-year period of 1984 to 1991 (Beck 1992). During these seven years the rate of incarceration again rose substantially (by 65 percent), but the "crime" rate, instead of falling, rose by 17 percent (Gainsborough and Mauer 2000). Thus, data from the initial time period no more show that incarceration causes crime than data from the latter period prove that it reduces crime (Mauer and Coyle 2004). These contrasting periods do not suggest that incarceration rates have no effect on crime rates, but they should make us extremely cautious about assuming that building and filling prisons will result in lower "crime" rates.

While criminologists may disagree on the degree to which incarceration affects "crime" rates, it is a commonplace view in criminology that this relationship is "considerably weaker than that promised by the political sponsors of 'get tough' policies" (Dillon 1998 and Mauer and Coyle 2004: 14). In fact, scholarship on "crime" rate reductions in the 1990s suggests that in the best case only 25 percent of the reduction in "violent crime" can be attributed to prison building (Spelman 2000 and Caulkins 1997).

Nevertheless, the dominance of the "tough on crime" phrase is unquestionable. The most cursory examination of news media immediately demonstrates its powerful currency. "Tough on crime" is especially prevalent in political circles to communicate a decisive response to "crime." It is frequently used as a construction upon which political candidates can base an entire election campaign (Dillon 1998). This is common both in local- and state-level elections (Stucky 2005) as well as in presidential elections (Anderson 1995). "Tough on crime" talk is, of course, always about being "tough" on people who "commit crimes"; as such it joins the long history of language used to define others as illegitimate, and therefore eligible for punishment, moral disapproval and the like (Becker 1963, Cavender and Mulcahy 1998, Ericson 1987, Erikson 1966, Goffman 1959 and 1971, Matza 1969 and Pfuhl and Henry 1993).

While the "tough on crime" discourse goes on unabated, many scholars have challenged it for being mythical (Elikann 1996), for fostering the criminalization of youth (Hogeveen 2005), and for obscuring the complexity with which the public views "crime" issues (Sprott 1999). For some time now, some scholars and public policy specialists have advocated for disassociating "tough" sentencing and "tough on crime" attitudes from "crime" control. They argue that the large number of people selected for prison and the length of their prison sentences reflect not how many people pose a significant threat to public safety, but how many people confront social structures, social forces and public policy gone awry (Mauer 1999). Frequently, elected representatives, law enforcement, and others respond to such an interpretation of "tough on crime" as being "soft on crime" (Garland 2000).

In my examination of "tough on crime" I have no intention to enter the ideological debate on whether we should incarcerate more or less. While I do find evidence that "tough on crime" discourse is substantially abused for political and rhetorical purposes, my interest in this discourse relates to the concerns of *Language of Justice* research, i.e. how social actors, "criminal" justice institutions and social policies and practices are meaningfully cast and shifted historically. To accomplish this task I undertake the straightforward research mission of tracing the phrase "tough on crime" over time in public discourse as represented in news media reports.

Tracing meanings in media documents

To trace the historicity and meanings of "tough on crime" I use the *LexisNexis* database and specifically the *majpap* subdivision, which catalogues and makes searchable the full content of English language newspapers.

In the "Interpretation of Documents and Material Culture," Ian Hodder describes documents as mute evidence (1998). While the phrase is catchy and draws seemingly appropriate images of still pages with dry ink, it is inaccurate. After years of research in documents, nothing surprises me more than how much is captured in the documents we construct. Thought of in another way, this is not so surprising: a document is a product of mind(s), of a setting, of a culture, of an age, which, no matter how insignificant or surpassing of its milieu, will always necessarily remain both in it and of it. My goal is to make documents speak, to make them spill their enclosed meanings.

My use of media documents makes qualitative document analysis central to my *Language of Justice* studies. Media analysis is an established method for investigating social meanings, e.g. in discerning ideology (Fowler 1991) and the social construction of meaning (Maines 1982). David Altheide's model of qualitative document analysis is critical to my task of deconstructing and finding meanings in media documents (1996, 1997, 2000), as is critical discourse analysis, which concerns itself with "notions such as power, dominance, hegemony, ideology, class, gender, race, discrimination, interests, reproduction, institutions, social structure or social order" (van Dijk 1988: 13).

Qualitative document analysis is distinguished by the high interactivity it promotes between data and researcher. Altheide argues that it ensures

> ... a recursive and reflexive movement between concept development-sampling-data, collection-data, and analysis-interpretation. ... Categories and variables initially guide the study, but others are allowed and expected to emerge throughout the study, including an orientation towards constant discovery and constant comparison of relevant situations, settings, styles, images, meanings, and nuances.
>
> (Altheide 1996: 16)

My *Language of Justice* studies begin with the close reading of texts, move to the development of emergent interpretations (Altheide et al. 2008), and then track the themes/frames/angles such interpretations suggest across documents in time and space – all of which is best described as a process of "tracking discourse" (Altheide 2000, 2002 and 2006).

This methodological process is best demonstrated with an illustration of such research. For example, in my study of "evil" (see Chapter 5) I first tracked how moral entrepreneurs use the word "evil" to describe "crimes" and "criminal actors." I began to closely read news documents (using the *LexisNexis* database) to track where and how "evil" and "crime" were discussed together. As I examined document data I developed interpretations (themes/frames/angles) of how these two concepts traveled together. I began a process best described as "a construction of interpretations" that emerged as I considered the data. Another way of saying this is that I tracked the discourse of "crime" as it relates to "evil" in search of emergent interpretations. One important interpretation that emerges is that when "crime" or "criminal actors" are discussed as "evil," the given "crime" causation factors disfavors social construction, communal responsibility for deviancy definitions and situational explanations. Another emergent interpretation is that "crime" causation factors favor metaphysical explanations. For example, both these interpretations are evident in the following *Toronto Star* headline: "Montreal Massacre Dead Killers are Evil not Insane" (December 7, 1996).

This example of my work highlights that in the qualitative investigation of documents, interpretation emerges through interactions with the material (Altheide et al. 2008). In this sense, qualitative document analysis treats documents as a community, which is best understood ethnographically. As the researcher immerses herself in a community of documents, she interrogates and listens to them as a community that can speak, and then tracks her emerging interpretations within the community of documents. Thus, a non-linear hermeneutic develops that focuses on returning again and again to the community of documents, much like an ethnographer would return to the village with her interpretations: immersion into the community, consideration of the community, interpretations of the community and a return to the community to inquire about the value of the interpretations made.

In qualitative document analysis, emergent methodology is the key to interpretation. This approach to research is defined by an ethnographic openness to those themes that "surface" in the encounter with data. In this approach I am less interested in reading to "uncover" or "displace," and I am more interested in construing to meaningfully encounter.

The historicity and meanings of "tough on crime"

My investigation of "tough on crime" (hereon TOC) meanings in media documents is an exploration of the contexts in which the phrase is employed. Early on I observed that TOC shares an important relationship with a second phrase, "smart on crime," and I found exploring these two in the context of each other to be rewarding.

My research into TOC highlights that as the political and economic context of our social life shifts, so does our justice discourse. For example, when federal and state budgets began to feel the crunch of a drop in economic prosperity coinciding with a rise in correctional costs, twenty-first-century "tough on crime" moral entrepreneurs were forced to find a way to discuss the unsustainable expense of a "criminal" justice system indebted to the incarceration boom of the 1980s and 1990s. They needed to find a way to language any decisions to change the TOC direction without appearing to have made a grave error by embracing it in the first place. While in substance many such moral entrepreneurs are arguing for "softening" incarceration policies, they are struggling not to be seen as "soft on crime" (a label and meaning reserved for discrediting liberal academics and reformers). To sidestep the perception of backsliding they argued for a new iteration of TOC to be conveyed by the phrase "smart on crime."

For example, consider a *Los Angeles Times* news story covering the shifting rhetoric of candidates in the city's district attorney race (Leonard 2012). Notably, the "story" is the candidates' shift in political rhetoric: "The race to become the first new Los Angeles County district attorney in more than a decade has veered away from the traditional campaign script of getting tough on criminals, with candidates instead touting a more nuanced approach to public safety." Leonard notes that the candidates first "tout their credentials" as crime fighters, "but then quickly stress the need to modernize the office, expand community outreach and add after-school programs." One candidate's political strategist accounts for this rapid transition by explaining that people "want the bad guys locked up, but they want the crime problem to be stopped before it can start." The author cites an academic expert who testifies to how greatly crime politics have changed from the norm of decades past, when "[y]ou could go as far on the toughness scale as you could go." Leonard then quotes one candidate's explanation of this shift: "Voters are sick and tired of our state's unsustainable addiction to spending gigantic sums of taxpayer money on prisons." The author ends his coverage by reporting that another candidate "is running on a platform of 'smart justice'," which, he notes, "echoes the 'smart on crime' message that Kamala D. Harris used to win the 2010 state attorney general's race."

The shift in discourse is palpable. Yesterday's TOC, which advocated for more severe and greater use of incarceration policies, has been replaced by today's TOC, which advocates for a more restrained use of incarceration policies while adding incarceration alternatives. In the careful tracking of media stories, I found that TOC rhetoric is not so much negated, as it is complimented with a new addition of "smart on crime." Evidence shows that while some moral entrepreneurs concerned with "crime" and incarceration have continued to embrace TOC language unabashedly, others have significantly changed their discourse and when they do use TOC, what they say when they employ the phrase changes its very meaning.

It is possible to observe how the meaning of "smart on crime" itself has changed with time. Media reports from the early 1990s feature speakers (such as the Director of the American Correctional Association) who declare that "smart on crime" means being smart with dollars, which in turn gets defined as building more prisons and doing less alternative programming. Twenty years later, this definition is turned on its head; "smart on crime" is taken to mean less dependence on the excessive use of expensive incarceration. In another media story from the early 1990s "smart on crime" is described as a gubernatorial package of new laws and sentences projected to increase both prisoner numbers and the length of sentences (Griffith 1990). Other media stories from the same time period define "smart on crime" as being too soft on crime – again the opposite of what this phrase means today (Baker 1995). In fact, more than half the TOC stories encountered in this early 1990s time period show that the use of the phrase "smart on crime" without simultaneous use of the TOC phrase carries a negative connotation, i.e. carries a "soft on crime" label.

The media stories from the mid-to-late 1990s show a change in focus. The "smart on crime" connotation of the early 1990s discourse is repurposed as a direct question: "are you 'smart on crime' or are you TOC?" In numerous stories various actors exercise this question (e.g. a judge, the Ohio Senate majority leader, bishops at a conference and a banker bemoaning business losses with mass incarceration). Of the 29 stories I encounter, ten call for being "smart on crime" and not being just TOC; the latter is credited for producing the – increasingly problematic – incarceration binge of the 1980s and early 1990s (editorial on Pataki, political platforms, etc.). Seven articles call for being "smart on crime" and TOC, and four stories call for not being "soft on crime" but being "smart on crime." Clearly, in the mid-to-late 1990s TOC meaning changes from advocating for greater use of incarceration policies to claims that incarceration policies need to be "smart on crime" and not only TOC.

With the turn of the century, media stories reveal yet another change in focus. For the time period up to 2005, the stance, "we need to be 'smart on crime' and not only TOC," that dominated the mid-to-late 1990s remains strong. However, a new emphasis in TOC discourse emerges and comes to prevail: namely, the standalone argument for being "smart on crime." Whereas during the previous period "smart on crime" was never referenced without also invoking a TOC attitude, now the argument for being "smart on crime" is made without reference to TOC. For example, this was done in various contexts including a Michigan election debate, as an argument for fiscal responsibility, in defense of alternative programming, and in coverage of US President Bush promoting the need to be "smart on crime." Perhaps most interesting for this time period is the rise of a new theme incorporating this phrase: "we must be 'smart on crime' and not TOC." The emergence of this combined phrase constitutes a complete reversal unimaginable two decades earlier: the negation of the TOC attitude in the face of a serious critique (interestingly the contexts here are letters to the editor, editorials, polls, stories on how Congress has failed, the insanity of three strikes, etc.). Another change of note in the discourse is the emergence of a new phrase, "strong on crime," which calls for taking on the TOC doubters and bravely supporting alternatives to incarceration that many will critique as "soft." Finally, after 2005 (and especially after the 2007 global economic crisis), the "smart on crime" meaning that comes to dominate is one that retains the "tough" on "criminals" stance but also includes a call for spending less on incarceration, i.e. incarcerating less.

The cycling of meanings across decades of "smart on crime" (hereon SOC) discourse shows how definitions have shifted in relation to TOC discourse. They travel from the equivalent "SOC means TOC," to the ambivalent "SOC means not just TOC," and finally to a "SOC means not being TOC." I theorize that part of what has happened is that the meaning of TOC itself has changed in time. Whereas TOC initially introduced "more punishment and being harsh on criminals to prevent crime," today, TOC alone may convey "punishing excessively" and "punishing as a solution which has failed over time." Perhaps it is that these two terms have changed together: while yesterday's phrase "SOC means TOC" has changed to today's "SOC means not TOC," what the terms "SOC" and "TOC" mean in each instance is different. Earlier, SOC meant "locking more people up for more time is the solution to crime," whereas today it means "locking up fewer people for less time and providing other programs is the solution to crime." Earlier, TOC meant "increased prosecution and sentencing/imprisoning of offenders," and now it means "maintain prosecution of offenders" which leaves the sentencing/imprisoning aspect up for grabs.

I present the above research to show that while some moral entrepreneurs concerned with crime and incarceration have continued an unabated embrace of TOC language, which calls for greater use of incarceration policies and the like, others have significantly changed their discourse and though they still use the language of TOC what they say when they use it changes what TOC means.

Conclusion

What, then, does this analysis of the "tough on crime" scheme reveal? I locate a series of implications which I present in 13 points.

1 My analysis demonstrates that the process of excluding, controlling and punishing the other is accomplished, reproduced and shifted inside of and through language. As the evolution of the "tough on crime" scheme shows, language choices in our social and "criminal" justice discourse have great impact; they affect not only how we interpret what is just, but also how we act in everyday life to create justice. For example, "tough on crime," "soft on crime" and "smart on crime" are shown to be parameters within which incarceration policy discourse occurs.

2 My analysis shows that in constructing justice in our everyday life, our speech reflects our justice claims (e.g. that we care about "equal justice for all") only some of the time. Moral entrepreneurs' work to demonstrate consistency of meaning in their use of "tough on crime" is a case in point. The importance of this cannot be overstated: public discourse leaders, i.e. moral entrepreneurs – whether progressive, conservative or other – shape justice discourse out of more than a motivation to argue for a particular justice scheme.

3 My analysis confirms that while moral entrepreneurs clearly acknowledge their justice actions some of the time, at other times, they attempt to conceal their justice actions through language. An example of transparency in language would be the early call for getting "tough on crime," which openly called for increased use of incarceration policies. By contrast, an example of obfuscation would be introducing a new discourse of "smart on crime" to hide the action of decreasing their reliance on incarceration policies when faced by a correctional situation they interpret as fiscally unsustainable. This maneuver allows them to claim sustained support for being "tough on crime," without too openly calling for a decrease in incarceration, which would seem to admit the failure of "tough on crime" policies. As my analysis demonstrates, the actions are deft, but result in an unacknowledged and complete transformation for the meaning of "tough on crime."

4 Fourth, my analysis illustrates that the words we use in our justice discourse influence how we think about justice. For example, the entire "tough on crime" discourse is produced, reproduced and shifted in the abstract universe of "crimes," "offenders" and "victims" and does

not engage the specificity and innate complexity of any one particular "crime situation."

5   My analysis exemplifies that our justice discourse is driven by a concern for social control and punishment rather than by the work of achieving the justice defined in our justice value claims. For example, the "tough on crime" discourse centers on social actors (moral entrepreneurs) highlighting activities to control "others," rather than activities to address or repair harms, to challenge "crime" causes or to address the new instances of harm created by incarceration and other policies.

6. My analysis of "tough on crime" provides empirical evidence in support of the argument that our failure to examine and evaluate our justice speech leads to confusion regarding our justice commitments. My exposition of how "tough on crime" discourse has changed over time shows that while we lay claim to a justice commitment by being "tough" on crime, our deeper commitment is maintaining control of others and that this control is determined by parameters other than justice (affordability, face-saving behavior). Thus, the examination of justice speech has the potential to clarify confusion and to locate our true justice commitments.

7   My analysis provides evidence for how our words create a justice system both intentionally and unintentionally. For example, my analysis of "tough on crime" discourse evinces that for at least some moral entrepreneurs, the "tough on crime" scheme has shifted from a model that is openly embraced, to a model that even when no longer embraced is difficult to disentangle from.

8   My analysis of "tough on crime" discourse demonstrates that the study of words associated with justice enables us to expose the social construction of our social and "criminal" justice system. For example, by examining the language of "tough on crime" I demonstrate how this justice scheme is constructed and transformed.

9   My analysis of "tough on crime" shows that examining our justice discourse provides an opportunity to interpret how we come to understand justice situations the way we do, i.e. we come to understand how agents act to shift the content of justice meanings such as "smart on crime" and "tough on crime." Such examination demonstrates the importance of carefully choosing our justice speech else we are fated to a social and "criminal" justice system created by moral entrepreneurs whose justice rhetoric may conceal agendas ranging from the regressive to the progressive. For example, this analysis reveals the ability of moral entrepreneurs to further a discourse agenda of "tough on crime" even when they conceal it with the language of "smart on crime."

10 This same "tough on crime" discourse dominance by moral entrepreneurs shows how successful they can be in influencing public opinion whether or not their work is aligned with broadly accepted justice

definitions and goals. It also shows how susceptible the public is to their individual politics, agendas and worldviews.

11 My analysis of the "tough on crime" discourse illustrates how the choice of an attitude, such as "tough on crime," leads us to reject another attitude, such as "soft on crime," or "smart on crime." This insight forces us to accept that we define the situations of social control and we decide who and what will be subject to such social control. Importantly, our "tough on crime" discourse commits us to the ideological choice that the individual is responsible to the society and deemphasizes the position that society has responsibility to the individual.

12 My analysis of "tough on crime" discourse illustrates that as an ideological vision, "tough on crime" is a justice scheme that targets the parties it does because those are the parties we target, and not because (as it is frequently argued), external reality so threatens our very existence that severe actions are required, such as having to be "tough" about "crime."

13 My analysis of the "tough on crime" discourse confirms that our language choices define how social actors ("crime" actors), "criminal" justice institutions (corrections) and social policies and practices (increased use of incarceration) are meaningfully cast and shifted with the passage of time. My research also confirms how such definition work is used to build entire justice recipes, such as "smart on crime" or "tough on crime," which come to encompass multiple meanings that eventually take on an existence and social life all their own, and that appear to be separate from recipe-making acts. This analysis shows that "tough on crime" comes to be seen as authorless because it takes on the appearance, for multiple audiences, of a justice notion that is true, objective and indisputable, e.g. a justice recipe defining the ways things are or need to be in the "criminal" justice system. As I have shown, "tough on crime" is not only a recipe, but can also be used as an ingredient itself in creating and communicating new justice recipes. Thus, one moral entrepreneur may use "tough on crime" to call for "a greater rate of incarceration and the building of more prisons," while another may use "tough on crime" to call for "the use of alternatives to incarceration that are more demanding on the offender," while a third may use "tough on crime" in a way that traverses the first two, or that introduces a third element, such as "smart on crime."

4 An ethnography of "innocent victim" language

As I suggested, however, a question remains and it is one that makes one suspect the characterization of the girl concerned and makes one wonder if after all she is really so innocent a victim. The question is: What was she doing at a Hell's Angels Convention?

John Lee
"Innocent victims and evil-doers"

Introduction

In this chapter I study the phrase "innocent victim" to ask what our use of it demonstrates. For example, what does our use of the term demonstrate about how we reflect on and implement justice? What does our use of it suggest about how we exclude, control and punish others, and how these efforts are accomplished, reproduced and shifted inside of and through language? Does our use of it reflect our justice claims (e.g. that we care about "equal justice for all"), or do the contexts of our use of it show we can have other concerns? What does our use of it demonstrate about how we talk about "victims"? Does our use reveal that we use "victim" for our own purposes or that we have hidden agendas? What are the implications of how we use the word "victim" in our social and "criminal" justice discourse? Does it suggest our discourse is oriented to producing justice, social control or to something other? Does it highlight confusion or lucidity within our discourse about our justice commitments? Does our use of "victim" demonstrate that we embrace some definitions of agency, i.e. victimhood, and reject others? Does our use of "victim" demonstrate the influence of public discourse leaders, i.e. moral entrepreneurs? If our discourse entails multiple meanings of "victim" do our uses demonstrate that we choose carefully among them, or that we choose thoughtlessly, or that we choose under the influence of others, such as moral entrepreneurs who bring their own agendas? Does our use of "victim" demonstrate that we take responsibility for choosing a definition of "victim" and an ideology of victimhood, or does our usage demonstrate that we operate as if an external definition of "victim" and ideology of victimhood are given? What does our use of "victim" demonstrate about how we meaningfully cast social actors, social and "criminal" justice institutions and social policies? Lastly, what justice recipes does our use of "victim" support, and how do different justice recipes use "victim" constructions as an ingredient?

Looking for "innocent victims"

I first noticed the term "innocent victim" in a news story that employed it to refer to people killed by airplanes flying through their Twin Towers' office windows during the 9/11 events. At the time I considered it odd that news workers thought it relevant or necessary to qualify persons attacked by airplanes as "innocent." I began to look at the use of "innocent victim" in media documents and quickly discovered that it appeared in coverage of a medley of circumstances and activities. The fact that I could not distinguish any patterns of use, especially as opposed to the use of "victim" without any qualifier, peaked my interest even more. I followed the methodological route described in the previous chapter (tracking discourse through qualitative document analysis), but was not able to arrive at inter-pretations that would answer my questions.

Stumped, I found myself in dusty library sections pouring over diction-aries dating from the 1700s to modern times – all in the hope of discovering insights into "innocent victim" by reading the history of definitions for "innocent" and "victim." Though I found many such insights there, it is important to note that I use dictionaries as places to inspire research direction and not as primary evidence for my arguments about the impor-tance of "innocent victim." While on occasion I use dictionary data for secondary support, I am very hesitant to do so because dictionaries are historical documents whose production and placement of individual entry meanings are linked to an array of historical meanings to which I do not have access. I also lack the training of a historian to fully appreciate the complexities of much that I encounter in these dictionaries.

Finally, I took the insights from my dictionary studies and returned to media documents and the wide array of contexts in which "innocent victim" occurs. I again used the *majpap* sub-database of *LexisNexis*, which indexes major English language newspapers. I used textual searches of "victim" and "innocent victim" with various other qualifications and considered newspaper articles from the years 1969 to 2012. The large amount of data generated by most textual searches indicated the need for a representative study. This was accomplished by retrieving data, annually, trimonthly or even one day per month for each month of each year (alternating date of month consistently), depending on the search. As a result, I have high confidence in the validity of my data. The research provided by the initial searches was printed and studied closely. Commonalities, themes, tensions, overlaps and gaps were developed in a comparative media discourse analysis study that suggested further research directions. These in turn developed into interpretations of the use of "victim" and "innocent victim" and inspired further searches that both strengthened and modified the interpretations.

The definition of "innocent" and "victim"

In my study of dictionaries I was careful to choose a variety of dictionary publishers to ensure that I would view disparate attempts of definition. I also viewed dictionaries across three centuries to ensure that I would develop understandings of these words' definitions across time.

"Innocent" as a simple and weak person

In 1780, Thomas Sheridan's *Dictionary of the English Language* defines "innocence" as "purity from injurious action, untainted integrity; freedom from guilt imputed; harmlessness, innoxiousness"; and importantly, "simplicity of heart, perhaps with some degree of weakness" (Sheridan 1780). Thirty years later, in 1810, Samuel Johnson's *A Dictionary of the English Language* repeats this definition, almost verbatim, including the entry of "simplicity of heart, perhaps with some degree of weakness" (Johnson 1810). In his 1852 *Dictionary of the English Language,* John Craig defines "innocence" similarly and also includes the "simplicity of heart, perhaps with some degree of weakness" in the entry (Craig 1852).

In 1911, *The Century Dictionary* marks two rites of passage for the word "innocence." The first has to do with the addition of legal entries (two of the four definitions given). The second is that although the definition contains an entry of "untainted purity of heart," it no longer carries the previously omnipresent "simplicity of heart, perhaps with some degree of weakness" (Century Dictionaries 1911). The 1942 edition of this same dictionary includes all the entries of the 1911 edition, omits the "simplicity of heart, perhaps with some degree of weakness" entry again and even entirely drops the modified version of "untainted purity of heart" (Emery and Brewster 1942).

I examined a broad chronological range of dictionaries for their definitions of "innocence," "innocency" and "innocent." I found that although these dictionaries expand on legal and other entries, none return to the "simplicity of heart, perhaps with some degree of weakness" entry. After 1911, the dictionaries I examined mostly define "innocent" as those "free of guilt." Some entries approach, but never reach, the older reference to a notion of "simplicity as weakness" (e.g. "tenderfoot," "naïve," "pure," "uncorrupted," "absence of guile," "artless" and "unsophisticated").

"Victim" as a person with or without agency

The Sheridan's 1780 *Dictionary of the English Language* defines "victim" in two ways. The first is as "[a] sacrifice, something slain for a sacrifice," and the second is as "something destroyed" (Sheridan 1780). Johnson repeats these two definitions for "victim" and also cites examples in his 1810 *Dictionary of the English Language*. For the first definition (sacrifice) the example is, "Clitumnus' waves, for triumphs after war, / the victim ox and snowy sheep prepare. *Addifon*" (Johnson 1810). For the second definition (something destroyed) the example is, "[b]ehold where age's wretched victim lies; / See his head trembling, and his half-clos'd eyes. *Prior*" (Johnson 1810). Though limited to the same two definitions, Craig's 1852 *Dictionary of the English Language* defines "victim" more extensively:

> A living being sacrificed to some deity, or in the performance of a religious rite, generally under the idea that the wrath of the god sacrificed to will be appeased by the offering; something destroyed; something sacrificed in the pursuit of an object, as Bonaparte was the *victim* of ambition.
>
> (Craig 1852)

In these definitions there is a palpable tension between "victim" as an object of sacrifice that has no agency (the ox as a "victim" of sacrifice for the deity), and "victim" as an object of sacrifice that has agency (Bonaparte as the "victim" of his own ambition). As defined here, then, "victim" inherently entails a tension between the absence and presence of agency.

Though *The Century Dictionary* of 1911 marks the introduction of new dimensions to the word "victim," it retains the entry on sacrifice as first and primary. New entries include "victimization," "victimize" and "victimizer." Examples given for all these emphasize a swindling transaction, cheating, being duped and the like (Century Dictionaries 1911). Additionally, there is a greater expansion of the notion of "victim" as "a person made to suffer in the pursuit of an object, or for the gratification of a passion or infatuation, or from disease or disaster." The 1942 edition of this same work integrates old and new notions of "victim" for the following definition (cited in full, excepting examples):

> *Victim*, (n). [L. *victima*, beast for sacrifice, victim.] A living creature sacrificed in religious rites; hence, a person or animal sacrificed, or regarded as sacrificed, in any undertaking or cause; a sufferer from any destructive, injurious, or adverse action or agency.
>
> (Emery and Brewster 1942)

This example portrays the development (blending) of what, prior to this, were disparate definitions of "victim." Following the textual order and citing some of the examples from the above definition, "victim" is developed in this order: (1) "victim" as the sacrifice of a living being in religious rites, to (2) "victim" as a person/being sacrificed in any undertaking or cause (militarism, vivisection), to (3) "victim" as a sufferer from any destructive or injurious action whether of agency or not (ambition, oppression, disease). This definitional development continues in dictionaries that follow historically and it becomes the standard definition. A few smaller, but important changes also take hold. For example, the primary entry for "victim" as sacrifice is subjugated and moved to third position in the 1966 edition of *The American College Dictionary*. Instead, "a sufferer from any destructive, injurious, or adverse action or agency" becomes the first entry, and "a dupe, as of a swindler" becomes second. This change remains fairly consistent. For example, throughout various editions of *The American Heritage Dictionary* (1969, 1980, 1992 and 2000) "victim" as sufferer of actions or agencies remains the primary entry, while "victim" as object of sacrifice shifts between either second or third entry.

In sum, what I took from my lexical studies of "innocent" and "victim" was a suggestion to examine my ethnographic data with two notions: "innocent" as somehow related to the notion of "simplicity as weakness" (the innocent as weak) and the idea of "victim" as related to the notion of agency (the "victim" as self-generated or other-generated, i.e. the "victim" as responsible or not for becoming a "victim").

"Innocent victim" in media documents

Equipped with new possibilities of interpretation, I returned to the investigation of "innocent victim" in media documents and found that in most searches, regardless of date, its use reveals a distinct pattern: the majority of articles using the term "innocent victim" reference themes that occur in one of three contexts: incidents involving children, incidents involving actors infringed upon by the state and incidents involving actors in current affairs refuting responsibility.

A typical example of this finding is illustrated in the results of a search in the first four years of the *majpap* database's use of the *New York Times* (1970–73). In this search 23 articles are cited to include the use of "innocent victim" and 13 match the above profile. Here, in greater detail, are the incidents where "innocent victims" are claimed:

1   Persons as IV ("innocent victims") of an infringing state: less developed countries as IV of strong US dollar; Turkish prime minister and his party as IV of military; persons not involved in IL drug rings as IV of federal raids; person killed as IV of drug raid in CA; persons killed as IV of drug raids; Palestinian guerrilla as IV of Israel; anarchist as IV of political trial in Italy; public as IV of police allowing radical groups to proceed; Pope John Paul as IV of Vietnam War.
2   Persons as IV of an attributed responsibility: failed Nixon appointees as IV of Watergate; Vice-President Agnew as IV of conspiracy to receive kickbacks; Nixon as IV of overzealous aides; Nixon as IV of Watergate.

A similar pattern is seen in the results of a search for "innocent victim" in newspaper headlines during the years of 1987–88. This search returns 26 stories, 14 of which are distributed as follows:

1 Children as IV of various: children as IV of day-care crisis; children as IV of sex crimes; children as IV of divorce; children as IV of parents' conflict.
2 Persons as IV of an infringing state: persons as IV of justice system; persons as IV of Tamil government feud; hemophiliacs as IV of government blunder that gave them HIV; Panamanians as IV of US invasion; homeless as IV of city's plan; residents of Washington, DC as IV of drug war; Israelis as IV of Arab nations; Vice-president Mondale as IV of Iran Scandal; teen as IV of Drug War.
3 Persons as IV of an attributed responsibility: Princess Anne as IV of accused failures.

Finally, a third example of a search for "innocent victim" from the period of October through December 1996 provides 25 stories of which 16 are distributed as follows:

1 Children as IV of various: children as IV of a bad marriage; children as IV of separation and divorce; boy as IV of gang members.
2 Persons as IV of an infringing state: Englishmen as IV of war-buried in Westminster Abbey; persons as IV of state war and oppression; persons as IV of state violence; persons as IV of civil war and tyranny; persons as IV of war and hostilities; PLO as IV of Israeli peace; civilians as IV of Liberia; Muslim government as IV of Serbia; persons as IV of civil war and violence; refugees as IV of Sudan, Ethiopia, and Somalia; Alger Hiss as IV of the cold war; persons as IV of the bail referendum; Vicki Oyston's husband as IV of the "criminal" justice system.

These examples reveal a recurrent logic in the use of "innocent victim": most frequently, a "victim" is "innocent" when a child, when overpowered by the disproportionately stronger state or when falsely accused. Some media articles make the first scenario of children as "innocent victims" particularly clear. Consider, for example, articles whose heading carries "the most innocent victims" label. Here I found articles discussing crack cocaine addicted babies and children killed in the Soviet–Afghan war as "the most innocent victims." The second scenario, "innocent victims" as persons overrun by an all-powerful state, frequently appears in the recurrent stories of civilians killed in police chases, in drug raids and in war-torn areas. In the third scenario, where persons claim that they are falsely accused, they are treated either with irony (Nixon, Charles Keating, Enron executives, etc.) or with great sympathy (Nelson Mandela, those convicted of rape but freed by DNA evidence, etc.).

In striking contrast to "innocent victim," the category "victim" references a seemingly unending (and expanding) list of contexts. Most salient is the dearth of the contexts that were encountered in the examination of "innocent victim." While references to children with "victim" labels are encountered, they are significantly diminished, as are contexts of being a "victim" of an all-powerful state and those claiming to be falsely accused. Instead, there is a plethora of other contexts. Some are omnipresent, such as "victims" of crime, disease or prejudice. For example, a search of "victim" in December 1970 unveiled 30 articles using the word "victim." Of these, four were in the context of disease (cancer, heart disease and muscular dystrophy), six were in the context of crime (rape, assault, political crime) and the remaining 20 were distributed across a host of contexts (negligence, incompetence, cyclone, etc.).

In another sample, a search of "victim" on May 29 and 30, 1985 unveiled 25 articles in the following contexts: crime (murder, abuse, soccer hooliganism), physical disease (rare aging disease, legionnaire disease, agent orange disease), death (by trampling, Satanism and starvation) and various other. Above all, "victim" is used in an array of seemingly unrelated contexts (airlines, dolphins, athletes, AIDS, etc.). The only exception to these patterns is the increased concern for topics that emerge within specific timeframes, e.g. earthquakes, "crime sprees," widely spread infections, etc. The latter phenomenon is also observable in "innocent victim" searches where some topics appear with high frequency in media articles only to significantly decrease after a certain period of time, such as articles discussing 9/11 events.

The relationship of agency to "innocent victim"

My lexical studies of "innocent" and "victim" highlight two interpretive notions that are relevant to my ethnographic data. The first is the idea of "simplicity as weakness" for the term "innocent": in other words, the "innocent" as weak. The second is the implication of agency for the term "victim": in other words the "victim" as responsible for becoming a "victim." As I will next demonstrate, these interpretations highlight a striking set of assumptions that lie behind the use of "innocent victim."

The *LexisNexis* data on "innocent victim" clearly indicates that agency is a critical issue. My research shows that "innocent victim" is more frequently than not (65 percent of the time) used in just three contexts: (1) incidents involving children, (2) incidents of actors being infringed upon by the power of a state and (3) incidents of actors refuting responsibility for an act they are charged with. Each of these cases is characterized by an implicit (in the case of the first two) or a declared (in the case of the third) lack of agency. In the media articles I reviewed, children are defined by their lack of agency due to their age, those overrun by state actions are depicted as having little agency (e.g. to stop a drug raid or a military invasion) and those denying responsibility for certain events are doing just that: denying any agency at all. Clearly, the issue of agency is critical to these instances.

The *LexisNexis* data on "victim" presents an interesting contrast. On the one hand, the potential for "victims" to exercise agency is always present. For example, each news story with a context of a "crime" "victim" provides the opportunity to declare the presence or absence of agency. However, this is not done with any frequency. Instead a person is declared a "victim" of their context (disease, crime or other) without qualification as to innocence, responsibility or other. On the other hand, the absence of the contexts that were observed as central in the examination of "innocent victim" is striking: while references to children with "victim" are encountered, they are significantly diminished, as are any claims to being a "victim" of an all-powerful state or of being falsely accused.

Viewed this way, one interpretation the data support is that when "innocent" immediately precedes or follows the term "victim," a suggestion of lack of agency (lack of responsibility) in becoming a "victim" is being argued. Additionally, the absence of "innocent" immediately preceding or following the term "victim" suggests that agency (responsibility) in being a "victim," though not assumed or insisted, is possible.

In my lexicon study of "innocent" I discuss how dictionary entries define "innocent" as those free of guilt and that once there existed (a now absent) entry of "innocence" as "simplicity of heart, perhaps with some degree of weakness." I assert that the association of "simplicity as weakness" with the word "innocence" has remained, despite the disappearance of the association in twentieth-century dictionaries. I further argue that the contexts in which "innocent victim" appears connotes such usage, i.e. that the use of "innocent" in the phrase "innocent victim" encourages the interpretation of a "victim" as someone who has a "simplicity of heart, perhaps with some degree of weakness." These contexts favor the definition in which innocence implies weakness. The distinction is important because the most common use of "innocent victim" is for children, those overpowered by the state and those refuting responsibility in actions – in other words, for those who are defined by the fact that they are in a situation where they are weak and unable to impact the situation. "Weakness" here is associated with agency; the greater the agency in the individual, the greater the power of that individual, and the lesser the agency, the weaker the individual. Hence, the use of "innocent" alongside "victim" underscores an individual's lack of agency. If my interpretation is correct, those ascribed with lesser responsibility (lesser agency) in their "victim" situations are more likely to be labeled "innocent victims." As I have shown, the ethnographic data on "innocent victim" support this conclusion.

Remembering the need for caution in using historical lexicons, it is of great interest to now reconsider how – as I showed in my lexical studies – the history of the definition of the word "victim" entails a definitional tension: sometimes "victims" are not agents in their victimhood (the ox at the deity's altar) and sometimes "victims" are characterized as the architects of their victimhood (Napoleon in his ambition). My lexicon study of "victim" shows that while the emphasis of one interpretation over another has changed over time (historically, lack of agency in becoming a "victim" was the primary definition, whereas now agency in becoming a "victim" is the primary definition), the dual aspects of agency are always present. It is possible that this is important in the following sense: when ascribed to a subject, the word "victim" in and of itself does not inherently communicate whether or not the subject has agency (responsibility) in becoming a "victim."

In other words, the lexicon data suggest a venue for research: does the word "victim" by definition carry a mixed sense of agency (i.e. that one may or may not have agency in being a "victim"), and does the phrase "innocent victim" by definition imply an absence of agency (i.e. that one does not have agency in becoming a "victim")? Beginning with the later question, the ethnographic data on "innocent victim" demonstrate that in great measure the phrase is used in contexts where agents refute agency in being a "victim." In the ethnographic data on "victim," little can be read to suggest either the assignment of, or the refusal to, assign agency. The absence of any consistently used label in contrast to "innocent victim" (such as "guilty victim," "responsible for being a victim" or other) suggests many questions. Given that the definition of "victim" is inherently open to suggesting responsibility for becoming a "victim," might this mean that when we declare persons as "victims" we are claiming that they have (or may have) agency in becoming "victims"? Might "victim" be useful as a term for describing a person whose level of agency in becoming a "victim" we are unsure of? Might "victim" be useful as a term for describing persons whom we suspect of having agency in becoming "victims"? Might "innocent victim" have use for describing or declaring those whom we feel confident bear no responsibility for becoming "victims"? Might we call some persons "victims" in order to imply that they have (or may have) responsibility for becoming "victims" without ever actually having to declare it outright? Might the last two questions explain why those who were killed at their desks by airplanes on 9/11 are most frequently described (interpreted) as "innocent victims," whereas those who are killed by opposing gang members or by their spouses are most frequently described (interpreted) as "victims"?

Innocent or not?

With the completion of my lexicon studies and ethnography, what can I claim? To begin with, though in our public discourse we could scarcely be accused of pointedly, directly and clearly doing so, our use of "victim" and "innocent victim" suggests that we have distinct notions of "innocent" and not "innocent" "victims." In other words, we tend to think of "victims" as bearing varying levels of responsibility for becoming such. We are more easily inclined to think of, or at least consider, the following as "innocent victims": children, those overpowered by the state and those loudly proclaiming innocence. Regarding all other "victims," my evidence suggests, the question of their "innocence" is not resolved either way. The definitions of both words that make up the phrase "innocent victim," in conjunction with the media contexts in which the phrase occurs, suggest that the use of "innocent victim" absolves an individual of any responsibility in becoming a "victim." Equally importantly, the definitions of "innocent" and "victim" and the media contexts in which they occur demonstrate that the use of "victim" without a qualifier such as "innocent" may include the implication of having agency in becoming a "victim" – and this is important – *regardless of circumstance.*

The use of "victim" also reveals that we embrace some definitions of agency and reject others. Though unexplored here, in my research I encountered other categories of "victim," such as "accidental victim," "actual victim," "false victim," "true victim" and more. While I have not studied these latter uses, their mere presence underscores what I have already argued about "innocent victim": we assign legitimacy and illegitimacy to "victims." These uses of "victim" demonstrate how we meaningfully cast certain social actors through language, and how we subsequently use these characterizations to construct justice recipes of innocence achieved or innocence lost.

The frequency with which certain social actors are labeled "victims" as opposed to "innocent victims," shows fertile ground for further research. I briefly studied corollary cases and found interesting results. For example, consider "rape victim" and "victim of prejudice." While the claim that "victims" of rape or prejudice are "innocent" appears intuitive, the scholarship in gender and race studies argues that in popular perception, more frequently than not, the opposite is the case (e.g. Reasons et al. 2002). *LexisNexis* data show that female persons raped by males and persons experiencing racial prejudice are, in their majority, described as "victims" and not as "innocent victims." Other searches informed by gender concerns reveal similar data. For example, a search for the phrase "not an innocent victim" shows that the overwhelming majority of uses are reserved for women as compared to men.

One media story nicely ties together many of these themes. An article titled, "Homicides, Lifestyles Linked in Police Data," features an interview with Phoenix, Arizona Police Lieutenant Benny Piña, commander of the homicide unit (Cieslak and Konig 2005). After reviewing the entire 2004 Phoenix murder list, Piña says: "In all honesty, we probably have a dozen innocent victims, everyone else at some point was involved in a high-risk lifestyle." In plain English, Lieutenant Piña says that of all murders committed in Phoenix in 2004 "only twelve are innocent victims." What, one might ask, does that imply about the remaining 209 persons murdered?

To my reading, the implication is evident: these others are – to one extent or another – responsible for their own murder by the active choice of their "high-risk lifestyle." As the reporters summarize, "police and national experts believe many murder victims could have avoided their fate by simply cleaning up their lives."

Conclusion

These examples foreground the preoccupation with social control over "equal justice for all" because, as my evidence suggests, a "victim," whether of rape, prejudice, murder or other, is not automatically deemed "innocent." Instead, "innocence" for "victims" may be assigned, or it may not, and as such, their "innocence" in becoming "victims" may be legitimated, or it may not. As Thomas' research demonstrates about general social situations, these examples demonstrate about justice situations: they are already defined before actors step into them (1923). For example, some "victims" have a greater prospect of being deemed innocent (e.g. children) than others (e.g. women raped by men). These examples demonstrate how "victim" discourse takes place within a body of interpretations, metaphors, rhetorical strategies and ultimately ideologies that are rarely acknowledged. Furthermore, my case study reveals that justice constructions can be hidden from sight. The constructed and contingent nature of our assumptions about "innocence" are seen only when we disrupt our "victim" discourse. When we unpack the "victim" language that appears seamless or homogeneous, we uncover that an underlying set of assumptions constitute an ideology with far-reaching justice implications. For example, "victim" discourse occurs in a narrative where responsibility for victimhood can be shifted to the "victim." Blaming the victim is very possible.

The emergent theme of "victims" as agents of their victimhood has far-reaching implications. I can only begin to suggest the relevance to certain recurring scenarios in discussions of "crime" and justice. For example, what I highlight here reinforces the findings in studies of rape (that women are broadly held to be responsible for their rape) and "crime" victimization (that "crime" victims are broadly held to bring it on themselves) (Summers and Miller 2007). In essence, my study demonstrates that through the use (and manipulation) of "victim" language it is possible to privilege or marginalize certain "victims" as better or worse by the control of their "innocent" status. Furthermore, this status may be ascribed regardless of exterior circumstances. Lastly, our use of "victim" shows that in our work to produce justice, our method cannot so honestly be described as the result of applying fixed and constant terms to assess fault or responsibility. Rather, my study of "victim" exposes the complex process by which social and "criminal" justice discourse reinforce bias and prejudice. Some of this is so thoroughly embedded in language that even before certain agents can act they are assigned value and quality in their acts. For example, "innocence" in being a "victim" can be in part defined by age, gender or race location, and not only by action.

Our use of "victim" in our social and "criminal" justice discourse demonstrates that our "criminal justice" talk creates injustices. While assigning children "innocence" may appear harmless, can the same be said for assigning less to women who are raped or persons on the receiving end of racial prejudice? My research demonstrates that words are not descriptors of external realities. Instead, *words are worlds of interpretation*. When we treat the words we use as if language is representational we are missing much of what is being said and what is being done. This means that the study of language is by definition a study of interference, i.e. an investigation of meaning making that lives below the surface. To produce the just society we must be devoted students of our language as it will always tell us where we succeed and where we fail.

5 Delineating the "evil," "criminal" other[1]

According to this view, the word "evil" is seen as a holdover from metaphysical and religious vocabularies that have been revealed by postmodern thought to be oppressive, binary, totalizing, and exclusionary. The word "evil," should be discarded, it is argued, because it has been used so often in oppressive ways. The act of identifying something as evil, of naming it "evil," actually promotes suffering, and in no small part by continuing ways of thinking that lead to violence and destruction.

Jennifer L. Geddes
Evil After Postmodernism: Histories, Narratives, and Ethics

Instead, *evil* is a label we reserve for those worse than bad. "Badness" we expect to find in many people, but evil relegates individuals to a special classification that suggests some form of satanic affiliation.

Eric W. Hickey
"Cultural Development of Monsters, Demons and Evil"

Introduction

In the previous chapter I examined an aspect of our "victim" discourse to ask some *Language of Justice* questions about modern social and "criminal" justice discourse as a whole and its relationship to social control and moral entrepreneuring. The goal of this chapter is to ask the same questions by completing an empirical examination of our use of the word "evil" in relationship to the notion of "crime." Simply put, I am interested in doing a *Language of Justice* study on "evil" as it relates to "crime" to ask what our use of it in our justice discourse demonstrates.

My interest in "evil" has to do with the observation that on occasion I encounter descriptions of "criminals" as "demonic" or as "participants in plans of evil." This use of metaphysical language to explain "crime" made me wonder when in our social and "criminal" justice discourse we opt for that choice, and when we opt for others, such as medical language ("insane") or sociological language ("poor").

In this chapter I have three tasks. The first is to complete a lexicon study of the words "evil" and "crime." This study is not intended to be exhaustive

or definitive, but an overview of how these words have been defined historically and how (if at all) patterns of definition have changed in the course
of time. My objectives here are the same as they were in my study of
"innocent victim": not to make historical assessments or interpretations
of lexical meanings, but to show how I went about my research and building
my interpretations of "evil" as it relates to "crime." The second task is to
study the contexts in which "evil" as it relates to "crime" is commonly used
by examining its employment in English-speaking communities (as in the
two previous chapters, I accomplish this by studying the contexts in which
we use the word "evil" in media documents). Finally, the third task is to
consider the findings of the first two tasks in light of criminology research
already linking the notions of "evil" and "crime" to a process of social
construction.

My study of "evil" and "crime" in dictionaries and media documents
follows the exact research process discussed in the previous two chapters. As
with the case of my exploration of "tough on crime" and "innocent victim,"
this study allows the gathering of independent authors' (journalists, editors,
letter-writers, etc.) decisions on how to use the word "evil." At the same
time, as members of wider communities, these writers are participating
in both the maintenance and creation of terms and are part and parcel of
the social construction process of language.

A lexicon study of "evil"

My first task is the completion of a lexicon study of the word "evil." This
study, like that of "innocent victim," while not intended to be exhaustive,
is intended to be comprehensive. To accomplish this I complete a sample
examination of dictionaries covering the last 300 years. I begin with
the *Oxford English Dictionary* (1971), which ascribes two derivations for
the word "evil." The first derivation is attributed to the Goths of the fourth
century ACE, and here "evil" is defined as the Gothic meaning of "exceeding due measure" or "overstepping proper limits." The second derivation
given is Teutonic, and is attributed to this family of languages circa 1,000
ACE (Oxford Dictionaries 1971). In this case, "evil" is defined as "the
antithesis of GOOD in all its principal senses," which is explained "as an
expression of disapproval, dislike, or disparagement (modern equivalent
of bad)" (Oxford Dictionaries 1971).

One of the earliest published dictionaries is the John Kersey's *Dictionarium Anglo-Britannicum*, which was issued in 1708. Here "evil" is given
three definitions: "Ill," "Mischief" and "the King's Evil, a Disease" (Kersey
1708).

In the eighteenth century, "evil" begins to be defined in three distinct
ways. Importantly, each of these is given a separate lexical entry. For example, in Sheridan's 1780 dictionary, the three categories of definition are
as follows:

1   Evil = "Having bad qualities of any kind; wicked, corrupt; miserable; mischievous, destructive."
2   Evil = "Wickedness, a crime; injury, mischief; malignity, corruption; misfortune, calamity; malady, disease."
3   Evil = "Not well in whatever respect; injuriously, not kindly" (Sheridan 1780).

This divergent path of definition into three directions is found in various dictionaries over the next 100 years. For example, in the 1810 edition of Johnson's dictionary, "evil" is again defined in these three ways:

1   Evil = "Having bad qualities of any kind; not good; wicked, bad, corrupt; unhappily, miserable, calamitous; mischievous, destructive, ravenous."
2   Evil = "Wickedness, a crime; injury, mischief; malignity, corruption' misfortune, calamity; malady; disease."
3   Evil = "Not well in whatever respect; not well, not virtuously, not innocently; not well, not happily, not fortunately; injuriously, not kindly; it is often used in composition to give a bad meaning to a word; but in this, as in all other cases, it is in the modern dialect generally con-tracted to ill" (Johnson 1810).

The 1837 edition of Johnson's dictionary keeps the same definitions without variation.

With the turn of the twentieth century dictionaries become more varied as available publications multiply and begin to serve a variety of purposes (collegiate, desk reference, concise, comprehensive, etc.). While some dic-tionaries have shorter definitions for "evil," others maintain the richer series of definitions. Regardless, the definitions of "evil" follow the pattern of the previous century. However, new definitions for evil are added with the result that modern comprehensive dictionaries can have definitions of evil several pages long (see for example *The Oxford Universal Dictionary on Historical Principles*, which contains more than three pages of definitions [Oxford Dictionaries 1955]).

Using sample references, I cite these new definitions below as I encoun-tered them in my research:

1   *Standard Dictionary of the English Language, Funk & Wagnalls Company* of 1894: "contrary to divine or righteous law," "sinful or depraved," "unwholesome," "hostile to the welfare of any creature," "poor, unskillful," "that which hinders prosperity, diminishes welfare, or prevents the enjoyment of a good," "affliction."
2   *The Encyclopedic Dictionary* of 1898 (Hunter 1898): "cruel."
3   *Chamber's Twentieth Century Dictionary* of 1901: "sin."
4   *The Oxford English Dictionary* of 1933: "misleading."

5   *The Concise Oxford Dictionary of Current English* of 1934: "The evil one, the Devil."
6   *The New Century Dictionary* of 1942 (Emery and Brewster 1942): "due to (actual or imputed) bad character or conduct."

I now turn to a discussion of these definitions.

"Evil" in the context of "crime"

This chapter is a particular investigation of "evil." I am concerned with the relationship of "evil" to the notion of "crime." Specifically, I want to underline how "evil" is part of three different processes of social construction having to do with "crime": how certain acts are defined as "crimes" or as "criminal"; how "evil" describes that which is "criminalized"; and how "evil" is the result of a discursive construction.

In thinking about the above definitions I have found connections between the two notions "crime" and "evil" that are alternatively both intuitive and surprising. Perhaps most striking is the original derivation of the word "evil" from the Gothic definition "exceeding due measure" or "overstepping proper limits" (fourth century ACE). Here "evil" is a descriptor for exceeding that which is defined as an appropriate measure, or that which is defined as a proper limit. Such a definition matches how we think about crime acts: as acts that similarly "exceed due measure" and "overstep proper limits." Importantly, the right "measure" or the "proper limit" is of course a matter of social definition and construction.

In *The Compact Edition of the Oxford English Dictionary* (Oxford Dictionaries 1971) the second derivative definition (Teutonic, circa 1,000 ACE) characterizes "evil" as "the antithesis of GOOD in all its principal senses." The full entry then goes on to explain: "In Old English, as in all the other early Teutonic languages (except Scandinavian), this word is the most comprehensive adjectival expression of disapproval, dislike, or disparagement." Here, again I see a relationship between the definition of "evil" and the notion of "crime." After all, "crime" is more commonly met with disapproval, dislike and disparagement than any other response. Importantly, what is disapproved, disliked or disparaged is once again a matter of social definition, of social construction.

As I showed above, in the eighteenth century, "evil" begins to be defined in three distinct ways. As I described, from this point in time onward the definition of "evil" in three directions is common if not ubiquitous. On one level, this change might reflect an explosion of the ways in which evil becomes used. This argument is strengthened by the observation that a pattern of ever-increasing growth and diverse definition of "evil," as we saw in the previous section, continues to this day. All the examples of the three categorizations I cite above, and for that matter all other ones I encountered but did not reproduce, display a similar pattern:

1   For Category 1 = Evil as having bad qualities of any kind, e.g. "wicked, bad, corrupt, mischievous, destructive, ravenous."
2   For Category 2 = Evil as the presence of products of such qualities, e.g. "wickedness, a crime; injury, mischief; malignity, corruption, misfortune, calamity; malady, disease."
3   For Category 3 = Evil as not well in whatever respect, e.g. "not well, not virtuously, not innocently;" "not well, not happily, not fortunately."

"Evil," then, takes on more meanings, but the various definitions also take on group identity. In terms of groupings, "evil" is a behavior quality, as in acting in a fashion that is wicked, bad, corrupt, mischievous, destructive, etc. (Category 1). "Evil" is also a product of such a behavior, as in the results of wickedness, injury, corruption, malady, disease and, interestingly, "crime" (Category 2). Finally, "evil" is a description of the absence of wellbeing, as in not virtuously, not happily, not fortunately, etc. (Category 3).

Perhaps the most important characterization to be made of all these definitions is that, be they definitions of qualities, products or states of being, they are all socially constructed and socially defined. Behaving evilly, producing evil and being evil are radically social processes where (1) actors are in socially destructive behaviors (wicked, bad, corrupt, mischievous), (2) actors are producing socially ruinous products in a social context (wickedness, crime, injury), or (3) actors are in states of being that are socially destructive and socially ruinous (not well, not virtuously, not innocently).

Noting the appearance of "crime" in Category 2, I now turn to a lexical examination of "crime," and its first appearance in the 1780 *General Dictionary of the English Language* (Sheridan 1780):

Crime = "An act contrary to right, an offense, a great fault."
Crimeful = "Wicked, criminal."
Crimeless = "Innocent, without crime."
Criminal = "Faulty, contrary to right, contrary to duty; guilty; tainted with crime; not civil, as a criminal prosecution."
Criminal = "A man accused of a crime."
Criminally = "Wickedly, guiltily."
Criminalness = "Guiltiness."
Criminous = "Wicked, iniquitous."
(and more)

I notice that in these definitions of "crime" there is no reference to "evil." According to these dictionary listings, though evil acts can be defined as crime acts, crime acts are not defined as evil. Beyond this, looking at the language used to distinguish these two words one is hard pressed to find a difference because both "evil" and "crime" are defined in moral language: right/wrong, good/bad, wicked, faulty, guilty, iniquity, etc. Most of the descriptors for both these meanings are actually the same.

Despite the fact that both "crime" and "evil" are defined in moral language, and despite the fact that even the moral distinctions used to define "crime" are all used to define "evil" (and importantly not the other way around), they are far from synonymous terms. As I have shown, "evil" has a plethora of definitions, and they only grow in time. Yet a survey of definitions of "crime" show the definition remains remarkably consistent with one important exception. Consider:

1 *General Dictionary of the English Language* of 1780 (Sheridan 1780): Crime = "An act contrary to right, an offense, a great fault."
2 *Dictionary of the English Language* of 1810 (Johnson 1810): Crime = "An act contrary to right; an offense, a great fault; an act of Wickedness."
3 *The Century Dictionary* of 1914: Crime = "1. An act or omission which the law punishes ... " and "2. Any great wickedness or wrong-doing; iniquity; wrong."
4 *Webster's New World Dictionary of the American Language* of 1951: Crime = "1. An act committed in violation of a law prohibiting it ... " "2. Extreme violation of the law," and "3. An offense against morality; serious offense; sin."

In all these definitions, only one significant change occurs in the definition of "crime": it goes from being defined primarily in moral language to being defined primarily in legal language.

The timing of the change of the definition of "crime," somewhere in the nineteenth century, coincides with the emergence of a whole new set of definitions for "evil" (listed in the six categories above). There I showed that while "evil" was strictly defined within moral language, suddenly a wave of definitions belonging to entirely other languages appears. The first thing to note is that half of these new entries easily fit in the categories of moral language or the previously encountered metaphor of disease ("cruel," "mis-leading," "due to bad character or conduct," and "unwholesome," "hostile to the welfare of any creature," "affliction"). The other half, however, introduces new language definitions of "evil." Four of these are theological ("contrary to divine or righteous law," "sinful or depraved," "sin" and "The evil one, the Devil") and two of them refer to measures of class ("poor, unskillful" and "that which hinders prosperity, diminishes welfare, or prevents the enjoyment of a good").

The theological entries are of special interest because despite the fact that prior to this point nearly all examples of early usage are drawn from biblical anecdotes to illustrate the plethora of definitions of "evil," these definitions did not once introduce notions of sin, the Devil or divine/righteous law. I find this absence counterintuitive and puzzling, and I only become more perplexed with these omissions when I consider the entry of "sin" as a definition for crime (as in *Webster's New World Dictionary of the American Language* 1951).

This oddity would be less puzzling if we see the modern era as having turned the tables in the definition of both words. In later times, "evil" and "crime" are connected to theological metaphors. Not only can "evil" acts be "crimes," but what connects "evil" acts and "crime" acts is a shared meaning of a theological "evil," which partakes of "sin," "the devil," "the disobeying of divine or righteous law" and "sinful and depraved nature."

I make this the last stop of the lexicon study, as this is the place where it all ends in our modern lexical era. In the next two parts of this chapter I will demonstrate what I have only hinted at in the end here: that in our age, "crime" acts have the capacity to be "evil" in a sense of "evil" that is beyond the classical moral language definitions. Now, "crime" acts have the capacity to be "evil" in a sense of theological language definitions. What currently defines "crime" acts labeled as "evil" is how they can partake, not only in a definition that is socially constructed (as seen in the above new definitions of "poor, unskillful" and "that which hinders prosperity, diminishes welfare, or prevents the enjoyment of a good"), but also in a definition that links "crime" to "sin," the "devil," the "disobeying of divine or righteous law" and "sinful and depraved nature," i.e. in a definition that is theologically constructed.

The complexity of the relationship between these two words showed further layers that strengthen my points. However, I will stop here in the hope that with this lexicon study I have begun to make clear the following:

- The meaning of words such as "evil" and "crime" may change in time and hence social context.
- The definitions of "evil" and "crime" illustrate that they may be productions of social construction processes, but also that their changing definitions may reflect changing social uses of the terms.
- "Evil" may describe a plethora of social qualities and products as well as ways of being that only multiply over time.
- "Evil" is a result of discursive construction.
- "Evil" acts are defined as "crimes" or as "criminal."
- The social construction of "crime" can occur in moral language, legal language or theological language.
- "Evil" may at times define a "crime" and that which is "criminal."
- Behaving "evilly," producing "evil" and being "evil" are radically social processes where (1) actors are in socially destructive behaviors (wicked, bad, corrupt, mischievous), (2) actors are producing socially ruinous products in a social context (wickedness, crime, injury) or (3) actors are in states of being that are socially destructive and socially ruinous (not well, not happily, not fortunately).

- A clear change of language occurs in definitions of both "evil" and "crime," and these definitions can be distinguished by an early period and a late period.
- In the early period both "evil" and "crime" are defined in moral language: right/wrong, good/bad, wicked, faulty, guilty, iniquity, etc.
- In the late period new language definitions of "evil" emerge. The most interesting of these are:

  ° Theological: "contrary to divine or righteous law," "sinful or depraved," "sin" and "[t]he evil one, the Devil."
  ° Measures of class: "poor, unskillful" and "that which hinders prosperity, diminishes welfare, or prevents the enjoyment of a good."

- In the late period "crime" acts become "evil" in a sense that is beyond the classical moral language definition. What currently defines "crime" acts labeled as "evil" is how they partake, not only in a definition that is socially constructed (as seen in the above new definitions of "poor, unskillful" and "that which hinders prosperity, diminishes welfare, or prevents the enjoyment of a good"), but more importantly in a definition that links "crime" to "sin," "the devil," "the disobeying of divine or righteous law" and a "sinful and depraved nature."

Most importantly, the changes from the early to the late period shift not only the definition of "evil," but also the relationship of "evil" to "crime" such that we now describe socially inappropriate acts by calling them "evil" (i.e. "criminal"), and we also use the word "evil" (in its theological sense) to qualify certain attributes of "crime" acts (e.g. sinful). *This process changes the meaning of the word "crime" and moves it from a socially constructed domain to a domain of imbued characterizations that point to "crime" acts as defined by powers beyond social construction.*

"Evil" in newspapers

In this section I put all lexicon definitions aside to study the contexts in which "evil" is currently used in the contemporary life of English-speaking communities. One way of completing such a study of contexts is by looking at popular media and their use of "evil" in news-story headlines (by using the *majpap* database of *LexisNexis*, as I did in the previous two chapters). Having completed this study I have three findings to report.

The first finding is that much like the ever-expanding definitions of "evil" that I discuss above, in time there is an ever-expanding use of "evil" in newspapers. For example, while in the early 1980s it occurs roughly 30 times a year, only three decades later, usage is well over 1,000 a year.

The second finding is that there is evidence of an amazing amalgam of contexts in which "evil" is used. Consider the following (small) sample of contexts where "evil" appears: government waste, abuses in nursing homes, factories without unions, fixing of horse races, nature of a church announcement, Israelis' treatment of Palestinians, plan to end civil-service job duration, the opposing sport team, the Soviet Empire, the Nazis, a mother-beater, various violent or other "crimes," money in politics, moral failure, small towns, drugs, toxins, newspapers, psychologists, eating, power, bombing, theatre, abortion, genocide, unemployment, Hollywood, rumours, racism and poverty. Detailed study shows that the use of "evil" becomes attached to particular world events or everyday situations and is consistently used to describe them. Examples are Ronald Reagan's "evil empire" (the Soviet Union), George Bush's "axis of evil" (Iraq, North Korea and Iran), or the general usage of "evil" to describe communists, genocide, terrorist actions, etc. The latter are yet more evidence for the ongoing and growing body of definitions for "evil."

Finally, my third finding relates to what I called in the previous section the (addition of a) definition of "crime" in theological language.

To review, in the first section I argued that while in the early period of definitions both "evil" and "crime" are defined in moral language, in the late period new language definitions of "evil" and "crime" emerge that are theological. In the late period "crime" acts have become "evil" in a sense that is beyond the classical moral language definition. I argue that currently "crime" acts labeled as "evil" can be defined by how they partake, not only in a definition that is socially constructed, but also in a definition that links "crime" to "sin," "the devil," "the disobeying of divine or righteous law," and a "sinful and depraved nature." I went on to argue that the changes from the early to the late period shift not only the definition of "evil," but also the relationship of "evil" to "crime" such that we can now describe socially inappropriate acts (i.e. "crime" acts) by calling them "evil," and we also use the word "evil" (in its theological sense) to qualify certain attributes of "crime" acts (e.g. "sinful," of "the devil," etc.). As I concluded, this process changes the meaning of the word "crime," because they move from acts that are socially constructed and defined to acts that can be defined as imbued with characterizations and powers beyond social construction.

Were this interpretation correct, one would expect to find evidence for it in the everyday life of English-speaking communities. This is exactly what I have found in my media study. For example, consider this sample of newspaper headlines from the last three decades:

1   September 30, 1992, *Chicago Sun Times*: "Defense Rips Witness as 'Diabolical Evil'."
2   December 7, 1996, *The Toronto Star*: "Montreal Massacre Dead Killers are Evil not Insane."
3   April 15, 2001, *The Indianapolis Star*: "The Execution of Timothy McVeigh: As the Oklahoma City Bomber Lives out his Final Days,

Still-struggling Survivors Take Some Solace in Knowing Evil did not Triumph."

4. July 22, 2012, *Sunday Telegraph* (Australia): "Slaughtered in their Seats: How this Evil Loner Planned his Crime – Dark Knight Massacre."

In these stories a trial witness is compared to diabolical evil, murderers are defined as imbued with "evil" rather than lacking mental health, Timothy McVeigh is placed in a greater design of evil and the Aurora, Colorado (Batman movie) shooter is described as "macabre" and "evil." There is something categorically different about these stories, and it is as simple as that they do not read, for example, "Defense Rips Witness as Lying" but do read, "Defense Rips Witness as 'Diabolical Evil'." A moral language defined "crime" and a moral language defined "evil" have moved from being easily identified as social constructions of a moral language. Instead a theological language of "sin" can now color "crime," and a theological language of "the devil" can now color "evil." In all, what used to be acts defined by their absence of positive moral choice can now be seen as acts imbued by characterizations that point to powers beyond social construction. As Hickey writes: "[E]vil is a label we reserve for those worse than bad. 'Badness' we expect to find in many people, but evil relegates individuals to a special classification that suggests some form of satanic affiliation" (2003: 285).

"Evil" and the construction of "crime" in criminology

In this third study my task is to connect the previous two studies with criminological scholarly literature already linking the notions of "evil" and "crime" to a process of social construction and theological language.

European and American criminology emerge from a worldview that has always been in deep part theological (e.g. the Inquisition, witch hunts, etc.). In criminology there is a small body of literature linking the use of theological "evil" as part of the construction project of "crime." Perhaps the best example of this is Theodore Sarbin and Jeffrey Miller's study, "Demonism Revisited: The XYY Chromosomal Anomaly" (1970). In this research the authors argue that the first (and still prominent) theory of crime causation is a belief that one who engages in "criminal" behavior is either possessed, driven by internal entities, forces, demons, humors or is driven by id impulses. The authors of course have no problem finding evidence in such events as the Inquisition and witch hunts, nor do they shy from presenting the historical belief that murderers were possessed by the devil, and the subsequent psychological evaluations of the "criminal" by Freud and Jung, which bring us to today's wide consideration of "crime" acts as failures of id impulses, i.e. of human persons improperly controlling their impulses.

A fascinating accompanying study is Ronald Lee Boostrom's 1971 study, "The Personalization of Evil: the emergence of American criminology: 1865–1910." This author argues that, historically, "crime" is conceived of as an alien phenomenon in American society, and as a consequence is seen as a (theologically) "evil phenomenon" to be controlled and which rigorously connects "crime" acts to (theologically) "evil identity."

Conceptions of "crime" as alien and "criminals" as "evil" have a long history that modern scholars argue vociferously. Esther Madriz, in "Images of Criminals and Victims: a study on women's fear and social control" has convincingly showed that women perceive "criminals" as "out of control evil strangers randomly attacking their victims" (1997: 345). As Madriz demonstrates, the image of the "evil stranger" is ubiquitous, and I would add, uses the theological connotations of "evil" (devil, demonic, etc.) to inflate the perceptions of dangerousness.

Similarly, in "Media Trials," Ray Surette demonstrates that trials in the US are generally portrayed in entertainment themes that emphasize (1) abuse of power and trust, (2) "sinful" rich persons and (3) "evil" strangers (1989). The author's characterizations neatly unpack three themes I have already discussed: "crime" as moral language, "crime" as "sin" and "crime" as "evil." In "Scared Straight: ideology and the media," Gray Cavender demonstrates how "criminals" are portrayed in a one-dimensional manner as "evil," vicious and barely human (1981). In *At Stake: monsters and the rhetoric of fear in public culture*, Edward Ingebretsen discusses how persons are created as other-than-human "monsters" in mass media and popular culture (2001). In his aptly titled, *Black Demons: the media's depiction of the African-American male criminal stereotype*, Dennis Rome extensively portrays how African-American males are painted as "demons" and "devils" (2004). A review of such literature would be worthwhile in its own right, but my purpose is simply to establish the depth of scholarly interest with this representative sampling.

As I highlight here, criminology, the study of "crimes" and "criminals," has always had and continues to maintain a body of research that links the use of theological "evil" to our notions of "crime" and "criminals." This work points to behavior that denies human agency in defining what constitutes "a crime" and therefore who is and who is not a "criminal." The denial of our agency in constructing "crimes" and "criminals" means that in such work we relieve ourselves of responsibility for the definition and construction of what is a "crime" and who is a "criminal." *In a consequential sense, such theological language work and such theological construction work allows us to wash our hands of "criminals" and what we do to them.*

Conclusion

My three studies in this chapter demonstrate a common (popular and academic) conception of "crime" and "criminal" as socially constructed as well as theologically constructed. I am particularly struck by the notion that "criminological" thinking is, in important ways, built on top of a model that rejects the social construction of "crime."

Social constructionists argue that meanings always necessarily arise and change within a social context (Berger and Luckmann 1966). My study brings evidence that while sometimes we seem to understand that "crime" and "criminals" are socially constructed categories, we also sometimes think of them within a theological paradigm. This suggests a level of denial about human agency, i.e. the inherently human-constructed character of what is and what is not a "crime" or a "criminal." Our uses of "evil" demonstrate that we connect human acts defined as "crimes" to theological language and metaphysical causation that frees us from the judgment that is used to exclude, control and punish others; it gives us the opportunity to be free of responsibility for the definition and construction of what is a "crime" and who is a "criminal." As seen in media presentations of "crimes" and "criminals" portrayed in "evil" terms, we use theology and metaphysics in our language to transform people into "diabolical evil." This allows us to operate as if definitions of "crime" and "criminal" are given to us, rather than defined by us, which frees us from the knowledge that it is we who meaningfully cast social actors, social and "criminal" justice institutions and policies.

Broader critiques of "evil" within postmodernist scholarship similarly identify "evil" as inherently imbued with theological hues. Jennifer Geddes argues that the word "evil" is "metaphysically and theologically burdened" (2001: 2). As she writes:

> [T]he word "evil" is seen as a holdover from metaphysical and religious vocabularies that have been revealed by postmodern thought to be oppressive, binary, totalizing, and exclusionary. The word "evil," should be discarded, it is argued, because it has been used so often in oppressive ways. The act of identifying something as evil, of naming it "evil," actually promotes suffering, and in no small part by continuing ways of thinking that lead to violence and destruction.
>
> (Geddes 2001: 1)

The evidence suggests that it would behoove us to abandon theological language when we discuss so-called "crimes" and so-called "criminals." The availability of more than the social construction option to think about how "crime" and "criminal" definitions are achieved makes us susceptible to the work of moral entrepreneurs who come with their own agendas, whether liberal or progressive. Few of us in everyday life are conscious of how we construct what is a "crime" and who is a "criminal." For most of us, moral entrepreneurs lead us daily in the dominant discourse of "tough on crime" that views "criminals" as the bad guys, the dangerous, the "evil," while overlooking that the vast majority of "crime" is non-violent (as are the vast amount of people in prison) and that the vast majority of "criminals" are our otherwise mostly boringly ordinary family members (and not strange, deranged or "diabolical" others). All the work that goes into these constructions is unnoticed, and even though it goes against the grain of our broadly accepted justice definitions and goals (such as equal justice for all), they result in gross inequities that are daily observable in our social and "criminal" justice system.

Our building of "crime" and "criminals" in theological language points to the value of investigating how we construct and practice social control. It also highlights at least part of how justice recipes, which are otherwise unacceptable to our sense of what is just or fair (the massive incarceration and control of millions in the US, most of whom represent racial/ethnic minorities, the poor and the least educated), become palatable and consumable. I find that the presence of such theological language highlights that our social and "criminal" justice discourse can be centered on producing more than justice, e.g. the control of such "other" populations. It also highlights our discourse as confused about our justice commitments, and not as lucid and unambiguous as we sometimes like to think it is.

6   Talking justice

Interviews with justice workers

Introduction

I began this work by demonstrating that language choices generate discourses. I went on to argue that "how we talk about things" is important because it reflects and creates "how we think about things." In *Language of Justice* research, then, I pursue how our language choices reflect and generate our justice discourse. In other words, I draw attention to how our word choices reflect and create how we think about justice. For example, I have highlighted that how we talk about "victims" reflects and re/creates our conception of who is and is not an "innocent victim," and that to talk about "crime" as "evil" is also to avoid talking about the human agency entailed in "crime" responses.

Our language choices impact how we think about justice issues, but they also impact how we act to achieve justice. How we talk about justice reflects and creates meanings that we frequently use to frame, debate and decide public policy. In turn public policy decisions, and especially the moral entrepreneurs pushing for them, create and reinforce (or shift) our available language and consequently our justice meanings regarding what are just or unjust situations. As I highlighted in my analysis of John Ashchroft's and George Soros' speech, their language – whether centered on "tougher federal sentencing guidelines" through battling "criminals who victimize," or calling for the "support of legal marijuana" in order to focus battling "serious crime" – is used to create meanings such as "taking a stand against crime," "protecting the public" and being "tough on crime." Wide political agreement on these meanings has led to the creation of public policy that has led to unprecedented growth of the US prison population and the number of prisons built. Policy decisions reinforce the use of language such as "tough on crime," and some of the meanings they create, e.g. "increasing prison sentencing laws."

Our social and "criminal" justice discourse is always undergoing change. As I highlighted in my analysis of "tough on crime," new associated meanings, such as "smart on crime," have strengthened as the capital and social costs of the growing numbers of people in prison have come under criticism.

I noted that this emergence has been significant enough to begin to shift the very meaning of the words "tough on crime." As I demonstrated, the words "tough on crime" increasingly are coming to be associated with being "smart on crime." Even the meaning of the latter phrase has experienced a shift: increasingly, it retains the association to the meaning "protecting the public" while it also shifts in meaning from a blanket commitment to "increasing prison sentencing laws" to the "use of alternatives to incarceration." This ongoing shift within language frequently entails that meanings lack uniform agreement. Much as with public policy, one decade's understanding of an issue may be turned on its head in the next decade.

My point is this: by studying the words we use to talk about justice and by studying how we use justice words we can distinguish things unknown about how we think and do justice in everyday life. This is the content and purpose of *Language of Justice* research. It follows that failure to attend to justice language hinders a complete understanding of the justice we are producing.

The interviews

My goal in this chapter is to examine the justice language of four interviewed moral entrepreneurs who are intimately involved in the world of social and "criminal" justice. In these interviews, I ask my subjects to freely and extemporaneously speak about "criminal" justice issues that they currently consider important. My analysis of the interviews does not aim to produce statistics of any type regarding language, meanings or other. My only purpose is to explore their justice speech from the point of view of someone interested in *Language of Justice*. In other words, I seek in my analysis to (1) examine my subjects' justice language, (2) explore how their justice language choices reflect or lead them to the constructions of certain justice meanings and (3) identify their moral entrepreneuring around justice issues. Rather than using the interview data to construct individual narratives or to expose moral entrepreneurs' motivation, I am using them to point to how they talk about social and "criminal" justice.

My interview subjects (of varying gender although they are all referred to as "she" to further protect their identities), come from diverse backgrounds and diverse ideological positions. They are a prominent state senator (one of the three most active in the formation of social and "criminal" justice policy in her state), a prominent state judge, a leading and seasoned social and "criminal" justice activist, and a prominent citizen voice with a long history of involvement with the social and "criminal" justice systems from both the inside (as a prisoner) and the outside (as a provider of expertise to state legislators and reformists). The ideological positions of my subjects range from the deeply conservative to the deeply liberal. Regardless of their experiences or ideology, the justice language of these speakers merits consideration as moral entrepreneuring because these are actors who intentionally construct justice perceptions, justice viewpoints and justice recipes that they wish to see more widely accepted.

My rationale to interview these particular individuals is driven by a variety of factors. Two factors are especially important. First, each is a moral entrepreneur in the domain of "criminal" and social justice. As such, they provide an excellent opportunity to investigate the relationship between the language of justice and the moral entrepreneuring of social and "criminal" justice discourse. Second, each individual represents a distinct ideological position (ranging from far right to far left) and perspective (government, judicial bench, activist and citizen voice). Thus, the interview subjects are selected to reflect a variety of voices, and consequently to provide a variety of speech, thereby permitting a rich examination of justice language.

My interview subjects entertain many rich notions about justice. As a student of justice language, I am curious about how they use particular words and reference particular meanings in discussing their ideas of justice. I am especially interested in pointing out the process by which they construct justice, their rationalizations for their ideological positions and of course, the consequences of their language choices. Fundamentally, I conducted these interviews in order to analyze how powerful social and "criminal" justice entrepreneurs talk about justice issues. My interest is in their use of language, the contexts in which they think about justice issues and the meanings that their speech constructs and communicates. I am further interested in examining how they frame social and "criminal" justice issues (what language is used to define the issues?), how they perceive such issues need to be framed in various settings and how they would shift the discourse if they could (what language would they use to frame these issues?). I interpret the interviews using the same methodology as in my analysis of media reports; that of emergent interpretation analysis. Both interview transcripts and media reports are documents and both are chosen for the same reason: to explore social and "criminal" justice discourse.

What matters most in my analysis is not the validation or evisceration of any particular justice construction. As a moral entrepreneur I have my preferred justice words, justice meanings and justice recipes. As a researcher I accept the unavoidable moral entrepreneuring consequence of my work. But I have research purposes that do not relate to defining justice situations for my reader, or to promoting justice goals that agree with or differ from the goals of those whom I interview. Rather, my agenda in these interviews is first to identify moral entrepreneurs as intentional actors. Second, through my analysis of these interviews I aim to distinguish methodologies that can uncover such moral entrepreneuring around justice and that can compare justice speech acts analytically. Third, my research aims to demonstrate how the words that we use to discuss justice permit – and often encourage – us to construct both meanings and persons in specific ways, as well as to attribute motives to those people who enable and empower constructs of/for social control.

Put differently, I seek to argue that justice language choices are significant by demonstrating how they are used to construct justice meanings that are, in turn, employed to build and present public policy options as palatable or meritless. Frequently, our meaning constructions complicate what happens in the real world as we enact them out of habit. As discussed earlier, contemporary constructions about justice promote social control in our social life and are used to justify punitive measures. Importantly, our justice constructions validate how we determine who is legitimate and illegitimate, whether a person is "good" or "bad," and what we decide about them. In this sense, our constructions serve to include or to exclude particular other people in our social life. Given the seriousness of such actions, the centrality and importance of close language study is apparent.

"Offenders," "criminals" and "prisoners"

The sociologist Alfred Schutz demonstrates that frequently we organize our ideas about people as "types" (1964). He argues that we construct categories of "kinds of persons" in order to accomplish a meaningful construction of the social world. He argues that we use particular cues (such as speech or dress), and mores (including definitions of appropriate behavior or styles of discussion), to think and treat individuals as "kinds of persons." For example, we are all familiar with typologies such as "liberal" or "conservative." Schutz shows how an individual gains a store of knowledge about "types of persons" from accumulated social interactions. For example, many individuals construct knowledge about "liberals" and "conservatives" from the experience of multiple interactions with media and conversational partners who discuss "liberals" as types of people who enjoy raising taxes and "conservatives" as types of people who deplore heavy taxation. Of course, upon closer examination such groupings of "types of people" frequently prove to be more complex. For example, any one "liberal" may prove to have conservative notions about taxation, as any one "conservative" may prove to have deeply liberal ideas about the same (Lakoff 2004).

Much as Schutz would predict, in the process of building our social and "criminal" justice system we have constructed various ideas about "kinds of persons." In our work to meaningfully order our various justice meanings, we have created categories of "types of people" who interact with the "criminal" justice system. For example, we use cues and definitions of situations to construct persons as "victims," "criminals" or "offenders." These typologies are of special interest in *Language of Justice* research because they are used to determine how to consider and treat (often to control) those people we interpret as belonging to them. For example, I have already explored several justice-related typologies in my examination of "victim"; I distinguished that we tend to think of "victims" as belonging to one of two main typologies: innocent or not.

My interview subjects prove to hold a variety of perceptions that populate the world of "criminal" and social justice with a variety of typologies. For example, typically they self-present their justice ideology within progressive or conservative parameters, display an understanding of what characterizes a "criminal," and note the differences between "good people" and "bad people."

Frequently, the words or metaphors employed by my interview subjects to discuss typologies reveal matters of interest for *Language of Justice* studies. For example, in discussing "offenders," one subject attributes that conservatives "want to be rid of probation/parole, take away their [prisoners] weights [exercise tools]," while moderates are projected as "not want[ing] to permanently disable these people," but as wanting to "give them a chance to be mainstreamed." By looking closely at the speaker's language I distinguish that her word choices go beyond the surface popular distinction of conservatives as "tough" and moderates as "soft," and that her words construct "conservatives" as takers and "moderates" as givers; to be more precise, conservatives are qualified as "taking" probation/parole and weights, while moderates are qualified as "giving" ability and opportunity. It could be beneficial to more widely explore how the construction of taking and giving occurs in moral entrepreneurs' descriptions of "prisoners" and other constructed types.

In this same phrasing, I find the wording, "permanently disable these people," to be extremely rich. The notion of "disabling someone" conveys two ideas: that our actions can impact "prisoners'" future actions and that we have a responsibility for "prisoners" as "made" or "created." The key here is the idea of responsibility. This phrase imputes that by our management of "prisoners," we can "able them" or "disable them." It also indicates (communicates) that we may relate to incarceration with a notion of responsibility or not. This raises the question of how moral entrepreneurs construct the problem of who is responsible either for what becomes of an incarcerated person or of what opportunities are given to a person while incarcerated? It would be interesting to see the results of *Language of Justice* research on this question.

Another rich phrase is "give them a chance to be mainstreamed." The use of "chance" (as in opportunity) implies that "prisoners" might change their ways and become "mainstreamed" given the occasion to do so. In this construction, the idea of "our" responsibility is present, as is again the idea that "our" actions have effects on "prisoners." It would be worth examining how, within a debate about the building of additional prisons for example, varying entrepreneurs cast the issue of "taking," "giving" and "responsibility."

Another issue raised by this interview subject's seemingly simple construction of moderates and conservatives, is the question of what philosophical anthropology (definition of human nature) operates in our discourse. Invoked in her definitions of moderates and conservatives are different political approaches to "crime," but also implied are different ideas about people who commit "crime." The range of definition in her construction is that conservatives view "offenders" as people from whom things must be taken away (rights/privileges), whereas moderates see "offenders" as people to whom things must not be taken away (ability) or to whom things must be given (opportunity). Inherent in the first is punishment and inherent in the latter is assistance. Operating in this debate (punish or assist?) are different ideas of what/who constitute human beings, and how a particular class ("offenders") is to be treated. It would be relevant to develop research that examines the range within which the correctional debate occurs: what are the assumptions about human nature in different correctional policies? Are they consistent? If not, where are they contradictory? When we discuss correctional policy how do our conceptions consider human nature? What are we assuming? What cultural biases do we follow? Whose definition of human nature never enters the discussion?

Many of these issues can be seen in a description given by an interview subject who is a self-declared Democrat:

> [T]he Democratic position has been yes, crime is bad, but the people who commit it for the most part are impoverished, inner-city dwellers who start out life with two strikes against them, and we don't want to excuse their behavior, but we want to give them the resources so that they can avoid a life of crime, before they commit crime, and also if they have committed crime, giving them the resources anyway so that when they get out, they can make something of themselves without indulging in crime. So there's an element of compassion and help I think in the typical Democratic approach to crime.

Not only are all the themes just explored present in this description, but so are several phrases that merit further study: the baseball metaphor of "two strikes," the attitude of "excusing behavior" (or not excusing it), and "a life of crime." What I find most interesting in this quote is that, in the midst of this decidedly "liberal" description of "offenders," appears the phrase "giving them the resources anyway so that when they get out, they can make something of themselves without indulging in crime." The phrase is as illogical and awkward as an earlier example of associating the meaning "country club" with "prison experience." To begin, it is self-contradictory: if one starts life "with two strikes against them" and "doesn't have resources to make something of themselves" it hurts one's logic/case to claim that such a party is "indulging in crime." The quandary becomes even more evident when later, in her description of the "Republican position," she ridicules the notion of "free will," or the idea that "we all can equally choose crime" (as in deciding whether or not to commit "crime"). Here is the full description:

> The Republican view has become predominant and that is the view that we all have free will, whether we live in [an upscale neighborhood] or whether we live in [a poor neighborhood], and we all can equally choose crime as opposed to making a million dollars, and if we make the wrong choice then you deserve to be punished for it, and so be it, because you're a drain on society, and you're a drain on the wealth maximization energies of the rest of society.

Is it possible that the meaning "indulging in crime" has taken deep enough roots, has enjoyed such predominance in our thinking of why people who commit "crime" do so, that even a speaker in the midst of developing an opposing view describes "crime" actors as "indulging themselves"? Only a greater investigation into how this phrase is used in a variety of contexts could answer this question or suggest other alternatives. Such work is future work for *Language of Justice* studies.

Another example for future work is embedded in another interviewee's description of "a young man who was speeding his car on the [freeway] and he crashed into another car and killed some people. It's a horrendous crime without a doubt. But the young man did not intentionally kill. He did not premeditate a killing." Here the juxtaposition of "horrendous crime" with the repudiation of "intentional killing" makes little sense and suggests another phrase worthy of a *Language of Justice* investigation.

A "worse murderer" and a "better murderer"

Everyday discourse on "criminal" and social justice overflows with the manufacture and reproduction of meanings and constructions related to justice. As I have already shown, my language studies consistently demonstrate that the words we use to discuss justice reveal that we act to control others and that we select "others" for exclusion, control and punishment. One example from my interviews seemingly attempts to describe a "worse murder" and a "better murder." This example is pulled from a point in the interview when the subject was discussing her views on mandatory sentencing:

> One of my favorite examples is first-degree murder, and a situation where let's say you got a gang member who kills somebody with torture and violence, and it is premeditated, and only minimally provoked, let's say, there's a verbal incident, that's first degree murder. And you can make an argument that that dude deserves a very, very severe sentence and if you believe in the death penalty, maybe even death. There's another person that you can conceive of who commits first-degree

murder, like a battered woman, in an abusive relationship, married or not, where the male, regularly beats up the woman, for whatever reason ... and this goes on for a long period of time, months or years, and the woman, because she's submissive or weak, or whatever, puts up with it and then reaches a point where she breaks down, she crosses the line, she loses self-control and she kills the batterer. That's first-degree murder as well. And in this state, and in many other states, there is no discretion; it's really a choice between 25 years, or life on the one hand, or death. The assumption that underlies that kind of philosophy is that everybody who commits first-degree murder is a horrendous animal, with equal culpability. My two examples show, at least to me, that that's false. These two murderers are not in the same category, psychology, but they're in the same legal category, and they don't deserve to be there.

I want to focus on her construction of these two murderers as "categorically" and "psychologically" different, or as I summarize them, the "worse murderer" and "better murderer." In this passage there are many language choices worth noting. For example, the description of the "worse murderer" focuses on the murderer as "offender": he is "a gang member," he kills somebody "with torture and violence," his murder act is "premeditated," "minimally provoked" and "deserves a very, very severe sentence and if you believe in the death penalty, maybe even death." In contrast, the description of the "better murderer" focuses on the murderer as "victim": she is "a battered woman," she is "in an abusive relationship" where "the male regularly beats (her) up," she suffers this "for a long period of time, months or years," she is "submissive or weak," and "puts up with it," until she finally "reaches a point where she breaks down, she crosses the line, she loses self-control and she kills the batterer." Though the description is of two murderers, the language choices have already constructed one as an "offender" and one as a "victim."

The interview subject indicates that she is concerned that two crimes, with what she considers different degrees of culpability, receive the same sentence. My arguments here should not be interpreted to argue one way or another about the balance of culpability between these two murders. What I want my reader to notice is that we do in fact think in these terms, i.e. that one murder carries more culpability than another; I also want my reader to notice that such difference is constructed. My point is not whether a particular construction is helpful or problematic, but that identifying and analyzing such constructions reveals how we think about and enact justice regardless of what we "seem" to be saying.

Given the crucial and unfavorable role that minority race status has played in jury members' determinations of who receives the death penalty, it is really important to ask about how we talk about murderers (Unah 2011).

How do we construct different kinds of murderers? Who gets portrayed as a murderer by nature of "finally breaking down"? Who gets portrayed as a murderer by less generous terms? What do our choices of description indicate? We might ask who ends up being described in our public discourse as the "worse murderer" and who as the "better murderer"? As I have not done this research, I am unable to answer these questions. It is nonetheless significant to ask, because the answers might be very telling – as I found in the "victim" chapter. My solitary interview example cannot convey who is and who is not considered a "worse murderer" in our social life, but it can convey that we operate with such a category, and its investigation might be worthwhile.

If one murderer is worse than another, then it seems reasonable to ask if one murder might be considered worse than another. How do we construct different kinds of murders? Is the death of a "gang-banger's" "victim" more or less significant than the death of a batterer? Would the answer to this question change if the "victim" of the first murder was "an innocent bystander" or "another 'gang-banger'"? If we were to compare media descriptions of black-on-black, white-on-white, white-on-black and black-on-white murders, what (if any) differences would emerge in how they are described as better or worse murders or murderers? Similarly, what might we find in exploring the murders of those who belong to groups traditionally ostracized or tightly controlled? Might the murders of "prisoners" be described in different terms? What of the murder of a transgender sex worker? What of persons in different settings or of different socioeconomic status? What differences might exist in describing "crimes" beyond murder?

This construction of murders and murderers brings many matters worthy of investigation to light. Among such matters are the series of other language choices and metaphors evident in the passage quoted above. For example, the "worse murder" description includes the killing method (torture) whereas the "better murder" does not include a killing method; the "worse murder" is described as being done with "violence" while the second is not described as such (it is hard to imagine a murder that does not include violence); the "worse murder" is described as "premeditated, and only minimally provoked," and by something as minimal as "a verbal incident."

Lastly, it is important to mention that my interview subject constructed the opposition between the two murders/murderers examples quite intentionally. She chose her examples, as she says, to register her opposition to thinking about the two acts in a similar fashion: "These two murderers are not in the same category (or) psychology." But matters are not this simple. Her choice of words and examples are hardly random. She chose from an enormous pool of available justice words and examples. Within a single description such choices may be said to lack import; however, we could not maintain such a claim if we found similar patterns in studying the larger discourse. In an important sense, this is the argument entailed in *Language of Justice*: the words that we choose to talk about justice issues matter. They matter because they convey, frequently unwittingly, a variety of justice positions, commitments and rationalizations that are otherwise not so obvious or plain to see. It may not be striking for a moral entrepreneur to describe a particular murder or murderer as deserving of "a very, very severe sentence." But what if we found that our language distinctions were predicated by identity distinctions and that one group of people versus other groups, or one gender versus another, is more frequently than not (1) described by "offender" versus "victim" language when committing murder, or (2) is described as "finally breaking down and killing" versus "violently killing," or is described as "a person" versus a "horrendous animal"?

"Kids who end up criminals," the "worst of the worst" and the "criminal production factory"

Another interview subject introduced the idea that education was a central concern for achieving social and "criminal" justice in public life. As she said:

> [M]y belief is, is that you have to, the education system is where the action is at. That if the average outcome is slightly negative for kids, for the kids who end up being criminals, it's horribly negative there, that they have a hateful relationship with school, they are undermining school while they're in it for other kids, and then when they get out, they're really struggling back in society.

In this construction there are at least two phrases of interest. The first is "kids who end up being criminals." The phrase raises various questions. How do we manage, if at all, the issue of "criminals who used to be kids"? Who does, and who does not, have their past (i.e. their childhood) re-examined when defined as a "criminal"? Does such re-examination occur in a blanket fashion, or is it reserved for certain people? Is it assigned differentially depending on the crime? Does this construction imply that "criminals" are "made" or "created," rather than persons "making the wrong choice"? What ideas do moral entrepreneurs pushing various "criminal" justice agendas employ to construct the relationships between childhood/adulthood and "criminality"?

The second meaning to which I want to draw attention is how the kids described as becoming "criminals" are found to be "undermining school while they're in it for other kids." The question to address is who do we identify as undermining whom? In other words, whom do we define as "criminal kids" and whom as "other kids"? The significance of such a question is underscored by recalling not only how desegregation of schools sparked intense debate and violence in the history of this country, but also that *de facto* re-segregation is a topic of concern to many in this country today.

One interview subject noted that the "people who are in prison right now are the worst of the worst." She also went on to observe that putting people in prison is "sort of like sweeping up the sidewalks for the neighborhood." It is striking how a description of "prisoners" as "the worst of the worst" differs from the description above that differentiated between the murderer who is a "horrendous animal" and the murderer who just "breaks down and crosses the line." It is striking how a description of putting people in prison as "sort of like sweeping up the sidewalks for the neighborhood" (with its implied metaphors of "prisoners" as disposable and "prisoners" as trash) differs from the above explanation, "yes, crime is bad but the people who commit it for the most part are impoverished, inner-city dwellers who start out life with two strikes against them." Such differences in description raise important questions. For example, when do we call people in prison the "worst of the worst" and when do we call them "inner-city dwellers who start out life with two strikes against them"? Are there groups of persons who earn that label more or less frequently? What is the range of our metaphors for responding to "crime" acts or actors? When do we speak of "cleaning up the neighborhood," and when do we speak of "helping those without sufficient resources"? Are these questions purely a matter of ideological divide, or will a closer investigation of our own words convey much more – as I have shown is so often the case?

Another interview subject notes that "crime" mapping can "tell us where all the criminals come from." She spoke about how such mapping lets policy makers know which areas are a "hot spot" and "a criminal production factory." One might stop to ask what it means to call a neighborhood with a lot of "crime" a "criminal production factory"? It behooves us to ask who would lose and who would benefit from such a description and who would and would not use it? The interview subject brought it all together as follows:

> Why does crime happen in society? A lot of it is income ... the poorer you are, the less you have at stake in society ... so, poverty causes crime. And the other thing that causes crime to me is an education system in which you're put in an environment that you consider hateful for four to six hours a day, and so if you cannot get any emotional sustenance through your educational environment, and you combine that with poverty, it's just a recipe for, to me that's the ingredients of a criminal production factory, poverty combined with a nasty education, environment.

Constructions such as "criminal production factory" suggest we need to be asking a lot of questions and doing a lot of *Language of Justice* research. What are the varying ways moral entrepreneurs construct the presence of "deviant" acts? What are the differing language choices in describing neighborhoods with a high number of "crime" instances? Do such descriptions shift when moral entrepreneurs argue for investing in neighborhood development instead of building additional prisons? If so, how do they language their position and what does that languaging demonstrate they think about "offenders" and "criminals"? Are moral entrepreneurs consistent in their work, or do they define the same parties as "worst of the worst" in one moment and as "victims without choices" in another? If there are differences, it would be relevant to know who is addressed in each version. When are different versions presented? How are different versions languaged and what does the study of the contexts in which each emerges tell us about how we construct the "criminal," "the offender" and the "prisoner"? When do we talk about people as problems of management and technology, when as public policy failures or missed opportunities, and when as individuals who need to be swept into the trash or who need our help? When do we stop talking about "offenders" as the "worst of the worst" and start talking about them as individuals "who start out life with two strikes against them"? When do we speak of "murderers" as "horrendous animals" and when as people who finally "break down and cross the line"?

"Bad people"

In this chapter, I have already indirectly discussed the construction "bad people." For example, as an interview subject claims above, not "everybody who commits first-degree murder is a horrendous animal, with equal culpability." In my analysis of this speech, I demonstrated how moral entrepreneurs may create types of murderers, characterizing some of them as more culpable or worse than others.

The distinction of people who come into contact with the social and "criminal" justice system as either "bad people" or "good people" has a variety of implications. For those on whom these labels are used, they can result in receiving harsher punishment or in avoiding a prison sentence. One example is the little-known practice of paying for a better jail experience. For instance, in Pasadena, California, $100.00 plus per day will buy you a jail cell that is isolated from the general population and hence safer and more comfortable. As Janet Givens, a spokesperson for the Pasadena Police Department, says of its early 1990s launch: "Our sales pitch at the time was, 'bad things happen to good people'," and as she clarifies, "[p]eople might have brothers, sisters, cousins, etc., who might have had a lapse in judgment and do not want to go to county jail" (Stienhauer 2007: 24). The construction of good "offenders" with family members who have suffered a "lapse in judgment" is required to maintain the image of a just social and "criminal" justice system that sells justice products for cash payments made in advance.

The construction of bad offenders, of "bad people," is to language a group of people as wholly other. Previously, researchers have focused on cultural meanings and methods for describing otherness as "monstrous," for example, the Gothic criminology comparison of serial killers to vampires (Picart and Greek 2003). Other research has explored the influence of popular film on the construction of "criminal deviance" as "monstrous" or "evil" (Halttunen 1998). These studies uncover efforts to place certain "crime" behavior in a category of subhuman acts. But such categorization results in a reification of human behavior and a denial of the very humanness of all "crime" acts.

Each of my interview subjects, directly or indirectly, presents "offenders," "criminals" and "prisoners," as "bad people." For example, one interview subject declares: "After all, these are really bad people and we really do need to get them off the street." Another interview subject proclaims: "I mean, as bad as these people may be for doing what they're doing, they still have a place in the community in someone's life."

Many interpretations can be made about the construction "bad people." This construction is a proper subject for a major in-depth research work. However, immediately evident in these examples are the many dimensions of meaning in the construction "bad people," regardless of a speaker's angle, perspective or politics. For example, in the instance, "these are really bad people and we really do need to get them off the street," we encounter "bad people" as a meaning to convey the legitimacy in designating a person as someone who deserves to be incarcerated. In the instance of "as bad as these people may be for doing what they're doing, they still have a place in the community," we encounter "bad people" as a meaning used to communicate the illegitimacy of describing a person as someone who deserves to be incarcerated.

I have argued that those justice constructions that win the day affect our perceptions, experience and imagination, and so determine how justice in everyday life is constructed and practiced. One interview subject points directly to this when she discusses her experience of knowing numerous prisoners, yet always encountering the same prisoner in the media:

> If they're going to interview a family of an inmate, about what it's like to visit at the prison, they're interested in talking to a biker chick, or someone that, for lack of a better descriptive term, is lower, you know, is White trash, or lower, or is poor Mexican, or is, not just Black, but poor, very Black, and those that fit the stereotypes. And if they're going to, and they're hoping that, you know, when they ask for a picture of their loved one, that they're gonna show someone with a lot of tattoos and a lot of, and who will quote unquote look like a prisoner, kind of a scary looking person. And so the media, I think, perpetuates those images, and since most people, the vast majority of people never go to a prison, and don't go sit in the courtroom and look at people who are being sentenced to prison, and don't have any perception of what a prison is like, that's the stereotype, the stereotype is very real for them.

Years ago I saw Mike Wallace interview a man who had been to prison, and the first thing Mike Wallace said was: "You don't look like a prisoner to me, you look like a college professor." Well? What's a prisoner supposed to look like? What's a college professor look like you know? But that was the first thing that kind of popped out of his head, and they used that, that was part of the interview, so it wasn't like it was just a side comment that he made, that someone was going to edit out of the tape, that was actually used.

This example of the search for a "representative prisoner" shows in some depth the impact of the construction "prisoner as bad person." According to the interview subject "prisoner as bad person" is a construction that has so powerfully affected perception, experience and imagination, that media constructions of the incarcerated seek out the "bad person" and willfully ignore the rich diversity of the more than two million persons finding themselves to be a "prisoner" today in the US.

Another interview subject points out that the construction of persons as "prisoners" requires acknowledgement of more:

You hear these enormously human stories about failure. A woman whose husband was killed by a violent crime, or by an accident, her mother and father are elderly and they are unable to care for themselves, and she provides their care, she has a child and the child is of, during, in its formative years, and under those stresses she drank alcohol, or she used drugs, or she did something that was inappropriate and she's very sorry about that, and what happens is that the human side of the story, which is supposedly incorporated into the concept of justice here, gets just shoved to the side and the person is sent to jail for 60 or 90 days, or for three months or for six months or for a year … Not because that serves the person, not because it makes them less likely that they will make a mistake in the future, not because it will increase the probability of success on probation and, therefore, be a success for everybody, not because the system demands it or because the public is outraged over someone taking a drink when their husband is dead and they are under these stresses, but because it serves their purposes to be seen as tough on crime.

In this exegesis is an argument about the impact of constructing persons "committing crime" in one way or another. The interview subject describes justice as "shoved to the side" when a woman who has committed a "crime" is constructed as a person deserving imprisonment. My interview subject interprets such action as bringing harm to everyone except those politicians concerned with appearing "tough on crime"; especially hurt, she claims, are the woman, her child, her parents and the community at large. This story raises many important questions. For example, how do language choices impact how persons are defined within the "criminal" justice system? How do moral entrepreneurs preoccupied with defining "offenders," "prisoners" and "criminals" employ "bad people" meanings (in this example: "she drank alcohol," "she used drugs" and "she did something that was inappropriate")? How do moral entrepreneurs using "bad people" meanings create and sustain justice constructions that promote social control and punishment?

The construction "bad people" proves to be multi-layered. In the story below an interview subject explains how people with family members in prison may use "bad people" for their own purposes:

> I'm always amused when someone contacts me, as an advocate for prisoners, and says, "my son, who's you know, 45, and he's now in prison for eight years because this is his third time drug offense, I'm really upset because he's in a prison and there are murderers there! And there are, you know, my gosh, there are real criminals in there! And my son isn't!" In my experience that goes all the way to death row where people will say, "Well, you know, my husband is next to a baby raper! Okay, you know, my husband killed a couple of drug dealers, that's not as bad"!

In this example we can see both the internalizing of and resistance to several justice meanings related to "bad people." The related (justice) meanings include: the "offense" (a drug offense indicates a better person than a murder offense), "criminal" ("not a real" criminal is better than "a real criminal"), and, of course, "bad person" (murdering a drug dealer is not as bad as raping a baby). The interview subject relating this story gave an interpretation worth repeating:

> People who are in prison, and it extends to their families, who tend to look down their noses at others who are also in prison, but for what they perceive to be a more serious or a more despicable, socially unacceptable crime. ... I think it's a coping mechanism, obviously, because when you're already down there at the bottom of the totem pole trying to support all that weight of the societal behavior that you've been judged on, then I think it's a natural tendency I guess, of human nature, to try and still remain in some level of dignity ... and unfortunately the choice is to remove yourself from, elevate yourself in a way that allows you to look down at someone else below you, and say, "Well, you know, at least I'm not down there."

In yet another interview, a subject further explores how the meanings of certain words (such as "responsibility") have become so intertwined with the meaning of "bad people," that entire levels of obfuscation have entered our justice discourse. The quote is long, but well worth citing:

I think this word "responsibility" is so overused I tend not to, I tend not to go there, because it's been so misconstrued. I mean people say, "look, you have to take responsibility for your acts, you robbed a bank," or "you robbed a convenience store." Well that's probably true, but that isn't the whole story is it? He can't take responsibility for the fact that there were no jobs in his neighborhood, he can't take responsibility for the fact that he grew up where the only people who had any kind of power in his community were the fucking drug dealers that drove around in fancy cars and had women and booze and all the rest of the stuff. How the fuck does he take responsibility for that? So, yes he did something that was wrong, and yes he's a drop out from school and yes, yes, yes, yes, yes, but he can't take responsibility for all the influences that were there. What he can do is he can finally, if we send him to prison and we're really lucky, this will be the one in a million who's going to say, "all of the rest of that stuff is true and I see how it influenced my behavior, but I recognize that I have to find some way to achieve an individual success by getting beyond all of it. I've gotta get, I have to do this leap frog routine, and I have to get completely to a different level in order to get over it." That's not taking responsibility that's fucking performing a miracle! Now, is there a sacrifice that's involved? Yeah. For the kid who doesn't go that route and who takes on his peers and who has to put up with all kinds of pressure and stresses and humiliation and the people who are snickering at him and calling him a wimp and all the rest of that stuff because he doesn't carry a gun and he doesn't you know act aggressive, yeah, there's a sacrifice involved and that sacrifice is paid off ten years down the road when he's got a house and a wife and kids and a job and he's functioning in a place where he is doing some good and he's got a degree. His personal sacrifice can be seen as, "oh well I took responsibility for some shooting, against all odds." No, what he did was, he took some damn good advice and he was willing to eat a mile of shit in order to succeed. That's not really responsibility, that's just a smart kid who was able to get over it. The kid right next to him didn't.

In this quote, as in others, my interview subject does not discuss the construction "bad people" directly. She never says, "this is not a bad kid." Yet it is everywhere implied as she details all the challenges this hypothetical kid has encountered. With this example I am interested in pointing to how moral entrepreneurs use language in subtle ways to construct and shift the meanings operating in our social and "criminal" justice discourse. Debates about justice in social life are settled in public discourse through both direct and indirect dialogue. However, debate always occurs within constructions of speech that pack multiple justice meanings in layers and dimensions too dizzying for scrutiny in the moment. Therefore, it is worthwhile to take the time to deconstruct the everyday justice speech of moral entrepreneurs.

This is the point of entry for *Language of Justice* research. With such work, the construction "bad people" may be located, either when it is directly used or when it is implied; we can then analyze the numerous justice meanings that accompany its use. Having unpacked these meanings we will be better positioned to make the incredibly impactful decisions about how to respond to these "bad people." Here, I can only begin to point to how the meaning of "bad people" is produced in our discourse, its importance and suggest some avenues for further research.

Conclusion

In the beginning of this work, I argued that moral entrepreneurs use justice words to construct justice-related images and metaphors (e.g. "the criminal production factory," "the worst of the worst") and sometimes even use all such constructions as ingredients for putting together what are best called recipes for achieving justice, such as the "tough on crime" discourse.

My analysis in this chapter points to a variety of recipes. Some of them (e.g. "crimes," "bad people," "worse murderers" and "better murderers") are so entrenched in our way of thinking about and doing justice that we never recognize them as recipes, but rather accept them as factual descriptions of reality. As constructions, our justice recipes carry layers and dimensions of meaning that are deeply complex. For example, the construction "criminals" communicates meanings shared by many moral entrepreneurs ("persons committing acts we rather they would not"), but it also carries meanings that are a matter of disagreement ("bad persons" versus "persons needing resources"). Ultimately, we must come to terms with the fact that typologies such as "criminals" are necessarily always constructions. They may be complex constructions, ones that allow for simplistic or critical meanings, or ones that lend themselves to progressive or conservative meanings; regardless, they are always constructions.

Deconstructing justice recipes is a complex process. A justice recipe is more than its ingredients. Frequently, a justice recipe can hide complex meanings that are themselves constructs of other justice meanings. Any single justice meaning can and frequently does take on an existence and social life all its own, and may be difficult to recognize as being constructed. Thus, any meaning may appear to be separate from meaning making. The same holds true for recipe-making acts. In other words, the author of any justice recipe may be so obscured as to leave the recipe appearing to be true, objective or undisputed. In such fashion, a justice recipe can come to define the way things are and the way things need to be done in the social and "criminal" justice system. One example is the phrase "the prosecuting of criminals." We have seen, in this chapter, how complex and pregnant with layers and dimensions of meanings the construction "criminals" is. The recipe itself, "the prosecuting of criminals," is uniformly accepted as social fact and necessity, while its alternatives (such as not prosecuting, or using restorative justice conceptions) are rarely considered.

My interviews are exploratory research into the world of justice language. More than anything they indicate how much language work there is yet to do and how many questions we need to ask. My interview data cannot suggest justice trends or habits, nor do they prove any particular interpretation about justice in our social life. But they can and do suggest a fruitful direction for further research by pointing to the constructed nature of justice meanings.

My claim is that *Language of Justice* research matters because if language is ignored or appropriately manipulated it may hide moral entrepreneurs, their agendas and their attempt to convince that they speak for us. Importantly, if we do not carefully choose our justice speech we are subjected to a justice system created by moral entrepreneurs whose justice rhetoric may conceal agendas varying from the regressive to the progressive and *none of which necessarily corresponds to our espoused communal value of equal justice for all.* It should be clear by now that our language choices affect not only how we interpret what is just, but also how we act in everyday life to create a just community. Thus, in scrutinizing how we talk about justice, I repeatedly find that the words we use have implications about how we think about justice and how we work to achieve justice.

Ultimately, I map speech acts and draw focused and close attention to the specific language that various speakers use in order to outline how justice discourse develops and changes. I observe that, while our language choices sometimes reflect our claim that we value justice, at other times they do not. Finally, I see that in our attempt to build a just social life, sometimes our actions are clearly acknowledged, whereas at other times they are concealed in language.

Knowing that our language choices affect life deeply matters. By knowing the importance of language we are alerted to how – in contextually studying justice words – we can observe and evaluate the construction of justice meanings and justice policy. In other words, we are awakened to the power and impact that language choices have in constructing justice policy and consequently, justice outcomes. Tracking justice discourse illuminates that various justice ideas and practices are intentionally constructed to increase social control in both public and private life. Knowing that our language choices matter highlights how they form and inform public policy, which disproportionately affects the least powerful among us: the "deviant," the excluded, the underclass and various minorities (racial/ethnic, sexual orientation and other).

7 *Language of Justice* as critical criminology

Society punishes severely those who commit the crime which she has herself prepared.

W.A. Bonger
Criminality and Economic Conditions

All official institutions of language are repeating machines: school, sports, advertising, popular songs, news, all continually repeat the same structure, the same meaning, often the same words: the stereotype is a political fact, the major figure of ideology.

Roland Barthes
The Pleasure of the Text

Introduction

The epigraphs that open this book suggest that human beings do not live in the world of social activity alone, but are also at the mercy of the language they speak. Language is not incidental to who we are, and it is far more accurate to say that who we become is due in great measure to the daily language habits that use us as much as we use them (Cross 1979). From this perspective, I argue that the language we use when we do justice is important, and that the work of the moral entrepreneurs who push language frames, regardless of their politics, matters even more. For, as Orwell clarifies, it is these who name people killed by carpet bombing "collateral damage" and it is these who make the violence of war more consumable (2000). Equally, I argue that it is moral entrepreneurs who name social control as being "tough on crime" and name "criminals" as being the "the worst of the worst"; this work makes the cruelty and violence of imprisonment (which harms not only the millions inside but also their children, families and friends) more consumable. To recognize the parallels between these two constructions is to have digested the arguments and evidence I offer in this book.

Debating justice language is anything but extraneous or meaningless. A debate about justice language is actually a disagreement about what are appropriate social and "criminal" justice practices; often, embedded in these disagreements is actually a competition to establish whose justice language will define debate about the practices. This makes evident how central the words we use to think critically about social and "criminal" justice are, because our justice words convey both what practices we are actually committed to and what practices we are truly striving for.

My *Language of Justice* research matters because, as C. Wright Mills writes, "[t]he control of others is not usually direct but rather through manipulation of a field of objects," and "[w]e influence a man by naming his acts or imputing motives to them or to him" (1940: 907). As Mills describes, I have argued; we define and perform social control indirectly by manipulating language and naming others. It is with and through our language choices that we design, prepare and execute social control of entire populations of persons. These people, on the whole, belong to racial/ ethnic minorities, are economically underprivileged, and unduly represent uneducated groups. These two facts together make *Language of Justice* research important to the theoretical paradigm of critical criminology – which views most dominant social and "criminal" justice conceptions, institutions and practices as operating in unjust and unequal playing fields.

Language of Justice and critical criminology

My purpose in this final chapter is to summarize the most important findings of this book, and in the process place *Language of Justice* research in the context of critical criminology.

Critical criminology is best understood as a response to classical criminology. Scholars of the latter argue from a macrosociology perspective and stress structural functionalism; they consider society's parts to be interdependent and organic, view society as stable and slow to change, and assume a wide consensus among members on norms and values (Parsons 1954 and Merton 1968). In contrast, critical criminologists travel in the tradition of conflict theory, which emphasizes the relation of society's parts as contentious and competitive, see society in a constant flux and conflict, and direct attention to social inequalities (Coser 1967 and Dahrendorf 1968).

Critical criminologists argue that many modern societies are defined by large and far-reaching systems of social control (law, police, prisons). They see these systems as maintained by the organizational work of those who disproportionately own community resources and who benefit most from the structures that protect their advantages (Ferrell 1993 and 1998). Consequently, the central concern of critical criminologists is the distribution of power and resources among social groups. The names given to various critical criminologies point to substantive concern for the distribution of political power (anarchist criminology), the unexamined benefit to privileged groups resulting from a positivist worldview (critical-radical criminology), the hegemony of some cultural groups over others (constitutive–cultural criminology), gender inequity in power and resource distribution according to gender group (feminist criminology), the absence of humanistic concerns (humanistic criminology), class antagonism (Marxist criminology), the power and control of media as a voice to maintain the status quo (newsmaking criminology) and the violence of punishment and how it perpetuates and expands "crime" (peacemaking criminology).

Critical criminologies offer unique insights by sharpening the focus on social, political and economic inequality as a defining reality and on the impact social–structural forces have in defining processes of social control. For example, in their study, *Under Siege: Poverty and Crime in a Public Housing Community,* Walter Dekeseredy and his coauthors demonstrate that the problem of "crime" can only be effectively addressed by comprehensive political, social and economic solutions to decades (if not centuries) of accepted inequities (2003). The authors convincingly argue that moral entrepreneurs of the modern "criminal" justice system proffer few solutions to problems of inequity (which disproportionately impact the definition and prosecution of "crime" acts). They complain bitterly about a self-righteous discourse, which they see as amounting to no more than band-aid solutions and cosmetic patchwork masquerading as social and "criminal" justice.

My *Language of Justice* research explores Dekeseredy and his coauthors' assertions: if the justice meanings that dominate our "criminal" justice discourse are interactional products promoted by moral entrepreneurs, then how are these meanings institutionalized in our public discourse and how are they maintained? If Dekeseredy and his co-authors are correct that these justice meanings promote a culture of selfishness, greed and indifference, and, if they are correct that this culture forces millions into wasted lives of incarceration, while providing little public safety to the rest of the population, then how are these justice meanings crafted, how are they introduced and how is their fabrication disguised? If Dekeseredy and his co-authors are correct in all this, how do we explain that most people seem to accept the dominant public social and "criminal" justice discourse, which claims we (at least broadly) accomplish "equal justice for all"?

My *Language of Justice* research contributes to an understanding of how the discourse distinguished by Dekeseredy and his co-authors is normalized by exposing the words we use in our social and "criminal" justice speech. I use the word "exposing" because, when I study seemingly ordinary words and phrases (as I did in Chapters 3, 4 and 5), or when I analyze the language of moral entrepreneurs discussing justice issues (as I did in Chapter 6), I find the same thing. I find that our language choices hide commitments that have little to do with our espoused ideals. I further find that these commitments frequently lead to the social control of "others" in socially disadvantaged positions. I find that our language also masks the work that we do to rationalize our justice actions. In my research, I show that not only is the process of selecting "others" for social control not acknowledged, but also unacknowledged is that they are left (at best) undiscussed and (at worst) framed to suggest that they are to blame for the condition we have chosen them for.

In my analysis of "tough on crime," I expose an underlying justice scheme that targets the parties that it targets because these parties are chosen to fulfill the role of target. I expose that this phrase does not refer, as is frequently argued, to an external reality which so threatens our existence that severe sentencing/punishment actions are required. Nor does this phrase disclose something particularly horrible about some persons or groups of persons ("evil"), or something particularly wonderful about others we must protect ("innocent victims"). Instead, we construct "others" as "evil" or "non-innocent victims" who must be handled "toughly" to justify and make more palatable the "tough on crime" sanctioning choice we seem unable to accept as just that: a choice.

As discussed earlier, when we choose one body of attitudes, values and laws we cannot avoid that by so doing we subordinate other candidates. The schemes we construct from such choices are the tools we then use to define situations and construct what we come to recognize as the seemingly independent "reality" of social control. As the architects of social control (even if we are inspired by the noble goals of determining an ideal social organization), we must accept that it is we who single out certain persons as "unadjusted" or "deviant." "Tough on crime" can never be a justice scheme demanded by external phenomena; it is condemned to be our choice for controlling populations we deem desirable to control. As critical criminologists argue, and the "tough on crime" rhetoric and agenda highlights, the unavoidable fact is that the populations we deem desirable to control are seldom the ones who prevent our ideal social organization. For example, although we view populations using recreational drugs as dangerous and in need of control, the damage they contribute to social inequities is miniscule as compared to the vast inequities those who design, produce and manage our social control are contributing.

The discourse tracking favored by *Language of Justice* research to analyze phrases such as "tough on crime" makes it possible to expose how the process of excluding, controlling and punishing the other is accomplished, reproduced and shifted within and through language. As I demonstrate by tracing the historical evolution of the "tough on crime" scheme in media reports, language choices in our social and "criminal" justice discourse have great impact. Language choices affect not only how we interpret what is just, but also how we act in everyday life to create the "just." While sometimes our speech acts reflect our justice claims (e.g. that we care about "equal justice for all"), at other times the contexts of our speech acts betray other concerns. For example, moral entrepreneurs' work to demonstrate consistency of meaning in their use of "tough on crime" highlights that their justice discourse is shaped by more than simply arguing for a particular justice scheme.

My analysis of "tough on crime" exposes that sometimes our justice actions are clearly acknowledged, as in the early call issued by some moral entrepreneurs to get "tough on crime," which openly called for expanding incarceration policies. But sometimes attempts are made to conceal our justice actions in language. For example, in the face of a fiscally unsustainable correctional situation, some moral entrepreneurs introduce a new discourse of "smart on crime" rather than admit the failure of "tough on crime" policies and/or openly call for a reduction of incarceration practices. The new discourse hides the justice action to decrease reliance on incarceration policies while allowing these moral entrepreneurs to claim sustained support for "tough on crime" policies. As my analysis demonstrates, the shift is impeccably deft, but nonetheless results in an unacknowledged, complete transformation of the meanings on which the "tough on crime" discourse rests. This analysis also shows that, absent a transparent justice discourse, moral entrepreneurs can run into significant challenges to alter the terms of the social and "criminal" justice discourse even when they want to.

My analysis exposes that the entire "tough on crime" discourse is produced, reproduced and shifted in the abstract universe of "crimes," "offenders" and "victims" and does not engage the specificity and innate complexity of particular "crime situations." In other words, abstract categories become the terms of social and "criminal" justice discourse, and they replace any candid acknowledgement of the constructed character of social control and the policies and practices resulting from it. Thus, our justice discourse is centered on a concern for social control and punishment and not the work of achieving justice as defined by our justice value claims. For example, the "tough on crime" discourse is perpetuated by social actors (moral entrepreneurs) who seek to emphasize activities whereby they control "others," rather than any activities undertaken to address or repair harms, challenge "crime" causes or address the new circumstances of harm that incarceration policies of "tough on crime" create for new "others" (e.g. families of the incarcerated). This same "tough on crime" discourse leadership by moral entrepreneurs illustrates how their work can be successful while going unnoticed (whether or not it is aligned with broadly accepted justice definitions and goals); it also reveals how susceptible discourse is to their individual politics, agendas and worldviews.

The *Language of Justice* frame is substantiated by exploration of the "tough on crime" example. My analysis of this discourse exposes that language choices define how social actors (crime actors), "criminal" justice institutions (corrections) and social policies and practices (increased use of incarceration) are meaningfully constructed and shifted with the passage of time. My research also unveils how such definition making is used to build entire justice recipes, such as "smart on crime" or "tough on crime," which come to encompass multiple meanings that eventually take on an existence and social life all their own, and appear to be separate from recipe-making acts. This analysis shows that eventually "tough on crime" is authorless because it exists for multiple audiences as a justice notion that appears true, objective and for many, undisputed, i.e. a justice recipe defining the ways things are and need to be in the social and "criminal" justice system.

Research into the term "victim" reveals commitments that have less to do with our espoused ideals and more to do with the "others" we choose to place at the center of our social control work. I also expose how, hidden in our very language, is the work we do to justify our justice actions. As I demonstrate in Chapter 4, though we could scarcely be accused of pointedly, directly and clearly doing so, our use of "victim" frequently demonstrates that we discriminate between "innocent" and not so "innocent victims." Our own use of the word "victim" highlights that we are frequently inclined to think of, or at least consider, the following as innocent: children, those overpowered by the state and those loudly proclaiming innocence. All others, my evidence suggests, remain suspect and we may doubt their innocence should they become "victims."

My study of "victim" demonstrates that, in our social and "criminal" justice discourse, we are ready to believe, by and large, that women are "not innocent victims." My study also shows how we are ready to believe that male-to-female raped persons are in their majority "not innocent victims," and that most targets of racial prejudice are "not innocent victims" either. Thus my study demonstrates that, within (and through) "victim" language, we can exclude and control others as better or worse "victims," as innocent or not innocent, and at times do so regardless of exterior circumstances. The popular use of "victim" further demonstrates that our justice claims (e. g. equal justice for all) may be summarily relinquished in our willingness to find fault with those others to whom we assign responsibility for becoming "victims."

A *Language of Justice* analysis of "victim" in our social and "criminal" justice discourse exposes that we create inequity. While imputing to children innocence may appear innocuous, can the same be said for assigning suspicion to racial minorities when they claim prejudice, or assigning deficiency of innocence to women when they claim rape? My analysis demonstrates that these agendas are hidden, and that, as witnessed by the words that betray us, we are unjust. The implication of how we use the word "victim" in our social and "criminal" justice discourse is that we are preoccupied by concerns other than that of producing justice. At best, our use of "victim" highlights us as confused about our justice commitments, which no longer seem, in this light, as lucid and unambiguous.

Further, my analysis of "victim" use demonstrates that legitimacy in being a victim is not necessarily given by external designations, but by a complex process of social and "criminal" justice discourse that belies a variety of justice commitments. Some of these justice commitments are so well defined that, even before agents can act, they are assigned value and quality. For example, one's innocence in being a "victim" may be determined by one's gender or racial identity more than one's action.

My analysis of our use of "victim" also exposes how we come to embrace some definitions of agency while rejecting others. Sometimes our decision to assign legitimacy or illegitimacy in victimhood is not the result of willful cognizant choice, but derives from social patterns entrenched in linguistic habits or pre-patterned thoughts. Our use of "victim" demonstrates that we operate as if the designation "victim" and the ideology of victimhood are external givens; we take no responsibility for selecting a definition of "victim" or an ideology of victimhood. Lastly, our use of "victim" demonstrates how we use language to add meaning (as having agency in becoming "victims") to certain social identities (such as women and racial minorities); it further shows how we then use these modified identities to construct justice recipes of innocence achieved or innocence lost.

My analysis of our uses of "evil" exposes that we use language to exclude, control and punish others by connecting human acts defined as "crimes" to theological language and (hence to) metaphysical causation, thereby freeing ourselves from responsibility for the fact that our judgment has excluded, controlled and punished others. As seen in media presentations of "crimes" and "criminals" portrayed in "evil" terms, we use theological and metaphysical categories in our language to transform people into "diabolical evil." Such evidence suggests that while we may espouse "equal justice for all," our actions do not always correspond to such justice claims, but rather that they are driven by other concerns.

My study of the relationship between the terms "evil," "crime" and "criminals" in criminology literature carries important implications for our social and "criminal" justice discourse. As I highlight, criminology has always had and still maintains a body of research that links the theological construct "evil" as part of how we socially construct "crime" and "criminals." Such work points to behavior that absolves humans of agency in defining what constitutes a "crime" and therefore who is and who is not a "criminal." The denial of our agency in constructing "crimes" and "criminals" means that in such work we free ourselves of responsibility for the definition and construction of what is a "crime" and what is a "criminal." Our use of "evil" as it relates to "crime" indicates that we can proceed as if external definitions of "crime" and "criminal" are given to us, rather than defined by us, which further frees us from recognizing our agency in meaningfully casting social actors, social and "criminal" justice institutions, and policies.

A *Language of Justice* analysis of "evil" as it relates to "crime" exposes the role of moral entrepreneurs in defining social and "criminal" justice language. Few of us in everyday life are aware that we construct what is a "crime" and who is a "criminal." For the most part, moral entrepreneurs lead us daily in a dominant discourse of "tough on crime," and "criminals" as the "bad guys," the "dangerous" and "the evil." Inundated by the repetition of such discourse, we quickly forget that most "crime" is non-violent as are the majority of people in prison. Most of this construction goes unnoticed, and although it goes against the grain of broadly accepted justice definitions and goals (such as equal justice for all), the gross inequities of our social and "criminal" justice system are daily observable.

A *Language of Justice* approach to "crime" and "criminals" brings the context of theological language to light and exposes how an attitude is created that allows us to wash our hands of "criminals" and of what we do to them. This attitude also leads us to accept justice recipes, such as three-strike sentencing, that would otherwise be unacceptable to our sense of what is just or fair. In looking at how such thinking relates to the massive incarceration of "others" in American society (two million and counting), or to the fact that most of those "others" represent racial and ethnic minorities, the poor and the least educated, I find that theological language highlights how our social and "criminal" justice discourse privileges objectives other than justice, namely social control.

A *Language of Justice* analysis of interviews conducted with moral entrepreneurs of justice exposes similar issues. Though my findings from these interviews are suggestive rather than conclusive (my sample is restricted to the language of a few individuals), the findings do resonate with the results of my other language studies. In my analysis of these speakers I show that operant in moral entrepreneuring around justice are different ideas about people who commit "crime." While terms such as "offenders," "criminals" and "prisoners" are common, there is a range of definition that constructs such people in vastly different ways: "offenders" as people who ought to have things taken away (rights/privileges), "offenders" as people from whom things must not be taken away from (ability) or as people to whom things must be given (opportunity). Inherent in the first is punishment and inherent in the latter two, assistance. Whether to punish or to assist is likely to be determined by different ideas of what/ who human beings are by definition of being human, and of how a particular class of them ("offenders") is to be treated. All these terms are used varyingly to construct some people as "dangerous" and some as "innocent." The question of immense import is which "offenders" do we construct as "dangerous," which as resembling "victims" and which as "innocent"?

The interview research underscores that the words we use to discuss justice unveil much about how we act to control others and about how we go about our process of choosing "the other" who is to be excluded, controlled and punished. Analysis of the language of one moral entrepreneur revealed a hierarchical conception of a "worse murderer" and a "better murderer." Such distinctions are themselves acts of social control that justify by escalating or de-escalating the severity of response. In the first case, social control escalates in response to the person who kills as an "offender," who is "a gang member," who kills somebody "with torture and violence" and whose murder is "premeditated," "minimally provoked" and "deserves a very, very severe sentence and if you believe in the death penalty, maybe even death." In the second case, there is the attempt to mitigate and de-escalate the punitive response to another person who kills as a "victim," who is "a battered woman," "in an abusive relationship [where] the male regularly beats [her] up," she suffers this "for a long period of time, months or years," she is "submissive or weak" and "puts up with it," until she finally "reaches a point where she breaks down, she crosses the line, she loses self-control and she kills the batterer." Though the description is of two murderers, the language choices have already constructed one as an "offender" and one as a "victim."

My analysis exposes that the construction of one person who kills as an "offender" and another person who kills as a "victim" is built on a body of undisclosed assumptions about who is a worthy candidate of our social control efforts and to what degree. The abstract categories of "gang member" and "battered woman" carry social meanings that have constructed the first as dangerous and violent and the second as vulnerable and breaking down. Yet it would be equally difficult to produce sociological evidence (with any consistency) that persons in gangs who commit murders are not "vulnerable" and "broken down," as it would be to produce evidence that battered women committing murders do not act in ways that are dangerous and violent. That we can construct a gang member who kills as "a worse murderer" and a battered woman who kills as a "better murderer," relates to something other than the act of murder or the chosen descriptors of the person committing the act of murder. Who is constructed as "worse," "dangerous" and the like is related less to external measures, than to who is defining the situation.

The justice language in these interviews introduces multiple, varied constructions of "offenders" from "the worst of the worst" and "horrendous animals" to "the people who commit [crime] for the most part are impoverished, inner-city dwellers who start out life with two strikes against them." One moral entrepreneur wants to know "where all the criminals come from" so she may control a "hot spot" as "a criminal production factory." To another interview subject, "offenders" are "really bad people and we really do need to get them off the street." While to another, "as bad as these people may be for doing what they're doing, they still have a place in the community in someone's life." In choosing their words, these moral entrepreneurs use meanings to construct and communicate the legitimacy of describing a person as someone who deserves to be incarcerated or the illegitimacy of describing a person as someone who deserves to be incarcerated. To one moral entrepreneur, "offenders" need to be picked up, "sort of like sweeping up the sidewalks for the neighborhood" and to another "they still have a place in the community in someone's life."

From the perspective of *Language of Justice* research, these interviews reveal that our social and "criminal" justice discourse is built, in part, by the intentional and unintentional work of moral entrepreneurs who use justice-related images and metaphors (such as "kids who end up criminals") to construct and boost the appeal of particular justice recipes. My research exposes that some of these justice recipes are so entrenched in our way of thinking about and doing justice that we no longer recognize them as recipes, but rather see them as self-evident (e.g. "victims," "crimes," "bad people"). As constructions, our justice recipes convey layers and dimensions of meaning that are deeply complex. For example, the construction "criminals" carries meanings that varying moral entrepreneurs share ("persons committing acts we rather they would not"), but also carries meanings that are a matter of disagreement ("bad persons" versus "persons needing resources"). Ultimately we must come to terms with the fact that typologies such as "criminals" are necessarily always constructions. They may be complex constructions, ones that allow for simplistic or critical meanings, or ones that allow for progressive or conservative meanings, but they are nonetheless always constructions.

Language of Justice research exposes that deconstructing justice recipes is a complex process. A justice recipe is more than its ingredients. Frequently, a justice recipe may hide complex meanings that are themselves constructs of other justice meanings. Any single justice meaning can, and frequently does, take on an existence and social life all its own; and it may then be difficult to see it as constructed. Thus any meaning can appear to be separate from meaning making. The same holds true for recipe-making acts. In other words, a recipe author may disappear leaving the recipe to appear self-evident, objective or undisputed. In such a fashion a justice recipe can come to define "the ways things are done" or "the way things need to be done" in the social and "criminal" justice system. One example is the phrase "the prosecuting of criminals." As just evinced, the construction "criminals" has complex levels of meaning. The recipe itself, "the prosecuting of criminals," is widely accepted as social fact and necessity, and its alternatives (such as not prosecuting, using restorative justice recipes or practices) are rarely, if ever, heard or considered.

Thus, in *Language of Justice* research I contribute to critical criminologies by drawing evidence to the argument that what defines "crime" and the "criminal" is not some "natural" or "criminogenic" status of personhood. Rather, I bring evidence to the argument that "crime" and the "criminal" are socially constructed definitions and situations, introduced and maintained by both intentional and unintentional acts of social control. By highlighting social and "criminal" justice discourse, my language studies identify how social control and social oppression occur as a result both of intentional moral entrepreneuring and of unreflective repetitive daily language use. Thus, my work demonstrates that both "crime" and the "criminal" are products that divide powerful from powerless, controller from controlled, oppressor from oppressed, and that represent the sense of "dangerous" and "threat" experienced by the former rather than the latter. Finally, with *Language of Justice* research I highlight that any solution to our current justice predicaments can only be resolved when social and "criminal" justice are conceived of as one field (and not as two). Beyond a concern for "criminal" justice institutions and practices of social control, the work must move into thinking through social policy that recognizes whom it targets and whom it does not.

The argument I wish to make with *Language of Justice* studies is that human meaning making is exploitable. By this I mean to say that moral entrepreneurs may act as social control agents by creating or promoting social meanings, which when normalized have the power to transform one thing into another. This transformation is clearly demonstrated in the preliminary research on the term "victim"; when this word is used in media documents the context reveals that we impute responsibility and agency to a person for becoming a "victim." Similarly, I would argue that, as my study of "crime" and "evil" show, the definition of "crime" as anything other than radically socially constructed (e.g. as theologically ordained) serves the interests of powerful social, political and other moral entrepreneurs in distancing themselves from the failure of the social control system known as the "criminal" justice system.

These conclusions support David Garland's argument that, in the current historical period, social, economic and political forces have built a culture of deep social control (2001). Garland argues this is evinced by the construction of pervasive systems of "crime" control and a sprawling "criminal" justice system. Garland's argument regarding a culture of social control seems plausible enough but, as with all macro-sociological enterprise, his argument needs some grounding. Such grounding is provided by Tonry who demonstrates, much as I have argued, that the moral entrepreneuring of politically motivated decision makers (i.e. Presidents Nixon, Reagan and Bush) has shifted particular social meanings in order to promote harsh drug and sanctioning policies that have, in turn, increased the culture of control that Garland describes (Tonry 2004). Cavender has modified Garland's argument by drawing attention to the moral entrepreneuring role of media (Cavender 2004). Cavender argues that media play a far more powerful, entrepreneurial role in the construction of those public attitudes that support the growth of a culture of control than Garland is willing to acknowledge. Cavender's argument fits squarely into my notion that social meanings, moral entrepreneuring and social control are intimately related.

In addition to supporting Garland's argument of a massive structure of social control, *Language of Justice* findings clearly demonstrate how social control is built, maintained and changed at least in part by the labor of moral entrepreneurs. Previous work has argued for the powerful presence of social control in US society (Rothman 1971 and Simon 1993); however, my investigation details the processes at work. My findings expose how social meanings are created around issues of "criminal" and social justice and how these meanings become symbolic in the entire discourse about "crime" and justice in our society. In this sense, my work demonstrates the power moral entrepreneurs have to define situations in everyday life when they frame the language used to discuss, interpret and understand issues in social and "criminal" justice.

Language of Justice studies enable identification of our blind spots about the social meanings we have created around justice and allow us to reflect on the words we use to define and describe justice. My examination of justice words demonstrates how many such meanings are beneath the surface of our awareness, as is the influence of moral entrepreneurs in making and enforcing the rules of our justice codes. For example, in my study of the term "evil" as it relates to "crime," I find that in the context of news stories, some "crime" acts are not defined in moral language but in theological language. This finding supports Marxist criminology, which argues that current definitions of crime are overlooking the most important definitional elements, namely, that "crime" occurs, is defined, monitored and punished within a social context and is impacted by deeply embedded social structures (Akers 1979 and Hinch 1983). As I additionally show in this research, modern criminological literature has, in some places, reflected discourse that derives from social perceptions of "crime" acts and "crime" actors as "evil men" or "evil strangers" "randomly attacking their victims" (see for example, Cavender 1981, Boostrum 1971, Madriz 1997, Sarbin and Miller 1970 and Surette 1989). Either way, the social definitions of acts as "morally reprehensible choices" or as "evil partaking in the metaphysical" are the result of a discursive construction.

Language of Justice research compliments the work of another critical criminologist, Richard Quinney, and particularly his arguments about "crime" (1980). Quinney argues that "crime" is only what we define as "crime," that behaviors which create conflict with those segments of society that wield power are the ones defined as "criminal," and that "criminal" definitions are applied by those segments of society with the power to shape the enforcement and administration of criminal law (Quinney 1970). In the media document analysis above, I found that when accounts use metaphysical language to redefine "crime" from being a product of social action to being the result of something beyond merely social action, the moral entrepreneurs making these claims represent exactly those segments of society that Quinney identifies: those who wield power, who define "crime" and who enforce the "criminal" definitions of law (e.g. legislators, political figures).

Classical criminologists often criticize critical criminology as a theory devoid of empirical evidence. However, my research demonstrates the salience of critical criminology theory (the effect of power on social life) by showing how moral entrepreneurs create, maintain and alter the definitions of issues in the everyday public discourse of social and "criminal" justice. My work exposes the process and procedure of power in social life and demonstrates the importance and use of language in the formation and deconstruction of power.

My *Language of Justice* research is a critical language theory, which argues that our justice discourse is a compilation of linguistic meanings that have become structurally hegemonic and that have colonized our social and "criminal" justice discourse. I argue that frequently moral entrepreneurs create and build language to promote a discourse of social control about social and "criminal" justice matters in our social life. I also argue that such language enters our linguistic pool and, with continued use, comes to dominate and suppress other languages or discourses of justice.

Much like George Orwell and many of the others examined in Chapter 2, I argue that some varieties of justice language have greater impact than others on what becomes the justice discourse of our social life. Specifically, control language, frequently propagated by leading moral entrepreneurs, dominates other justice language options and defines our social and "criminal" justice discourse. Moral entrepreneurs by definition have the power to not only encode their language in discourse, but also to replicate the language and enforce its content. Like these authors, in *Language of Justice* research I argue that not all justice language is cognitively equivalent and that differences are not merely stylistic. In fact, differences in justice language determine justice discourse parameters, i.e. determine the potential expression of justice concepts and thus the availability of justice concepts for debates about social and "criminal" justice. In this way, we arrive at how one form of language (control language) exerts greater influence and dominates discourse.

Here is the hot seat for moral entrepreneurs: when their work leads to the dominance of their justice concepts, other concepts remain largely unknown or disappear without ever being widely heard; the available pool of justice concepts shrinks. For example, the debate about prisons in the US ranges from a conservative discourse (build more) to a progressive (create reform programs). Widely unheard and almost entirely unpromoted by powerful moral entrepreneurs are calls to close prisons on a massive scale or to use entirely different paradigms for facing issues of social and "criminal" justice and injustice. Thus, moral entrepreneurs of our public justice discourse wittingly or not, be they defined by conservative or progressive ideologies, create, maintain and in ongoing work build a social reality defined by significant inequalities.

Language of Justice research is a critical linguistics. I look at dominant justice language to argue that it operates hegemonically, that it colonizes and suppresses other justice language and alternative justice discourses, and that it perpetuates social control formats and frames. I argue that our justice discourse reflects linguistic categories (such as "tough on crime," "criminals") that lack meaning unless an entire paradigm of assumptions, interpretations and ideology is accepted about human nature, human action and the meaning of social and "criminal" justice. I also argue that our everyday justice discourse takes place within a body of interpretations, rhetoric and metaphors that many accept as self-evident rather than acknowledge how deeply ideology informs them. In my research I also go further to explore how justice language choices connect to social control purposes, permit political actions (such as suppressing others through imprisonment) and relate to the behavior of moral entrepreneurs whose work dominates public life.

Critical criminology has established that the study of order is as important as the study of disorder. In *Language of Justice* research, I work to interfere with what I find is the disturbing trend in our justice discourse to uncritically accept a supposedly seamless and homogeneous language that defines social and "criminal" justice as the domain of social control: "criminals" are "offenders" to be "treated tough" by being "imprisoned at severe length." I argue that what we recognize as social and "criminal" justice situations and what we recognize as definitions of persons involved with the social and "criminal" justice system are constructs of a discourse (social control), which is built with language choices (such as "criminals," "tough on crime") and promoted by powerful agents (moral entrepreneurs). This is what Michel Foucault calls a "panopticon society," which supports a culture of "governmentality" (1977 and 1991). Jock Young identifies this phenomenon as the building of an "administrative control" society (1986), and Jonathan Simon warns that it develops a social reality whose inequities are pushing the US toward a civil war (1993).

Directions for future *Language of Justice* research

The opportunities for further *Language of Justice* research are numerous as so little of this work has been done. Many of the discussions in this book point to rich possibilities, as exemplified by the better and worse "crime," "criminal," "murderer" typologies I discuss in the previous chapter.

Research is also needed to distinguish how moral entrepreneurs construct the problem of who is responsible for what becomes of an incarcerated person, or for what opportunities are given to a person while incarcerated. A larger project, much needed, is an investigation into the philosophical anthropology (i.e. definitions of human nature) operating in our social and criminal justice discourse. One place to examine the range of arguments about human nature is within the discourse of corrections: what assumptions about human nature guide different correctional policies and the different moral entrepreneurs who promote them? Are they consistent? If not, where are they contradictory? When we discuss correctional policy, how do our conceptions take human nature into account? What range of human nature definitions never enters the discussion? What do we assume? What cultural or other biases are we following?

Another large *Language of Justice* project that we need is a study of the dominant metaphors of our social and "criminal" justice discourse. Aristotle defined a metaphor as a transference that allows us to understand one thing in terms of another (1995). What are the topics and themes of such transferences in social and "criminal" justice discourse? Given that metaphor is a fundamental mechanism for both our minds and language itself, what metaphors emerge in social and "criminal" justice discourse (Lakoff and Johnson 1980)? Nietzsche famously described language as an army of dead metaphors, which raises another important question: what are the keywords of our justice discourse that no longer resonate as metaphors, and what light is shed on our discourse if we recapture their metaphorical content (Gilman et al. 1989)? While neither a study of this depth or of this discipline, Raymond Gozzi's *The Power of Metaphor in the Age of Electronic Media* points us in the direction we need to travel (1999).

A *Language of Justice* research project focusing on those who are most deeply controlled is of special importance. When do we call people in prison the "worst of the worst" and when do we call them "inner-city dwellers who start out life with two strikes against them." Are there groups of people who earn that label more or less frequently? What is the range within our language for responding to "crime" acts and actors? When do we speak of "cleaning up the neighborhood," and when do we speak of "helping those without sufficient resources"? Are these questions only a matter of ideological divide, or will a closer investigation of our words reveal something more?

Constructions such as "criminal production factory" suggest we need to be asking a lot of questions and doing a lot of *Language of Justice* research. By what various ways do moral entrepreneurs explain the presence of "deviant" acts? What differing language choices are explored to describe neighborhoods with a high number of "crimes"? Do such descriptions shift when moral entrepreneurs argue for investing in neighborhood development as opposed to building additional prisons? If so, how do they language their position and what does that languaging demonstrate they think about "offenders" and "criminals"? Are moral entrepreneurs consistent? Or do they label people as the "worst of the worst" in one moment and as "victims without choices" in another? Who hears which versions? When are different versions presented? How are different versions languaged and what does the study of the contexts in which each emerges tell us about how we construct the "criminal," "the offender" and the "prisoner"? When do we talk about such people as problems of management and technology, when as public policy failures or missed opportunities, when as persons who need to be swept into the trash and when as needing our help? When do we stop talking about "offenders" as the "worst of the worst" and start talking about them as persons "who start out life with two strikes against them"? When do we speak of "murderers" as "horrendous animals" and when as people who finally "break down and cross the line"?

Conclusion

My interpretation of modern social and "criminal" justice discourse is that it highlights a collective either in denial or in hiding from the constructed character of social and "criminal" justice. Without a doubt, to a significant degree, we operate as if the categories of "crime" and the persons characterized as "criminals" are givens and not our own creations. We operate as if such definitions are handed to us from another source (whether from ontological definitions about human nature, from epistemological definitions given by theological language or other). In our social and "criminal" justice discourse we daily live a lie, thereby ensuring continued injustice toward "others," and then use language to hide from ourselves and others what it is that we do in our social and "criminal" justice system.

What we do in our social life is not subject to any debate or doubt. It is a matter of undisputed record that is daily discussed online, on our TVs and in our newspapers. It is also daily suffered by the targets of our social control: we hold more than two million people in prisons and jails, most of them men, disproportionately racial and ethnic minorities, disproportionately poor and disproportionately uneducated. These persons are the targets of our social control, not because they need to be or ought to be, but because they are chosen to be. These are the targets of our social control work not because they cause the most economic "crime" (the far less prosecuted white collar "crimes" cost far more than blue collar "crime") (Conklin 1977), not because they cause the most violent "crime" (industrial and environmental "crime" kills more persons than the sum of violent individual acts) and not because they are the most dangerous to the individual or the collective (the "crimes" of the mostly unprosecuted or pardoned power elite are more dangerous to both) (Reichel 2005). The social control mechanisms of law, law enforcement through monitoring and imprisonment, the indoctrination and propaganda supported by lobbyist-dominated representative government, and the free movement of mass media communications that work to promote the interests of a minority (super-wealthy class) have reshaped a larger community such that most members no longer have the information or understanding to make decisions that relate to their espoused and shared values (Bagdikian 2004).

I perform *Language of Justice* studies to expose our social and "criminal" justice discourse. I also do such research with the hope that the more conscious and intentional we are about our justice language choices, the more we can design justice policy in alignment with our claimed justice ideals, such as having an equitable society with justice for all. Above all, I want to alert the reader to how language choices impact the building of a justice schema, regardless of its content. I have gone to great lengths to openly present my theoretical, methodological and, by consequence, substantive justice positions. Like any moral entrepreneur, I work in my life to promote the justice ideology my values embrace. I offer *Language of Justice* research not as a tool for ideology, but as a tool for recognizing ideology. The goal we can all aim for is not escape from ideology, but honesty about the ideology we manifest in our own social and "criminal" justice practices, and through our words. When we have matched the ideological claim that we value an equitable society with justice for all, with the practices and language that demonstrate its existence, then we will have arrived at the justice we speak of. At least until then, the process of examining language employed in social and "criminal" justice discourse remains a vital and necessary ally to all friends of justice.

Notes

Introduction

1 Howard Becker argues that rules/laws are made as the result of a "moral enterprise" effort and calls such efforts the work of "moral entrepreneurs" (1963: 145–47). Moral entrepreneurs cover the entire spectrum of political and moral opinion and include political actors, government administrators, various law-enforcement agents or representatives, courts and numerous public voices ranging from the Sunday preacher to the national or local journalist, activist and more.

5 Delineating the "evil," "criminal" other

1 Previously published as "Language, Metaphysics and Deviancy: Delineating the 'Evil' 'Criminal' Other," in *Transnational Criminology Manual*, edited by Martine Herzog-Evans, Nijmegen: Wolf Legal Publishers, 2010: 127–44 (Coyle 2010a).

References

Akers, R.L. (1979) "Theory and Ideology in Marxist Criminology," *Criminology* 16 (4): 527–44.

Altheide, D. (1996) *Qualitative Media Analysis*, Thousand Oaks, CA: Sage Publications.

—— (1997) "The News Media, the Problem Frame, and the Production of Fear," *The Sociological Quarterly* 38 (Fall): 647–68.

—— (2000) "Tracking Discourse and Qualitative Document Analysis," *Poetics* 27 (May): 287–99.

—— (2002) *Creating Fear: news and the construction of crisis*, New York: Aldine de Gruyter.

—— (2006) *Terrorism and the Politics of Fear*, Lanham, MD: Alta Mira Press.

Altheide, D. and Coyle, M.J. (2006) "Smart on Crime: the new language for prisoner release," *Crime, Media, Culture* 2 (Fall): 286–303.

Altheide, D., Coyle, M., DeVriese, K. and Schneider, C. (2008) "Emergent Qualitative Document Analysis," in S.N. Hesse-Biber and P. Leavy (eds) *The Handbook of Emergent Methods*, New York: Guilford Publications.

American Heritage Dictionaries (1969) *The American Heritage Dictionary*, first edition, Boston, MA: Houghton Mifflin Company.

—— (1980) *The American Heritage Dictionary*, second edition, Boston, MA: Houghton Mifflin Company.

—— (1992) *The American Heritage Dictionary*, third edition, Boston, MA: Houghton Mifflin Company.

—— (2000) *The American Heritage Dictionary*, fourth edition, Boston, MA: Houghton Mifflin Company.

Anderson, D. (1995) *Crime and the Politics of Hysteria: how the Willie Horton story changed American justice*, New York: Random House.

Archer, M. (1995) *Realist Social Theory: the morphogenetic approach*, Cambridge: Cambridge University Press.

Aristotle (1995) *Poetics*, S. Halliwell (trans), Cambridge, MA: Harvard University Press.

Arpaio, J. (2004) "Personal notes from Joe Arpaio presentation to students in *Corrections and Justice* course", presented at Arizona State University, Tempe, AZ, March 15.

Arrigo, B.A. (2001) "Transcarceration: a constitutive ethnography of mentally ill 'offenders'," *The Prison Journal* 81 (2): 162–86.

Arrigo, B.A. and Schehr, R.C. (1998) "Restoring Justice for Juveniles: a critical analysis of victim–offender mediation," *Justice Quarterly* 15 (December): 629–66.

Ashcroft, J. (2005) "Prepared remarks of Attorney General John Ashcroft," *U.S. Department of Justice*, February 1, www.usdoj.gov/archive/ag/speeches/2005/02142005aggheritage1.htm (accessed June 30, 2006).

Atkinson, J. and Drew, P. (1979) *Order in Court: the organization of verbal interaction in judicial settings*, London: Macmillan.

Austin, J.L. (1962) *How to Do Things with Words*, New York: Oxford University Press.

Bagdikian, B.H. (2004) *The New Media Monopoly*, Boston, MA: Beacon Press.

Baker, P. (1995) "Allen to Get Tougher on Teen Crime: plan also targets family violence," *The Washington Post*, October 14, C1.

Barthes, R. (1964) *Elements of Semiology*, A. Lavers and C. Smith (trans), London: Jonathan Cape.

—— (1972) *Mythologies*, A. Lavers (trans), New York: Hill and Wang.

—— (1975) *The Pleasure of the Text*, R. Miller (trans), New York: Hill and Wang.

—— (1986) *The Rustle of Language*, Richard Howard (trans), New York: Hill and Wang.

Bavelas, J. and Coates, L. (2001) "Is it Sex or Assault? erotic versus violent language in sexual assault trial judgments," *Journal of Social Distress* 10 (November): 29–40.

Baynham, M. and Slembrouck, S. (1999) "Speech Representation and Institutional Discourse," *Text* 19 (4): 439–57.

Beck, A. (1992) "Jail Inmates, 1990," Washington, DC: Bureau of Justice Statistics Bulletin.

Beck, A.J., Karberg, J.C. and Harrison, P.M. (2002) *Prison and Jail Inmates at Midyear, 2001*, Washington, DC: Bureau of Justice Statistics Bulletin.

Becker, H.S. (1963) *Outsiders: studies in the sociology of deviance*, New York: The Free Press.

Beetham, M. (2002) "Speaking Together: heteroglossia, translations and the (im)possibility of the just society," *Women's Studies International Forum* 25 (2): 175–84.

Berelson, B. (1952) Content Analysis in Communication Research, Glencoe, IL: Free Press.

Berger, P. and Luckmann, T. (1966) *The Social Construction of Reality: a treatise in the sociology of knowledge*, New York: Anchor Books.

Blackledge, A. and Pavlenko, A. (2001) "Introduction," *International Journal of Bilingualism* 5 (September): 243–57.

Blakemore, D. (1990) *Understanding Utterances: the pragmatics of natural language*, Oxford: Blackwell.

Blumer, H. (1962) "Society as Symbolic Interaction," in A.M. Rose (ed.) Human Behavior and Social Process: an interactionist approach, Boston, MA: Houghton-Mifflin.

—— (1969) Symbolic Interactionism: perspective and method, Berkeley, CA: University of California Press.

Bonger, W.A. (1916) *Criminality and Economic Conditions*, H.P. Horton (trans), New York: Agathon Press.

Boostrom, R.L. (1971) "The Personalization of Evil: the emergence of American criminology, 1865–1910," unpublished dissertation, University of California, Berkeley.

Bosmajian, H. (1960) "The Rhetoric of the National Socialist Speakers," unpublished dissertation, Stanford University.

—— (1983) *The Language of Oppression*, Lanham, MD: University Press of America.

—— (1992) *Metaphor and Reason in Judicial Opinions*, Carbondale, IL: Southern Illinois University Press.

Bowers, F. (1989) *Linguistic Aspects of Legislative Expression*, Vancouver, BC: University of British Columbia Press.

Brown, G. (1998) *Discourse Analysis*, Cambridge: Cambridge University Press.

Brown, P. and Levinson, S. (1978) "Universals in Language Usage: politeness phenomena," in E. Goody (ed.) *Questions and Politeness: strategies in social interaction*, Cambridge: Cambridge University Press.

Burgin, V. (1982) *Thinking Photography*, London: Macmillan.

Burney, E. (1999) *Crime and Banishment: nuisance and exclusion in social housing*, Winchester: Waterside Press.

Burton, F. and Carlen, P. (1977) "Official Discourse," *Economy and Society* 6 (November): 377–407.

Burton, T., Dollery, B. and Wallis, J. (2000) "A Note on the Rhetorical Patterns at the 1999 New South Wales Drug Summit," *Current Issues in Criminal Justice* 12 (2): 207–15.

Carley, K. (1990) "Content Analysis," in R.E. Asher (ed.) The Encyclopedia of Language and Linguistics, Edinburgh: Pergamon Press.

Carston, R. (2002) *Thoughts and Utterances: the pragmatics of explicit communication*, Oxford: Blackwell.

Caulkins, J.P. (1997) "Mandatory Minimum Drug Sentences: throwing away the key or the taxpayer's money?" Santa Monica, CA: RAND Corporation.

Cavender, G. (1981) "'Scared Straight': ideology and the media," *Journal of Criminal Justice* 9 (6): 431–39.

—— (2004) "Media and Crime Policy: a reconsideration of David Garland's *The Culture of Control*," *Punishment and Society* 6 (3): 335–48.

Cavender, G. and Mulcahy, A. (1998) "Trial by Fire: media constructions of corporate deviance," *Justice Quarterly* 15 (December): 697–717.

Century Dictionaries (1911) *The Century Dictionary: an encyclopedic lexicon of the English language*, New York: The Century Co.

—— (1914) *The Century Dictionary: an encyclopedic lexicon of the English language*, New York: The Century Co.

Chambers Dictionaries (1901) *Chamber's Twentieth Century Dictionary*, Edinburgh: W. & R. Chambers.

Chandler, D. (2002) *Semiotics: the basics*, New York: Routledge.

Charon, J.M. (1979) *Symbolic Interactionism: an introduction, an interpretation, an integration*, Englewood Cliffs, NJ: Prentice-Hall, Inc.

Chilton, P. (1985) *Language and the Nuclear Arms Debate: nukespeak today*, London: Frances Pinter Publishers.

Chomsky, N. (1975) *The Logical Structure of Linguistic Theory*, Chicago, IL: University of Chicago Press.

Christie, N. (2000) *Crime Control as Industry*, London: Routledge.

Cieslak, D.J. and Konig, R. (2005) "Homicides, Lifestyles Linked in Police Data: many Phoenix victims had ties to gangs, drugs," *The Arizona Republic*, February 14.

Cisneros, H.G. (1995) *Defensible Space: deterring crime and building community*, Washington, DC: U.S. Department of Housing and Urban Development.

Clinard, M.B. and Yeager, P.C. (1987) "Illegal Corporate Behavior, 1975–76," ICPSR07855-v3. Ann Arbor, MI: Inter-university Consortium for Political and Social Research.

Cobley, P. and Jansz, L. (1998) *Introducing Semiotics*, Mulgrave, VIC: McPherson's Printing Group.

Cohen, E. (1989) "Symbols of Culpability and the Universal Language of Justice: the ritual of public executions in late medieval Europe," *History of European Ideas* 11: 407–16.

Cole, P. (1978) *Pragmatics*, New York: Academic Press.

Colvin, M. (1997) *Penitentiaries, Reformatories, and Chain Gangs: social theory and the history of punishment in nineteenth-century America*, New York: St. Martin's Press.

Conklin, J.E. (1977) *Illegal but Not Criminal: business crime in America*, Englewood Cliffs, NJ: Prentice-Hall.

Conley, J.M. and O'Barr, W.M. (2005) *Just Words: law, language, and power*, Chicago, IL: University of Chicago Press.

Cooley, C.H. (1983) *Human Nature and the Social Order*, New Brunswick, NJ: Transaction Books.

Coser, L.A. (1967) *Continuities in the Study of Social Conflict*, New York: Free Press.

Cotterill, J. (2004) *Language in the Legal Process*, New York: Palgrave Macmillan.

Coupland, N. and Jaworski, A. (1997) *Sociolinguistics: a reader*, New York: St. Martin's Press.

Coyle, M.J. (2010a) "Language, Metaphysics and Deviancy: delineating the 'evil' criminal other," in M. Herzog-Evans and I. Dréan-Rivette (eds) *Transnational Criminology*, Nijmegen: Wolf Legal Publishers.

—— (2010b) "Notes on the Study of Language: toward a critical race criminology," *Western Criminology Review* 11 (1): 11–19.

Craig, J. (1852) *A New Universal, Technological, Etymological, and Pronouncing Dictionary of the English Language*, London: Routledge.

Crampton, J.W. and Elden, S. (2007) *Space, Knowledge and Power: Foucault and geography*, Burlington, VT: Ashgate Pub Co.

Cross, D.W. (1979) *Word Abuse: how the words we use use us*, New York: Coward, McCann & Geoghegan.

Cullen, F.T., Maakestad, W.J. and Cavender, G. (1987) *Corporate Crime under Attack: the Ford Pinto case and beyond*, Cincinnati, OH: Anderson Publishing Company.

Culler, J. (1985) *Saussure*, London: Fontana.

Dahrendorf, R. (1968) *Essays in the Theory of Society*, Palo Alto, CA: Stanford University Press.

Danet, B. (1980) "'Baby' or 'Fetus'? language and the construction of reality in a manslaughter trial," *Semiotica* 32 (3/4): 187–219.

Dekeseredy, W.S., Alvi, S., Schwartz, M.D. and Tomasxewksi, E.A. (2003) *Under Siege: poverty and crime in a public housing community*, Boulder, CO: Lexington Books.

De Landtsheer, C.D. and Feldman, O. (2000) *Beyond Public Speech and Symbols: explorations in the rhetoric of politicians and the media*, Westport, CT: Praeger.

Denzin, N. and Lincoln, Y.S. (1998) *Collecting and Interpreting Qualitative Materials*, Thousand Oaks, CA: Sage Publications.

Derrida, J. (1976) *On Grammatology*, G.C. Spivak (trans), Baltimore, MD: Johns Hopkins University Press.

Descombe, V. (1980) *Modern French Philosophy*, Cambridge: Cambridge University Press.

Dillon, D.J. (1998) *The Politics of Prison Expansion: winning elections by waging war on crime*, Westport, CT: Praeger.

During, S. (2003) *The Cultural Studies Reader*, New York: Routledge.

Durkheim, E. (1964) *Rules of Sociological Method*, New York: The Free Press.

Eco, U. (1976) *A Theory of Semiotics*, Bloomington, IN: Indiana University Press.

—— (1984) *Semiotics and the Philosophy of Language*, London: Macmillan Press.

Elikann, P.T. (1996) *The Tough-on-Crime Myth: real solutions to cut crime*, New York: Plenum Press.

Emery, H.G. and Brewster, K.G. (1942) *The New Century Dictionary of the English Language*, New York: P.F. Collier & Son Corporation.

Ericson, R.V. (1987) *Visualizing Deviance: a study of news organization*, Toronto: University of Toronto Press.

Erikson, K.T. (1966) *Wayward Puritans: a study in the sociology of deviance*, New York: John Wiley and Sons.

Evans, J. (2002) "Indigenous Australians: language and the law," *International Journal for the Semiotics of Law* 15 (January): 127–41.

Fairclough, N. (1992) *Discourse and Social Change*, Cambridge: Polity Press.

Fairclough, N. and Chouliaraki, L. (1999) *Discourse in Late Modernity: rethinking Critical Discourse Analysis*, Edinburgh: Edinburgh University Press.

Ferrell, J. (1993) *Crimes of Style: urban graffiti and the politics of criminality*, New York: Garland.

—— (1998) "Against the Law: Anarchist Criminology," *Social Anarchism* 25: 1–16.

Fish, S.E. (1980) *Is There a Text in This Class? the authority of interpretive communities*, Cambridge, MA: Harvard University Press.

Fisher, B.S., Cullen, F.T. and Turner, M.G. (2000) "The Sexual Victimization of College Women," Washington, DC: National Institute of Justice and Bureau of Justice Statistics.

Flavin, J. (2000) "(Mis)representing Risk: headline accounts of HIV-related assaults," *American Journal of Criminal Justice* 25 (1): 119–36.

Foucault, M. (1973) *The Order of Things: an archaeology of the human sciences*, New York: Vintage.

—— (1975) *The Birth of the Clinic: an archaeology of knowledge*, London: Tavistock.

—— (1977) *Discipline and Punish: the birth of the prison*, A. Sheridan (trans), New York: Vintage Books.

—— (1991) "Governmentality," in G. Burchell, C. Gordon and P. Miller (eds.) *The Foucault Effect: studies in governmentality, with two lectures by and an interview with Michel Foucault*, London: Hawester Wheatsheaf.

—— (2003) *Society Must Be Defended*, D. Macey (trans) and M. Bertani and A. Fontana (eds.), New York: Picador.

Fowler, R. (1991) *Language in the News: discourse and ideology in the press*, New York: Routledge, Chapman & Hall.

Fowler, R., Kress, G., Trew, T. and Hodge, R. (1979) *Language and Control*, London: Routledge & Kegan Paul.

Friedrichs, D.O. (2009) *Trusted Criminals: white collar crime in contemporary society*, fourth edition, Belmont, CA: Wadsworth Publishing.

Funk and Wagnalls Dictionaries (1894) *Standard Dictionary of the English Language*, New York: Funk & Wagnalls Company.

Gabor, T. (1994) *Everybody Does It! crime by the public*, Toronto: University of Toronto Press.

Gainsborough, J. and Mauer, M. (2000) "Diminishing Returns: crime and incarceration in the 1990s," Washington, DC: The Sentencing Project.

Garland, D. (2000) "The Culture of High Crime Societies: some preconditions of recent 'law and order' policies," *British Journal of Criminology* 40 (3): 347–75.

—— (2001) *The Culture of Control: crime and social order in contemporary society*, Chicago, IL: University of Chicago Press.

Geddes, J.L. (2001) *Evil after Postmodernism: histories, narratives, and ethics*, New York: Routledge.

Gee, J.P. (2005) *An Introduction to Discourse Analysis*, Cambridge: Cambridge University Press.

Geertz, C. (1988) *Works and Lives: the anthropologist as author*, Palo Alto, CA: Stanford University Press.

Gergen, K.J. (1997) "Social Theory in Context: relational humanism," in J.D. Greenwood (ed.) *The Mark of the Social: discovery or invention?* New York: Rowman and Littlefield.

Giddens, A. (1979) *Central Problems in Social Theory: action, structure, and contradiction in social analysis*, Berkeley, CA: University of California Press.

—— (1984) *The Constitution of Society: outline of the theory of structuration*, Berkeley, CA: University of California Press.

Gilman, S.L., Blair, C. and Parent, D.J. (eds.) (1989) "On Truth and Lie in an Extra-Moral Sense," in Friedrich Nietzsche on Rhetoric and Language, D. Parent (trans), Oxford: Oxford University Press.

Goffman, E. (1959) *The Presentation of Self in Everyday Life*, Garden City, NY: Doubleday.

—— (1971) *Relations in Public: microstudies of the public order*, New York: Basic Books Inc.

Goldsmith, V. (2000) *Analyzing Crime Patterns: frontiers of practice*, Thousand Oaks, CA: Sage Publications.

Goodwin, M. (1990) *He-Said-She-Said: the interactive organization of talk in an urban Black peer group*, Bloomington, IN: Indiana University Press.

Gordon, R. (2012) "Jail's Demise Fine Farewell for Sheriff," *The San Francisco Chronicle*, January 4, C1.

Gottschalk, L.A. (1995) Content Analysis of Verbal Behavior: new findings and clinical applications, Hillside, NJ: Lawrence Erlbaum Associates, Inc.

Gozzi, R. (1999) *The Power of Metaphor in the Age of Electronic Media*, Cresskill, NJ: Hampton Press.

Gregory, M. and Holloway, M. (2005) "Language and the Shaping of Social Work," *British Journal of Social Work* 35 (1): 37–53.

Grice, H.P. (1975) "Logic and Conversation," in P. Cole and J. Morgan (eds) *Syntax and Semantics 3: speech acts*, New York: Academic Press.

Griffith, S. (1990) "Gondles Expected to Quit as Sheriff of Arlington," *The Washington Post*, June 14, B11.

Grossberg, L., Nelson, C. and Treicher, P. (1992) *Cultural Studies*, New York: Routledge.

Habermas, J. (1979) *Communication and the Evolution of Society*, T. McCarthy (trans), Boston, MA: Beacon Press.

Hall, S. (1980) "Cultural Studies: two paradigms," *Media, Culture, and Society* 2 (1): 87–96.

—— (1992) "Race, Culture, and Communications: looking backward and forward at Cultural Studies," *Rethinking Marxism* 5 (1): 10–18.

Halttunen, K. (1998) *Murder Most Foul: the killer and the American gothic imagination*, Cambridge, MA: Harvard University Press.

Haviland, J.B. (2003) "Ideologies of language: some reflections on language and U.S. Law," *American Anthropologist* 105 (4): 764–74.

Hawkins, L., Fook, J. and Ryan, M. (2001) "Social Workers' Use of the Language of Social Justice," *British Journal of Social Work* 31 (February): 1–13.

Held, D. (1980) *Introduction to Critical Theory: Horkheimer to Habermas*, Berkeley, CA: University of California Press.

Hepburn, J.R. and Griffin, M.L. (1998) "Jail Recidivism in Maricopa County: report to the Maricopa County Sheriff's Office," Tempe, AZ: Arizona State University.

Heritage, J. (1998) "Conversational Analysis and Institutional Talk," in D. Silverman (ed.) *Qualitative Research: theory, method and practice*, London: Sage Publications.

Hickey, E.W. (2003) "Cultural Development of Monsters, Demons, and Evil," in M. Silberman (ed.) *Violence and Society: a reader*, Upper Saddle River, NJ: Prentice-Hall Publishers.

Hinch, R. (1983) "Marxist Criminology in the 1970s: clarifying the clutter", *Crime and Social Justice* 13 (Summer): 65–74.

Hjelmslev, L. (1961) *Prolegomena to a Theory of Language*, F.J. Whitfield (trans), Madison: University of Wisconsin Press.

Hodder, Ian. (1998) "The Interpretation of Documents and Material Culture," in N. Denzin and Y.S. Lincoln (eds.) *Collecting and Interpreting Qualitative Materials*, Thousand Oaks, CA: Sage Publications.

Hodge, R. and Kress, G. (1988) *Social Semiotics*, Ithaca, NY: Cornell University Press.

Hogeveen, B.R. (2005) "'If We are Tough on Crime, If We Punish Crime, Then People Get the Message': constructing and governing the punishable young offender in Canada during the late 1990s," *Punishment & Society* 7 (1): 73–89.

Holsti, O.R. (1969) Content Analysis for the Social Sciences and Humanities, Reading, MA: Addison-Wesley.

Holzman, H.R., Kudrick, T. R. and Voytech, K.P. (1996) "Revisiting the Relationship Between Crime and Architectural Design: an analysis of data from HUD's 1994 survey of public housing residents," *Cityscape* 2 (1): 107–26.

Horkheimer, M. (1993) *Between Philosophy and Social Science: selected early writings*, G.F. Hunter, M.S. Kramer and J. Torpey (trans), Cambridge, MA: MIT Press.

Hunter, R. (1898) *The Encyclopedic Dictionary*, Philadelphia, PA: Syndicate Publishing Company.

Ingebretsen, E.J. (2001) *At Stake: monsters and the rhetoric of fear in public culture*, Chicago, IL: University of Chicago Press.

Ingram, D. (1990) *Critical Theory and Philosophy*, New York: Paragon House.

James, W. (1975) *Pragmatism*, Cambridge, MA: Harvard University Press.

Jameson, F. (1972) *The Prison House of Language*, Princeton, NJ: Princeton University Press.

"Joe Arpaio: tyrant of the desert" (1999) *The Economist*, July 31, 4.

Johnson, S. (1810) *A Dictionary of the English Language, 10th edn.*, London: [s.n.].

—— (1837) *A Dictionary of the English Language, abridged quarto edn.*, London: [s.n.].

Johnstone, B. (2002) *Discourse Analysis*, Oxford: Blackwell.

Jorgensen, M. and Phillips, L. (2002) *Discourse Analysis as Theory and Method*, Thousand Oaks, CA: Sage Publications.

Kasper, G. and Blum-Kulka, S. (1993) *Interlanguage Pragmatics*, Oxford: Oxford University Press.

Kelling, G. and Coles, C. (1997) *Fixing Broken Windows*, New York: Free Press.

Kellner, D. (1989) *Critical Theory, Marxism and Modernity*, Cambridge: Polity.

Kersey, J. (1708) *Dictionarium Anglo-Britannicum*, Menston: Scolar Press Limited.

Klemperer, V. (2006) *The Language of the Third Reich*, M. Brady (trans), London: Continuum.

Knox, G.W. (1995) *Gangs and Other Problems in Public Housing, a special report: preliminary results of the 1995 anonymous survey of Altgeld-Murray Homes residents*, Chicago, IL: National Gang Crime Research Center, Department of Criminal Justice, Chicago State University.

Kransky, M. (2011) "Exit Interview with Sheriff Michael Hennessey," *Forum*, KQED, December 15, MP3 audio file, www.kqed.org/a/forum/R201112151000 (accessed June 27, 2012).

Krippendorf, K. (2004) *Content Analysis: an introduction to its methodology*, second edition, Thousand Oaks, CA: Sage Publications.

Kristeva, J. (1980) *Desire in Language*, New York: Columbia University Press.

Labov, W. (1972a) *Language in the Inner City: studies in Black English vernacular*, Philadelphia, PA: University of Philadelphia Press.

—— (1972b) *Sociolinguistic Patterns*, Princeton, NJ: Princeton University Press.

—— (1994) *Principles of Linguistic Change: internal factors*, vol. 1, Cambridge, MA: Blackwell.

—— (2001) *Principles of Linguistic Change: social factors*, vol. 2, Cambridge, MA: Blackwell.

Lacan, J. (1968) *The Language of the Self: the function of language in psychoanalysis*, Baltimore, MD: The Johns Hopkins University Press.

Lakoff, G. (2004) *Don't Think of an Elephant!: know your values and frame the debate*, White River Junction, VT: Chelsea Green Pub. Co.

Lakoff, G. and Johnson, M. (1980) *Metaphors We Live By*, Chicago, IL: Chicago University Press.

Lakoff, R. (1975) *Language and Women's Place*, New York: Harper & Row.

Lasswell, H. (1950) *Politics: who gets what, when, how*, New York: P. Smith.

Lazar, M. (2005) *Feminist Critical Discourse Analysis: gender, power, and ideology in discourse*, Basingstoke: Palgrave.

Lee, J. (1984) "Innocent Victims and Evil-Doers," *Women's Studies International Forum* 7 (1): 69–73.

Lemert, C. (1979) "Language, Structure and Measurement," *American Journal of Sociology* 84 (January): 929–57.

Leonard, J. (2012) "In D.A. Contest, Severity is Passé," *The Los Angeles Times*, June 4, A1.

Levi-Strauss, C. (1963) *Structural Anthropology*, C. Jacobson and B.G. Schoepf (trans), New York: Basic Books.

—— (1966) *The Savage Mind*, J. Weightman and D. Weightman (trans), Chicago, IL: University of Chicago Press.

—— (1969a) *Elementary Structures of Kinship*, J.H. Bell and J.R. von Sturmer (trans), Boston, MA: Beacon Press.

—— (1969b) *The Raw and the Cooked*, J. Weightman and D. Weightman (trans), New York: Harper and Row.

Liebes-Plesner, T. (1984) "Rhetoric in the Service of Justice: the sociolinguistic construction of stereotypes in an Israeli rape trial," *Text & Talk* 4 (1–3): 173–92.

Luntz, F. (2007) *Words that Work: it's not what you say, it's what people hear*, New York: Hyperion.

MacIntyre, A. (1998) *Whose Justice? Which Rationality?* Notre Dame, IN: University of Notre Dame Press.

Madriz, E.I. (1997) "Images of Criminals and Victims: a study on women's fear and social control," *Gender and Society* 11 (3): 342–56.

Maines, D.R. (1982) "In Search of Mesostructure: studies in the negotiated order," *Urban Life* 11 (October): 267–79.

Mannheim, K. (1936) *Ideology and Utopia*, London: Routledge.

Manning, P.K. and Cullum-Swan, B. (1998) "Narrative, Content and Semiotic Analysis," in N. Denzin and Y.S. Lincoln (eds.) *Collecting and Interpreting Qualitative Materials*, Thousand Oaks, CA: Sage Publications.

Maricopa County Sheriff's Office (2006) www.mcso.org/ (accessed August 3, 2006).

Marion, N.E. and Farmer, R. (2003) "Crime Control in the 2000 Presidential Election: a symbolic issue," *American Journal of Criminal Justice* 27 (2): 129–44.

Mason, P. (ed.) (2006) *Captured by the Media: prison discourse in popular culture*, Portland, OR: Willan.

Matza, D. (1969) *Becoming Deviant*, Englewood Cliffs, NJ: Prentice-Hall.

Mauer, M. (1999) *Race to Incarcerate*, New York: The New Press.

—— (2006) *Race to Incarcerate*, New York: The New Press.

Mauer, M. and Coyle, M.J. (2004) "The Social Cost of America's Race to Incarcerate," *Social Thought* 23 (1): 7–26.

Mayr, A. (2004) *Prison Discourse: language as a means of control and resistance*, New York: Palgrave Macmillan.

McConnell-Ginet, S. and Borker, R. (1980) *Women and Languages in Literature and Society*, New York: Praeger.

Mead, G.H. (1934) *Mind, Self and Society: from the standpoint of a social behaviorist*, Chicago, IL: The University of Chicago Press.

Merton, R.K. (1968) *Social Theory and Social Structure*, New York: Free Press.

Mertz, E. (1996) "Recontextualization as Socialization: text and Pragmatics in the law school classrooms," in M. Silverstein and G. Urban (eds.) *Natural Histories of Discourse*, Chicago, IL: University of Chicago Press.

Mills, C.W. (1940) "Situated Actions and Vocabularies of Motive," *American Sociological Review* 13 (5): 904–09.

—— (2000) *The Sociological Imagination*, Oxford: Oxford University Press.

Mishler, E. (1984) *The Discourse of Medicine*, Norwood, NJ: Ablex.

Moerman, M. (1988) *Talking Culture*, Philadelphia, PA: University of Pennsylvania Press.

Morrison, K.M. (2002) *The Solidarity of Kin: ethnohistory, Religious Studies, and the Algonkian-French religious encounter*, Albany, NY: State University of New York Press.

Mouzelis, N. (1995) *Sociological theory: what went wrong?* New York: Routledge.

Mumby, D. (1993) *Narrative and Social Control*, Newbury Park, CA: Sage.

Newman, O. and Franck, K.A. (1980) "Factors Influencing Crime and Instability in Urban Housing Developments," Washington, DC: National Institute of Justice.

Obeng, S.G. (1997) "Language and Politics: indirectness in political discourse," *Discourse & Society* 8 (1): 49–83.

Office of National Drug Control Policy (1997) "The National Drug Control Strategy," Washington, DC: US Department of Justice, www.ncjrs.gov/htm/chapter2.htm (accessed October 22, 2012).

Olsson, J. (2008) *Forensic Linguistics*, London: Continuum.

Orwell, G. (1946) *Animal Farm*, New York: Harcourt, Brace and Company.

—— (1981) *1984*, New York: New American Library.

—— (2000) "Politics and the English Language," in S. Orwell and I. Angus (eds) *George Orwell: in front of your nose*, Boston, MA: Nonpareil Books.

Oxford Dictionaries (1933) *The Oxford English Dictionary*, Oxford: Clarendon Press.

—— (1934) *The Concise Oxford Dictionary of Current English, 3rd edn.*, Oxford: Clarendon Press.

—— (1955) *The Oxford Universal Dictionary on Historical Principles, 3rd edn.*, Oxford: Clarendon Press.

—— (1971) *The Compact Edition of the Oxford English Dictionary*, Oxford: Oxford University Press.

Parsons, T. (1954) *Essays in Sociological Theory*, Glencoe, IL: Free Press.

Peirce, C.S. (1960) *Collected Writings*, C. Hartshorne, P. Weiss and A.W. Burks (eds.), Cambridge, MA: Harvard University Press.

Pfuhl, E.H. and Henry, S. (1993) *The Deviance Process*, Hawthorne, NY: Walter de Gruyter.

Phillips, S.U. (1998) *Ideology in the Language of Judges: how judges practice law, politics, and courtroom control*, Oxford: Oxford University Press.

Picart, C.J. and Greek, C. (2003) "The Compulsion of Real/Reel Serial Killers and Vampires: toward a Gothic Criminology," *Journal of Criminal Justice and Popular Culture* 10 (1): 39–68.

Pohlman, H.L. (2004) *Constitutional Debate in Action: civil rights and liberties*, Lanham, MD: Rowman & Littlefield Publishers.

Pool, I. (1959) Trends in Content Analysis, Urbana, IL: University of Illinois Press.

Powers Stubbs, M.K. (2000) *The Nature of Language: rhetorics of environmental (in)justice*, unpublished dissertation, Miami, FL: Miami University.

Prus, R. (1996) *Symbolic Interaction and Ethnographic Research: intersubjectivity and the study of human lived experience*, Albany, NY: State University of New York Press.

Quinney, R. (1970) *The Social Reality of Crime*, Boston, MA: Boston, Little, Brown.

—— (1980) *Class, State and Crime*, New York: Longman Publishing Group.

Rangell, C. and Tomasch, M. (2011) "Your Tax Dollars: how much does it cost to defend the Maricopa County Sheriff's Office?" www.abc15.com/dpp/news/local_news/investigations/your-tax-dollars-being-spent-to-fight-sheriff-joe-arpaio%E2%80%99s-lawsuits (accessed on June 20, 2012).

Reasons, C.E., Darlene, D.J. and Debro, J. (2002) *Race, Class, Gender and Justice*, Boston, MA: Allyn and Bacon.

Reichel, P. (2005) *Handbook of Transnational Crime and Justice*, Thousand Oaks, CA: Sage Publications.

Reiman, J. and Leighton, P. (2010) *The Rich Get Richer and the Poor Get Prison: ideology, class and criminal justice*, ninth edition, Cambridge: Pearson.

Riffe, D., Lacy, S. and Fico, F.G. (2005) Analyzing Media Messages: using quantitative Content Analysis in research, Mahwah, NJ: Lawrence Erlbaum.

Ritzer, G. (2000) *Modern Sociological Theory*, New York: McGraw-Hill.

Robertson, D. (1976) *A Theory of Party Competition*, New York: J. Wiley.

Rogers, R. (2003) *An Introduction to Critical Discourse Analysis in Education*, Mahwah, NJ: Lawrence Erlbaum.

Rome, D. (2004) *Black Demons: the media's depiction of the African American male criminal stereotype*, Westport, CT: Praeger.

Rorty, R. (1989) *Contingency, Irony and Solidarity*, Cambridge: Cambridge University Press.

Rothman, D.J. (1971) *The Discovery of the Asylum: social order and disorder in the new republic*, Boston, MA: Little Brown.

Royce, T. (2002) "Gypsies and British Parliamentary Language: an analysis," *Romani Studies* 12 (1): 1–34.

Rusche, G. and Kirchheimer, O. (1968) *Punishment and Social Structure*, New York: Russell and Russell.

Samuels, W.J. (1990) *Economics as Discourse: an analysis of the language of economics*, Boston, MA: Kluwer Academic Publishers.

Sapir, E. (1921) *Language*, New York: Harcourt, Brace & World.

Sarbin, T.R. and Miller, J.E. (1970) "Demonism Revisited: the XYY chromosomal anomaly," *Issues in Criminology* 5 (2): 195–207.

Saunders, D.J. (2010) "Sheriff Joe Arpaio's Polar Opposite," "Token Conservative" blog entry, *The San Francisco Chronicle*, September 3, blog.sfgate.com/djsaunders/2010/09/03/sheriff-joe-arpaios-polar-opposite/ (accessed June 27, 2012).

Saussure, F. (2006) *Writings in General Linguistics*, S. Bouquet and R. Engler (eds.) Oxford: Oxford University Press.

Schiffrin, D., Tannen, D. and Hamilton, H.E. (2001) *The Handbook of Discourse Analysis*, Oxford: Blackwell.

Schutz, A. (1964) Collected Papers II: studies in social theory, The Hague: Martinus Nijhoff.

—— (1967) The Phenomenology of the Social World, G.Walsh and F. Lehnert (trans), Evanston, IL: Northwestern University Press.

Scully, D. and Marolla, J. (1984) "Convicted Rapists' Vocabulary of Motive: excuses and justifications," *Social Problems* 31 (5): 530–44.

Searle, J. (1969) *Speech acts*, Cambridge: Cambridge University Press.

Serrano, R.A. (2005) "Ashcroft Makes Plea for Sentencing," *The Los Angeles Times*, February 2, A17.

Sheridan, T. (1780) *A General Dictionary of the English Language, 1780*, reprinted 1967, Menston: The Scolar Press Limited.

Shotter, J. (1993) *Conversational Realities: constructing life through language*, Thousand Oaks, CA: Sage Publications.

Shuy, R.W. (1993) *Language Crimes*, Oxford: Blackwell.

—— (1998) *The Language of Confession, Interrogation and Deception*, Thousand Oaks, CA: Sage Publications.

—— (2005) *Creating Language Crimes: how law enforcement uses (and misuses) language*, Oxford: Oxford University Press.

Simon, J. (1993) *Poor Discipline: parole and the social control of the underclass 1890–1990*, Chicago, IL: University of Chicago Press.

Slembrouck, S. (2005) "Discourse, Critique and Ethnography: class-oriented coding in accounts of child protection," *Language Sciences* 27 (66): 619–50.

Sloop, J. (1996) *The Cultural Prison: discourse, prisoners, and punishment*, Tuscaloosa, AL: The University of Alabama Press.

Smart, C. (1989) *Feminism and the Power of Law*, London: Routledge.

Solan, L. (1993) *The Language of Judges*, Chicago, IL: University of Chicago Press.

Solan, L. and Tiersma, P.M. (2004) *Speaking of Crime: the language of criminal justice*, Chicago, IL: University of Chicago Press.

Soros, G. (2010) "Why I Support Legal Marijuana," *The Wall Street Journal*, October 26, A17.

Spelman, W. (2000) "The Limited Importance of Prison Expansion," in A. Blumstein and J. Wallman (eds.) *The Crime Drop in America*, New York: Cambridge University Press.

Sperber, D. and Wilson, D. (1986) *Relevance: communication and cognition*, Oxford: Blackwell.

Spierenburg, P. (1984) *The Spectacle of Suffering, Executions and the Evolution of Repression: from a preindustrial metropolis to the European experience*, Cambridge: Cambridge University Press.

Sprott, J.B. (1999) "Are Members of the Public 'Tough on Crime'? the dimensions of public punitiveness," *Journal of Criminal Justice* 27 (5): 467–74.

Steingraber, S. (1997) *Living Downstream: an ecologist looks at cancer and the environment*, New York: Addison-Wesley.

Stienhauer, J. (2007) "For $82 a Day, Booking a Cell in a 5-star Jail," *The New York Times*, April 29, A1.

Stoller, P. (1992) *The Taste of Ethnographic Things*, Philadelphia, PA: University of Pennsylvania Press.

Stucky, T.D. (2005) "Local Politics and Local Strength," *Justice Quarterly* 22 (2): 139–69.

Sturrock, J. (1986) *Structuralism*, London: Paladin.

Substance Abuse and Mental Health Services Administration (2012) "Results from the 2011 National Survey on Drug Use and Health: Summary of National Findings," Rockville, MD: Substance Abuse and Mental Health Services Administration.

Summers, A. and Miller, M. (2007) "A Social Psychological Model of Victim Blame in the Legal System," paper presented at Western and Pacific Association of Criminal Justice Educators Conference, Reno, NV.

Surette, R. (1989) "Media Trials," *Journal of Criminal Justice* 17 (4): 293–308.

Tannen, D. (1991) *You Just Don't Understand: women and men in conversation*, London: Virago.

The United States Department of Justice (2012) "Mission Statement," March, www.justice.gov/about/about.html (accessed June 19, 2012).

Thomas, W.I. (1923) *The Unadjusted Girl: with cases and standpoint for behavior analysis*, Boston, MA: Little, Brown and Company.

Tjaden, P. and Thoennes, N. (1998) "Prevalence, Incidence and Consequences of Violence Against Women Survey," Washington, DC: National Institute of Justice and Centers for Disease Control & Prevention.

Tonry, M. (2004) *Thinking about Crime: sense and sensibility in American penal culture*, Oxford: Oxford University Press.

Trudgill, P. (1995) *Sociolinguistics: an introduction to language and society*, London: Penguin Books.

Tyler, S.A. (1987) *The Unspeakable: discourse, dialogue, and rhetoric in the postmodern world*, Madison: University of Wisconsin Press.

Unah, I. (2011) "Empirical Analysis of Race and the Process of Capital Punishment in North Carolina," *Michigan State Law Review* 2011 (3): 609–58.

van Dijk, T.A. (1988) *News as Discourse*, Hillsdale, NJ: L. Erlbaum Associates.

—— (1993) "Principles of Critical Discourse Analysis," *Discourse & Society* 4 (2): 249–83.

—— (1994) *Elite Discourse and Racism*, Newbury Park, CA: Sage Publications.

Voloshinov, V. (1973) *Marxism and the Philosophy of Language*, M. Ladislav and I.R. Titunik (trans), New York: Seminar Press.

Wardhaugh, R. (1992) *An Introduction to Sociolinguistics*, Cambridge, MA: Blackwell.

Weber, M. (1949) *The Methodology of the Social Sciences*, E.A. Shils and H.A. Finch (trans), Glencoe, IL: Free Press.

Webster's Dictionaries (1951) *Webster's New World Dictionary of the American Language*, [s.l.]: [s.n.].

White, R. (2002) "Indigenous Young Australians, Criminal Justice and Offensive Language," *Journal of Youth Studies* 5 (1): 21–34.

Whorf, B.L. (1956) *Language, Thought, and Reality*, Cambridge, MA: The Technology Press of MIT.

Young, J. (1986) "The Failure of Criminology: the need for radical realism," in J. Young and R. Matthews (eds) *Confronting Crime*, London: Sage Publications.

Index